T0303988

ROUTLEDGE LIBRARY EDITIONS: TAXATION

Volume 1

ENGLISH TAXATION, 1640–1799

ENGLISH TAXATION, 1640–1799
An Essay on Policy and Opinion

WILLIAM KENNEDY

Routledge
Taylor & Francis Group

LONDON AND NEW YORK

This edition first published in 2019
by Routledge
2 Park Square, Milton Park, Abingdon, Oxon OX14 4RN

and by Routledge
711 Third Avenue, New York, NY 10017

Routledge is an imprint of the Taylor & Francis Group, an informa business

First published in 1913 by G. Bell and Sons Ltd
Second impression published in 1964 by Frank Cass & Co Ltd

British Library Cataloguing in Publication Data
A catalogue record for this book is available from the British Library

ISBN: 978-1-138-56291-2 (Set)
ISBN: 978-0-429-48988-4 (Set) (ebk)
ISBN: 978-0-8153-4960-0 (Volume 1) (hbk)
ISBN: 978-1-351-11738-8 (Volume 1) (ebk)

Publisher's Note
The publisher has gone to great lengths to ensure the quality of this reprint but points out that some imperfections in the original copies may be apparent.

Disclaimer
The publisher has made every effort to trace copyright holders and would welcome correspondence from those they have been unable to trace.

ENGLISH TAXATION
1640-1799

AN ESSAY ON POLICY AND OPINION

WILLIAM KENNEDY

FRANK CASS & CO LTD

1964

First published by G. Bell & Sons Ltd
and now reprinted by their kind permission

This edition published by Frank Cass & Co Ltd
10 Woburn Walk, London WC1

First Edition   1913
New impression 1964

Printed and bound in Great Britain by
Thomas Nelson (Printers) Ltd, London and Edinburgh

PREFACE

THIS book is a result of an attempt made several years ago to understand the grounds of English tax policy since the re-imposition of the Income Tax and the beginning of the reform of the tariff in 1842. That attempt was made in the expectation that, if at all successful, it would not only explain much that seems fortuitous in our present tax system, but would also throw light upon some important general questions which theoretical works on taxation appeared to me to treat superficially. The attempt was so far successful that this expectation became a working hypothesis, but so far unsuccessful that I was unable to understand with any assurance certain aspects of the policy of the period from the material which the period itself offered. This was particularly true of policy regarding the taxation of the wage-earning classes. In the hope that the history of the preceding period would help to resolve these doubts, I went back to the time of William Pitt. The material turned out to be in many ways more significant ; but I found myself still unable to interpret it as a whole with any certainty. In effect the doubtful aspects of the policy of Parliament were thrown into stronger relief, but not explained. In this difficulty I again went back to the period dealt with in this book, in the history of which, I believe, are to be found not only the main elements of the interpretation which was lacking, but also much assistance towards a realization of what is involved in the permanent general question of the distribution of taxation.

I have called the book an *Essay* with the intention

of suggesting its relation to histories of taxation. It is
not a history of taxation in the sense in which Dowell's
work on the same period is a history of taxation. Dowell
gives in detail a record of the tax enactments, but
makes comparatively little attempt to bring out their
general tendency and almost none to explain it. The
present work is an essay upon the basis of Dowell's
record—amplified on points, particularly as regards the
interregnum and the direct taxes of the seventeenth
century, on which Dowell is inadequate—and attempts
to get at the policy embodied in the record, and the
opinions and motives, supporting and opposing, which
lay behind the policy. On the other hand, neither is
the book a history of taxation in the sense in which
such a work may, perhaps, some day be written; it
can be, at best, but an essay towards such a history.
And this not merely because such a history would
necessarily deal directly with many questions which are
only touched on here by the way, but also because,
on those questions of the distribution of taxation and
the underlying political and social opinion with which
this book is chiefly concerned, such a history would
presuppose an assurance, demanding correlation of the
results of work on other fields of social history, which
at the present moment is unobtainable, and the lack of
which makes the conclusions of this study in a measure
provisional.

In issuing this essay, which from one point of view
is critical of the existing literature on the history of
taxation, I wish to acknowledge most fully my indebted-
ness to that literature, and particularly to two books.
The first is Stephen Dowell's *History of Taxation and
Taxes*, but for the existence of which it would have
been quite impossible to have attempted such a study
as the present. The second is Professor Seligman's
Incidence of Taxation (3rd edition), the historical
portions of which have been of constant service in
dealing with the pamphlet literature of this period.

I desire also to acknowledge with gratitude the help which I have obtained from fellow-students and teachers in working on this subject—from Professor Smart, under whose guidance I first approached it; from Professor Cannan, who has at different times read both the preliminary studies in which this book was first sketched and the final manuscript, and to whom I am indebted for many suggestions and much stimulating criticism; from Mr. J. B. Black, Miss M. D. Gordon and Mr. R. H. Tawney, with whom I have had the advantage of discussion of particular points, and from whom, along with Dr. Lilian Knowles, Mr. David Ogg, Mr. W. R. Scott and Professor Unwin, I have received much help regarding sources. I am also indebted to Miss Olivia Powell for her generous assistance in the labour of seeing the book through the press.

The historical research on which the essay is directly based was carried out during my tenure in sessions 1910–11 and 1911–12 of the Shaw Research Studentship at the London School of Economics and Political Science, and a course of lectures also based upon this work was delivered there in Michaelmas term 1913.

W. Kennedy.

CONTENTS

Note.—Where library press-marks are given in the footnotes, they refer to those of the British Museum, unless otherwise stated. With a few exceptions, quotations are given in modernized spelling.

I

INTRODUCTION

Taxation has had the misfortune to be identified in England with two great controversies in which very few of its own essential problems were involved. The first and greater of these dealt with the question of the authority by which taxes should be levied. This was merely part of the wider constitutional question of the body which should make law and control the administration of government. In its main features, the question was settled in the seventeenth century in favour of Parliament and those who at different times came to control Parliament; but its settlement in no way decided the question of the kind of taxation which this governing body should adopt. The second controversy was the tariff struggle, of the second quarter of the nineteenth century, over the use of Customs duties for protective and preferential purposes. The struggle resulted in the victory of the Free Trade doctrine that taxes should be imposed only for revenue. It is true that certain minor questions of the best form of Customs duties were also involved, but it is obvious that the controversy touched only a very small portion of the whole field of taxation.

Interest in these constitutional and tariff questions has tended to the neglect of the essential problems in taxation. Evidence of the neglect appears on all sides. In spite of the fact that these problems are raised every year in Parliament, nothing is more striking than the absence there of anything that could be called a theory of taxation. English text-book writers are useful on questions of incidence and administration ; on questions of distribution their discussions are, with few exceptions,[1] so little fundamental that they do not even recognize that questions of political philosophy are involved. But the most striking evidence is given by the two books upon which we chiefly depend for our knowledge of the history of English taxation—Stephen Dowell's large History (1884) and Mr. Sydney Buxton's study of the period 1783 to 1885.[2] Both are invaluable so far as they go, but in regard to strictly tax questions they give little more than an unilluminating record of the facts of tax legislation.[3] They do not even indicate a consciousness of what constitute the essential problems involved in the material with which they deal. Professor Seligman has more recently made valuable contributions to the history in his survey of theories of incidence [4] and his history of the Income Tax, but these are both sectional studies only, and the second and less sectional avoids a discussion of the most important, if least obvious, aspects of the period with which it deals (the nineteenth century).

The relatively superficial character of our histories of taxation [5] may indeed be considered the proximate cause of the neglect of essential problems. For these problems are difficult, and it is not at first obvious even what they are ; and it is just in such a situation that history can afford most help to present thought.[6] Over centuries these problems have been considered many

[1] The most prominent exception in England is Professor Edgeworth, who bases his theory of distribution on Benthamite utilitarianism. See *Economic Journal* (1897), vii. 550 *seq.*

[2] *Finance and Politics, 1783–1885,* 2 vols., 1888.

[3] This criticism is less fully applicable to Dowell's chapters on the medieval period.

[4] *Shifting and Incidence of Taxation,* 3rd edition, 1910 ; part i. book i.

[5] It is perhaps as well to say that local taxation or rating is not in view in this essay.

[6] Compare the comparative lack of suggestion to be obtained from the history of problems which have been sharply defined and well analysed in modern times,—*e.g.* problems of incidence of taxation.

times and by many men—not, it is true, systematically or as a whole, but one problem at one time and another at another time; and retraversing old practice and opinion we have laid open to view the elements and connections of many of them. Nor is the service which history may in this way perform for the present, vitiated by the fact that the situation in which the problems arose was different in important respects in the past; for the service we ask of history is not to provide models to copy in the present. History is the attempt to understand the past and to bring out, *inter alia*, the connection between the setting of a problem and its contemporary solution; and the more fully history succeeds in this attempt, the more assistance does it provide towards an understanding of the present, by indicating not only that the setting in the present is different as well as similar, but that it is similar and different in particular and defined respects.

In this essay, then, an attempt will be made to understand the way in which certain of the essential problems in taxation were dealt with and thought about in the seventeenth and eighteenth centuries in England. There are, moreover, two additional reasons for thinking that this subject is important in the present stage of historical and financial investigation. On the tax side, it is practically impossible to understand the history of taxation and of related opinion in the nineteenth century without grasping the outstanding features in the preceding century; and this not merely on the general ground that no period can be appreciated without knowledge of its antecedents, but chiefly on the particular ground that the nineteenth century (which may for our purposes be taken to begin with the imposition of the modern Income Tax in 1799) had a peculiar tendency to shut its eyes to certain forms of question and to ignore the motives and ideas which yet influenced its treatment of them. On the historical side, the tax policy of the period from the Civil War to the end of the eighteenth century is an important aspect, which still awaits interpretation, of the social and economic policy of the then governing landed class ; and it is an aspect which has the merit of forcing on the attention the wider question, to which comparatively little has yet been done, of the social attitude or what may be called the practical political theories of that period.

The essential questions in taxation may be grouped in three divisions, according as they treat of its purposes, its distribution, and the methods of attaining, by actual taxes, the purposes and distribution desired. The purposes for which taxes may be imposed are many. The provision of revenue to maintain certain common services, whether national or of a more restricted character, is a purpose of nearly all taxes and the sole purpose of the majority ; the repression of consumption (*e.g.* in spirit duties), the achievement of certain ends of commercial policy (*e.g.* in Customs duties), or of agricultural and land policy (*e.g.* in Australian land taxes), are instances of other purposes for which, alone or along with a revenue purpose, taxes may be levied. We shall, therefore, consider the state of opinion in this period on the question of the purposes of taxation, and shall note to what extent purposes other than that of revenue were embodied in actual taxes. But, while an attempt will be made to estimate the relative importance of these purposes and their influence upon other aspects of tax doctrine, no detailed discussion of the grounds on which they were based will be offered ; that would involve, among other things, an appreciation of the Mercantile System. The second group of questions— in the history of which our chief interest will lie—deals with the distribution of the total burden of taxation among the members of the community. The problem of distribution is the fundamental problem of taxation, in the narrow sense of taxation for revenue ; it is neces- sarily raised by it, and, speaking generally, it is not raised by taxes of which revenue is not the only or a main purpose.[1] It may be divided into two parts : first, should every member of the community pay taxation—a minor form of which is the question, should the poor man [2] pay taxation ? and second, what is the criterion or standard of distribution, according to which the burden is to be distributed among those who, it is considered, should pay taxation ? The third group of questions deals with methods of attaining the kind of taxation desired—that is, with the devising of actual taxes and of a taxing organization which will yield the necessary amount of revenue, distribute the burden in a satisfactory way and fulfil any other purposes intended. The many difficult and technical questions here involved may be roughly classified as follows : first, problems of incidence, dealing with the question upon whom and in what proportion different taxes will lay a burden ; second, problems of collection, dealing with the relation between the forms of taxes and the system of collection and supervision, with a view to prevention of evasion, cheapness of collection, and the like ; third, problems of the incidental features of taxes, dealing with the minimization of the ' necessary evils ' which always attend taxation, and which offend against opinions and prejudices on such subjects as personal liberty and restraint of trade. With the problem of incidence we shall be directly concerned here ; it provides the minor premiss in the argument that a particular tax or system of taxation is distributively

---

[1] Thus, for instance, a spirit duty imposed solely to reduce consumption (so far as consistent with the prevention of evasion) would involve no problem of distribution in any but the formal sense that it would be intended to make people pay in proportion to their use of the dangerous commodity. On the other hand, the problem of distribution *might* be considered in a Customs duty imposed solely or chiefly for protection, in the real sense of taking into account, in arranging the distribution of taxation as a whole, the burden involved on the consumers of the protected commodity. The statement in the text is, however, true for most cases and for this period.

[2] Unless otherwise stated, ' poor man ' in this essay always means the ordinary wage-earner, and never means pauper or destitute person.

just. The other problems of method will be treated more casually; but it will be necessary to notice the phases of them which were most prominent in this period, both because the policy of the period would otherwise be partly unintelligible, and because, as is less obvious, the exigencies of these problems usually force the taxing power to be content with taxes which fail in a degree to achieve the purposes and distribution which it would desire.

An illustration, in the form of a simple scheme of taxation, will make this description of the essential problems clearer; and will at the same time afford a useful background of comparison against which to throw up the features of the tax systems of the seventeenth and eighteenth centuries. The scheme which it is most convenient to take corresponds closely to the English tax system of the period 1860–1880, as it was conceived, with varying precision, by the men of that time.[1] The principles of this scheme were these: the only purpose of a tax is to produce revenue; every one, including the poor man, should pay taxation; taxation should be distributed in direct proportion to incomes; the roughly satisfactory method of achieving this result is by a compensatory system of taxes, each in itself distributively unfair, but in such a way that the unfairnesses cancel one another—on the one side the Income Tax and certain minor taxes which fall only on the rich and middle classes, and on the other Customs and Excise duties upon a small number of imported and native commodities of very general consumption, to which a poor man pays more, proportionately to his income, than richer people. This was not, in fact, a quite accurate account of the tax system of that time, nor was it perhaps ever so fully defined, but it was the account which was dominant in a somewhat vague way. It is, moreover

---

[1] If any one doubts this assertion, he may consider the scheme given as an hypothetical one for purposes of illustration and comparison. It is impossible to adduce the proof here.

still sufficiently familiar even now, in spite of its present inapplicability, and at the same time sufficiently comprehensive in its realization of the essential problems in taxation, to entitle it to be treated as a useful position from which to look either forward or backward.

But before we can go on to consider the way in which the questions thus answered in the Gladstonian epoch were dealt with between 1640 and 1799, it is necessary to sketch in outline the kind of tax system which the Long Parliament inherited.

II

THE INHERITANCE OF THE LONG
PARLIAMENT

THE Civil War involved the final breakdown of a financial
system which had ruled in England for about three
centuries.[1] In contrast with modern times, its most
striking feature was lack of homogeneity. We now consider the national expenditure as one whole, made up
of the cost of maintaining many different services ; and
the national revenue as provided almost exclusively by
a system of taxes of a proportionate aggregate yield.
But during these centuries, both revenue and expenditure were in theory divided into three separate sections,
and the total revenue was not derived from a system
of taxes.[2] The first section comprised the proprietary
revenue from Crown lands and feudal rights, which
constituted a varying but large proportion of the total
revenue,[3] and was supposed to provide for the ordinary
internal administrative expenditure of the State. This
was not a tax revenue at all. The second section com-

---

[1] For special sources of revenue in this period, such as benevolences
and monopolies, see Dowell i., books vi.–viii., and W. Hyde Price,
The English Patents of Monopoly. They are not discussed in this
outline sketch, partly because they were of minor financial importance, but chiefly because they had no importance as a part of the
tradition which the Long Parliament inherited.

[2] Fortescue, *Governance of England*, ed. Plummer, written 1471–6,
chaps. vi.–viii.

[3] *e.g.* in 1610, £144,000 out of an estimated ordinary revenue
of £461,500, which included Customs revenue £247,800. Gardiner,
History of England, 1603–42, x. 222.

prised the revenue from Customs duties, which was supposed to provide for the 'keeping of the sea' for the protection of merchants and the defence of the realm—that is, for expenditure on the Navy.[1] These duties, as we shall see, were not regarded as national taxes. The third section comprised the revenue from direct taxes, in the full modern sense of the word, which were levied usually on a grant by Parliament for special national purposes such as war.

This theory of a sectional financial system was in some ways realized, in others repudiated in practice. But, from the point of view of taxation, there was one important respect in which it was not, and another in which it was, carried out. In spite of the fact that Customs duties were explicitly granted for the maintenance of the Navy, there is no reason to suppose that the revenue derived was ever so allocated[2]; the Customs were treated by the Crown in practice as providing a portion of the ordinary yearly revenue, and the Navy as one of the objects of ordinary expenditure. On the other hand, direct taxes, since they were granted only for short periods, were kept closely in touch with the theory that they were levied to provide for special purposes of more or less intermittent occurrence. The result of these two circumstances was to produce an attitude to tax problems very different, in superficial ways, from that which is familiar nowadays. Tax problems did not arise, properly speaking, in connection with the ordinary yearly revenue of the State—for Crown lands yielded a property revenue and Customs

---

[1] It is not clear whether the ancient, and in the seventeenth century relatively unimportant, prerogative Customs duties were supposed to have this destination. The doctrine applied directly to the duties granted by Parliament, usually for the King's life, see *e.g.* 1 Eliz. c. 20 (in Prothero, *Select Documents*, p. 26) and 16 Chas. I. c. 8; also Rushworth, part iii. vol. i. pp. 21-2 for Pym's statement of grievances.

[2] Fortescue, p. 123, and Plummer's note, p. 232. *Debates in Parliament*, 1610 (ed. Gardiner), Salisbury's account of the reasons for increasing the duties in 1608, pp. 155-6. Prothero, p. 354, Commission to levy impositions, 1608.

were not considered as a national tax ; they were involved only in direct taxes, and presented themselves in the form how occasionally to raise revenue for national purposes. But to-day almost the whole of the national revenue is derived from taxes, and from taxes which are levied every year. The second half of the seventeenth century witnessed the transition from the first to the second of these tax situations.

What kind of taxes, we must then ask, were Customs duties considered to be, if they were not national taxes, and in what way was taxation raised by the direct taxes ?

Customs duties were imposed on ' all manner of goods and merchandise coming in and going out of the realm,' and were always thought of as a special charge imposed on imported and exported merchandise for the special service required from the Crown of the protection of such merchandise. Modern Customs duties are levied upon the citizen (through his consumption of certain imported goods) as taxes for general national purposes ; in the sixteenth century, Customs duties were levied on those (whether Englishmen or foreigners) who consumed the dutied goods, in theory as dues or fees for a special service performed, no doubt by the Crown, for their particular benefit. They were analogous to tolls on roads. Traded merchandise, and not the country at large, should pay for the protection of trade ; and hence exports as well as imports paid duty.

The theory is fully illustrated by the records of the controversy in the reign of James I. over the power of the King to impose duties without consent of Parliament. Both sides regarded the Customs in the way described. Hakewill thought that ' because the common law expecteth that the King should protect merchants in their trades . . . it also giveth him out of merchandises exported and imported some profit for the sustentation of this public charge,' but this sustentation, he contended, was a duty certain, not to be increased at the

King's will.[1] Baron Fleming, the chief of the Bench which supported the Crown in Bates' case, explained the reason for Customs duties in the same way, but argued that in order to protect merchants and regulate trade, the King necessarily had the right to alter the duties when necessary.[2]

It will be noticed that Customs are spoken of as paid 'out of merchandise,' and not by merchants. This distinction was intentional, for it was well recognized that, although advanced by merchants, the burden of the duties really fell on the consumers of the commodities. The interests, that is to say, which ultimately benefited by and paid for the special service of the Crown, were the consumers, home and foreign, and not the merchants. As John Hales[3] wrote in 1549, 'the merchante, if he bie dear, he will sell deare agayne.' Out of many illustrations of the doctrine in the first half of the seventeenth century, this from Fleming's judgment[4] is perhaps the clearest :

'It is well known that the end of every private merchant is not the common good, but his own particular profit, which is only the means which induceth him to trade and traffic. And the impost to him is nothing, for he rateth his merchandise according to that. The impost is imposed upon currants ; and he who will buy them shall have them subject to that charge. . . .'

Fleming denied that the duties injured the merchant

---

[1] See abbreviated speech in Prothero, pp. 343, 350.

[2] Hubert Hall, *Customs Revenue of England*, i. 155, gives a useful summary of this and other speeches. For another statement of the theory on the Royalist side, see Sir John Davies, ' *The Question concerning impositions* . . .' 1656 (written t. James I.), pp. 78–80.

[3] *A Discourse of the Commonweal of this Realm of England*, ed. Lamond, p. 33.

[4] *State Trials*, ii. 390. See also Clark's judgment, *ibid.*, ii. 386 ; Noy's view of incidence of Customs in 1629 (given in Gardiner, *op. cit.* vii. 60) ; and the implication of the desire to exempt necessaries in the interest of the poor. It should be pointed out that the instances of the doctrine all refer to duties on imports ; in the text I have generalised it to cover export duties also.

in any way, but the merchants were well able to assert their interest on the point. They contended that duties destroyed their trade or that the burden fell on them. The truth contained in this contention, namely, that duties restrict trade, was, however, a commonplace, and was recognized to be quite consistent with the doctrine that the consumer pays the duties. Thus in the time of Henry VIII., the speakers in Starkey's Dialogue [1] agree that by reason of heavy Customs merchants ' have less will to travail for the commodity of the rest of the Commons. Wherefore we lack many things that we might have or at least much better cheap than we have commonly.' So in a speech [2] in 1610 the inconveniences of recent impositions are summarized thus : ' How hurtful they are to the merchants in impoverishing them in their estates ; to the King in the decreasing his revenues by decay of traffic ; and to the whole people in making all commodities excessive dear, is confessed by all and therefore need no debate.'

The result of this view of the Customs as dues or tolls rather than taxes, was that the problem of distribution was not thought of as involved. The people who paid the dues paid for special benefit received. Nor was this result any the less definite because the theory was not put into practice. It was, indeed, untrue to the facts in a double way. On the one hand, the Customs revenue was not allocated to the Navy, and the duties were increased several times in the first forty years of the seventeenth century simply to add to the general

[1] Thomas Starkey, *England in the Reign of King Henry the Eighth*, ed. Cowper, p. 141.

[2] *State Trials*, ii. 480—a speech in Parliament attributed by Cobbett to Yelverton, but by Gardiner to Whitelocke (see *op. cit.* ii. 77 n.). Cobbett's text gives *in*creasing where *de*creasing is obviously meant. See also Salisbury's speech in *Debates in Parliament*, 1610, p. 158. It will be obvious that in its main elements the question of the incidence of Customs duties was understood in a practical way. The precise modern explanation of the consistency of the two points alluded to, viz., that for a time the merchant is positively injured by a new duty, is not given, however ; nor have I noticed a discussion of the various effects of protective duties.

resources of the Crown [1]; on the other, even in theory the duties were levied to enable the Navy not only to protect trade but also to defend the realm, that is, to provide a general benefit. The protection of trade, however, was the side emphasized, and the theory retained influence well into the second half of the century.

But while imposed for revenue—in theory for the protection of trade, in fact for general purposes—the Customs were also partly regulated by considerations of an entirely different character. The records of the impositions [2] indicate the general acceptance of two principles to be observed. The first dealt with the effect of import duties on the consumer, and laid it down as a rule that the necessaries of the people should be spared. Thus the instructions for the impositions of 1608 [3] gave special charge, in order to avoid inconvenience or grievance to the people, ' to exempt and forbear all such merchandises inwards as were either requisite for the food and sustenance of our people (as wheat, rye, barley, malt, oats, beans, peas, butter, cheese, lings, codfish, colefish, herrings, sprots, haddocks, newladfish, all sorts of salt and all sorts of fowls) . . .' Salisbury, in his defence of these impositions, [4] was careful to point out that one of the cautions adopted at a conference with merchants was ' that no victual, nothing necessary to munition or defence of the realm, should pay any impost inward'; and Fleming, in Bates' case, [5] rebutted the argument against the impost on currants, as articles of victual

[1] e.g. 1635, *Book of Rates*, prefaced letter patent, p. 2 ; and 1608, Impositions, Prothero, p. 354. The seventeenth-century Books of Rates can be seen, in London, most conveniently at the Goldsmiths' Library, South Kensington (Professor Foxwell's collection).

[2] The policy of the Long Parliament gives confirmation, see Giles Greene, *Declaration in Vindication of Parliament*, . . . 1647, E. 405 (8), pp. 4–5.

[3] Letter patent to Salisbury, 28th July 1608, as set out in one of 5th September 1610, prefaced to 1610 Book of Rates (513, a. 38). Original abbreviated in Prothero, p. 354.

[4] *Debates in Parliament*, 1610, p. 157.   [5] *State Trials*, ii. 390–1.

and necessary food, by pointing out that on the contrary they were 'nice and delicate things,' no more necessary than wine. In fact, of course, very few necessaries other than salt and fish (which, though not exempted completely, were rated very low to the old poundage duty) can have been imported ; and there was a tendency to regard imports in general as superfluities, and necessaries as 'that which ariseth from agriculture and of the earth within this land.' It was, therefore, 'only a small number of delicate persons and those also who are of most able and best estate' who were thought of as paying import duties.[1]

This principle of the exemption of necessaries, while not considered as a principle in the distribution of a burden imposed by taxation, was nevertheless adopted in order to exempt the poor, and obviously bordered on a distributive meaning.[2] It was the doctrine to which men appealed later, to condemn the taxation of the poor man through Excise duties on necessaries.

The second regulating principle in Customs duties was trade policy, dealing with their effect on the producer. The idea that it is necessary, in the industrial and social interest of the nation, to control the course of foreign trade, was inbred in the sixteenth and seventeenth centuries.[3] To encourage the im-

---

[1] *Ibid.* Salt was rated at 8d. (white or Spanish) and 6d. (Bay or French) per bushel, according to the Book of Rates of 1604 ; the rates were not increased in 1610, but in 1635 they were raised 50 per cent., and in 1642 reduced to the old level. The real prices were over 1s. 6d. in the east of England, and nearly 2s. 6d. in the Midlands, so that the nominal 5 per cent. tax at 6d. and 8d. amounted really only to 1 per cent. to 2 per cent. Rogers, *Hist. of Agric.*, v. 430, 441. The position was similar as regards fish.

[2] It might be stated as the importation of an idea of distributive burden into a scheme of benefit taxation. Cf. the principle in railway rating of charging what the traffic will bear.

[3] *e.g.* Starkey's *Dialogue*, pp. 93–4 ; Hales' *Commonweal*, pp. 61–2, 65–6, 68 ; King James I., *Basilikon Doron* 1599 (Edinburgh), p. 59 Bacon, Essay on *Seditions and Troubles* (works, ed. Spedding, vi. 410); Thomas Fuller, *Holy and Profane State*, 1642, book ii. chap. 17. Cf. Bodin, *Les six livres de la République* (Engl. tr. Knowles, 1606, pp. 662–3).

port[1] and discourage the export of material which might set the people on work, and to discourage the import of foreign superfluities or competing manufactures, and encourage the export of our surplus products, were the most important aspects of the doctrine. Such considerations did in fact influence the rates of the Customs duties, as is obvious from the Book of Rates of 1610,[2] but the extent of the influence is very difficult to estimate. It is scarcely doubtful, however, that the purpose of influencing the course of trade was small relatively to that of raising revenue.[3]

The Customs were thus not merely regarded as the charge for a special service or benefit, though that was their primary aspect ; they were also an instrument of trade policy. A suggestive analogy is found in special Convoy duties imposed in 1798, when Customs had long been looked upon as general taxes. In that year an Act [4] was passed 'for the better protection of the trade of this kingdom' by the provision of convoys during the continuance of the war, and for imposing duties both on exports and imports [5] 'in order to defray the extraordinary expense arising from the protection given.' It was natural, therefore, that the first intention, as we learn from George Rose,[6] was to lay a duty of $2\frac{1}{2}$ per cent. on all imports and exports ; but then trade considerations being raised, the uniform rate was regulated by ideas of trade policy, and the duty on exports to Europe, to take an instance, restricted to $\frac{1}{2}$ per cent. to meet the danger of foreigners underselling us there. The Stuart principle of exempting imported

---

[1] e.g. cotton wool, cotton yarn, raw silk, and raw hemp (1610, Book of Rates, preface pp. 3-4).

[2] Ibid., passim. Also Debates in Parliament, 1610, p. 157. It is possible that ideas of sumptuary policy may have also had some slight influence on the duties, but the point is practically negligible.

[3] The question is discussed below.

[4] 38 Geo. III. c. 76.

[5] Also on Ships.

[6] The Parliamentary Register (Debrett), 68, 156 (16th May 1798). Rose was one of Pitt's secretaries at the Treasury.

necessaries did not, however, reappear in these Convoy duties.

It was in the occasional direct taxes that the essential problems of national taxation, in the strict sense, were involved prior to the Civil War. These taxes were imposed simply to raise revenue for general national purposes,[1] and always defined a standard according to which the burden was to be distributed among the members of the community. To use a theoretical term, they were ability or faculty taxes, which should distribute a common burden according to some conception of the ability of different individuals to bear it, and in this light they were considered.[2]

The recognized direct taxes of the early seventeenth century were the Fifteenth and Tenth, and the Subsidy.[3] At that period they were both stereotyped taxes, assessed in practice in very different ways from those laid down in the authorizing statutes. No systematic study has yet been made of the actual methods of assessment, but fortunately the schemes of assessment intended to be observed, which are easily found from the Acts, are

[1] See the preambles to the Acts (*e.g.* 1 Eliz. c. 21 in Prothero, p. 27), and the recognition of the fact by Fortescue, chap. viii. (ed. Plummer, p. 127); Latimer, *First Sermon to King Edward VI.* (Everyman ed., p. 83); Thomas Becon, *Catechism* (ed. J. Ayre, p. 308–9).

[2] Debates in Elizabeth's Parliaments illustrate this, see *Old Parliamentary History*, iv. 337, 444–6. See also Miss M. D. Gordon, *Collection of Ship Money* (Trans. of Royal Hist. Socy., 1910, pp. 145–9); Gibbon, *The Order of Equalitie,* 1604, 8226, c. 14, *passim*; A *Discourse Touching the Diminution of the Subsidy,* t. James I., attributed to Wm. Tooker, Dean of Lichfield (Harleian MS 188 (1.), p. 5). It is worth while suggesting that the idea of ability is probably derived from an organic functional view of society, regarding individuals and classes on the analogy of organs of the human body (see chap. v.). The Discourse says : ' The life of the subsidy consisteth in a certain geometrical and proportional contribution, as of every member and part in the body organical and natural, so in the body politic, unto the head, and that according to the power and faculty, strength and ability of every part and parcel thereof. . . .'

[3] Benevolences and the ship money of Charles I. were not part of the ' canon ' to a sufficient extent to demand discussions here. For ship money, see Miss Gordon's article, which brings out clearly the distributive policy.

of much greater interest. It was only in the nineteenth century that any continuous and fairly complete success was attained in keeping actual taxes in touch with the intention of the taxing power. In earlier times, what happened was that a new direct tax was tolerably accurately assessed at first, but then fell away and was later stereotyped in some very deficient form; until, the yield becoming too small or the possibility of reforming it too remote, a new attempt was made to get a productive and equitable tax, which in its turn gradually passed through the same stages. The result is that, in order to understand the tradition of equitable taxation which the Long Parliament inherited, it is more important to go back to the intention of the Acts at different periods, than to the actual methods of levy in the early seventeenth century. In this way we may obtain a rough idea of the course of intended distribution over the three preceding centuries, first as regards the standard of distribution, and next as regards exemptions.

The tax which became stereotyped in 1334 as the Fifteenth and Tenth developed during the thirteenth century, and by the beginning of the fourteenth had superseded earlier partial taxes.[1] It was a tax on the moveable goods of all classes,[2] excepting certain personal goods such as clothes and armour.[3] The owner of land, the merchant and the poor man, all paid on the same kind of assessment, as two Colchester schedules which have been printed for 1295 and 1301[4] show. Thus in 1295 Master Simon of Neylond (probably a Churchman) paid on wheat, oats, oxen, ploughbeasts, cows and sheep in his manor in Miland;[5] a tanner on

---

[1] Dowell, i. 76, 95. The references here and elsewhere are to the first edition of Dowell's *History*.

[2] *e.g.* 1232, Grant of a Fortieth (*Foedera*, i. 207); 1297, Grant of an Eighth and a Fifth (*Parl. Rolls*, i. 239); 1307, Twentieth and Fifteenth (*Parl. Rolls*, i. 442); 1322, Tenth and Sixth (in Dowell, i. 259). [3] Dowell, i. 78.

[4] *Parl. Rolls*, i. 228 *seq.*, 243 *seq.*, abbreviated in Dowell, i. 251 *seq.*

[5] P. 236, cf. 1301, p. 259 (Dominus Robertus, in manerio suo).

(*a*) wheat, barley, oats, and pigs ; (*b*) tannery stuff and implements, and (*c*) sundry household effects ; a poor man (Hugo le potter) on a cow and a young ox.

After 1334, when the contribution of each district was fixed at a definite sum, not much is known of the actual method of assessment. It differed no doubt in different places, and the tax is said to have become in the end practically a local rate on fixed property.[1] In any case it ceased to be assessed according to a national standard,[2] and in the sixteenth century its yield was wholly incommensurate with the wealth of the country.

An important change in the standard of distribution characterized the next attempt at a satisfactory national direct tax. Income was substituted for moveable property as the standard in the case of the great mass of the taxpayers—landowners, yeomen (including copyholders), clergy, holders of offices, and wage-earners ; moveable property (and that in the sense of net capital) remained the standard for merchants, artisans, and doubtless tenant-farmers. In the intervening special land taxes [3] of the fifteenth century, it was the annual value which was rated, and in 1488 [4] an unsuccessful attempt was made to impose a general tax of the kind described above. Under Henry VIII. the attempt was successful, and the Subsidy, as it was called, represents the new scheme of distribution.[5] The rating provisions

---

[1] Dowell, i. 97 ; Cannan, *History of Local Rates*, 13–14 ; Prothero, Introduction, p. lxxxi.

[2] Not without attempts to prevent this, *e.g.* 1463, *Parl. Rolls*, v. 497.

[3] See Dowell, book v. chap. i. part iii., and book vi. chap. ii. In some cases the annual value of offices was also taxed, *e.g.* 1435 and 1450 (pp. 124, 127). These taxes were granted on several occasions in supplement of the Fifteenth and Tenth.

[4] *Parl. Rolls*, vi. 421 and Dowell, i. 169.

[5] Those rated on their lands included, besides copy holders, holders-at-will in 1514 (6 H. VIII. c. 26), 1523 (14 & 15 H. VIII. c. 16) and 1540 (32 H. VIII. c. 50), but by the time of Elizabeth holders-at-will were excluded (see 1 Eliz. c. 21, in Prothero, p. 30). A clergyman (through the subsidy granted specially by the clergy) paid 4s. per £ for every pound that he might yearly spend by reason of his spiritual promotion, according to the assessment of such promotion made for

varied considerably in the earlier Acts, but by the time of Elizabeth they had become practically fixed, the rates of a subsidy being 4s. per £ of income for those rated on income, and 2s. 8d. per £ of net capital for those rated on moveables.

Moveables still continued to be the standard of assessment for merchants and others, doubtless because there was no other way of testing their means ; though why they should have been charged at the rate just given is hard to understand. In practice, it is said, personal property escaped for the most part. But even as regards traders, it is clear that the idea of taxing according to income was coming to be familiar in the early seventeenth century. A project for raising money in 1628 [1] suggested that every person lending money at an interest of 10 per cent. should pay a tax of the 10th penny of the interest ; and in the 1635 edition of Dalton's manual for Justices of the Peace,[2] the author thought that in rating a man by his goods for the Poor, 'it seemeth reasonable that such goods be rated after the value of lands to be purchased, *sc.* one hundred pounds in stock or goods to be rated after 5 or 6 £ per annum in lands.'

Subsidy Rolls which have been printed for a Norfolk

the perpetual dime (32 H. VIII. c. 23, and cf. 5 Eliz. c. 29, in Prothero, p. 54). Yearly wage-earners of 20s. a year were taxed in 1514 at 6d. per £ ; in 1523, daily, weekly or yearly wage-earners of 20s. a year were taxed 4d. a head ; in 1544 (37 H. VIII. c. 25, § 5), yearly wage-earners were taxed only if earning 40s. (then at 2s. per £), and thereafter only king's servants earning £5 a year were to pay (*e.g.* Prothero, p. 30). The later subsidy Acts do not provide for taxing the *net* yearly value of lands, but that the idea of real income in this sense was familiar for tax purposes is clear from the Act of 1488 (*Parl. Rolls*, vi. 421), which provides for deducting 'the rents, fees and other services going out of the said lands,' etc. by the year, and from the Act of 1534, which taxes the *clear* yearly value (26 H. VIII. c. 19). Those taxed to moveables were charged on coin, plate, merchandise, 'cornes and blades severed from the ground,' household stuff, etc., *plus* debts due to them, *less* debts owing by them ; see 6 H. VIII. c. 26, 14 & 15 H. VIII. c. 16, and Prothero, p. 29.

[1] S.P.D. (1628), 126, 47.

[2] Michael Dalton, *Country Justice*, 1635, p. 136. See Cannan, *History of Local Rates*, pp. 85–7.

Hundred[1] show that an attempt was made to carry out the provisions of the earlier Acts, but already in the time of Elizabeth the tax was so unequal and so much a stereotyped assessment that it had very little connection with the prescribed scheme of distribution.[2] The standard which seems to have been in the minds of the local assessors and commissioners, when they were trying to distribute their quota fairly, was the undefined and non-rigid one of general ability or means. There is every reason to suppose that income would be the chief element in this standard, but the expenses of position and of large family were also taken into account.[3] In Gibbon's words, ' sessors ought to look into the charge of a man's family before they can well tell how to charge him by his ability. . . .'

Such was the tradition in 1640 in respect of the standard of distribution.[4] On the question whether every one should pay taxation, it was less definite. One point, however, stands out clearly. There was no tradition that either the rich or the landed nobility and gentry should bear all taxation ; the small landholder (and England was largely composed of such) was always rated in the tax Acts, and in fact paid subsidy in the seventeenth century. The important question is the treatment of the labouring poor (with or without small

---

[1] Walter Rye, *Rough Materials for a History of the Hundred of North Erpingham* (Norfolk), part ii.

[2] See Latimer, *Sermons* (Everyman ed. p. 261) ; Rye ; Gibbon ; *Discourse Touching the Diminution of the Subsidy* ; Dowell, i. 196 *seq.* ; Best's Farming Book (Surtees Society), pp. 85–91 ; *Considerations touching Trade with the Advance of the King's Revenue. . .* 1641 [E. 148 (1)], pp. 12–13 ; and *Old Parliamentary History*, iv. 446.

[3] Dowell, i. 199 ; Gibbon, pp. 23–4.

[4] The account given here of the English direct taxes between the fourteenth and seventeenth centuries differs somewhat from that given by Professor Seligman (*Essays in Taxation*, 5th ed. pp. 43–7, and *Income Tax*, pp. 47–9). It appears to me that to describe the Fifteenth and Tenth and the Subsidy as general property taxes, or as a combination of produce and property taxes, is misleading, and prevents Professor Seligman from realizing the significance of the seventeenth century direct taxes, and the relation to them of Pitt's Income Tax. See subsequent discussion.

land-rights) who depended chiefly on wages. The assessments of moveables in the thirteenth and fourteenth centuries, although they fixed a limit of exemption, made it so low as to bring in many and perhaps most poor people. This is quite clear from the Colchester assessments. The limit in the 1295 schedules was 7s., and people who were thus included had such moveables as Walterus Ferthing, 1 cow, 5s., and 1 young ox, 2s.; Walterus ate Noke, 1 cow, 5s., and 1 qr. oats, 2s.; Johannes Bungheye, tannery stuff, 7s.; Willelmus Molendarius, wheat, oats, and a pig, 7s. 4d. The limit of exemption varied, but in the fourteenth century, 10s. in counties and 6s. in towns, boroughs and ancient demesne[1] was about the average. It is easy to infer that only the very poor would escape. How long poor people continued to pay Fifteenth and Tenth is uncertain,[2] but a well-known instance of taxing them in the period prior to the sixteenth century subsidy occurred in the Poll Taxes imposed, on the plea of urgency, in 1377, 1379, and 1380.[3] The first was a simple poll tax of 1s. on every person over fourteen years, the second and third were graduated, but included a poll tax for the poor, of 4d. in 1379, and 1s. in 1380. When we turn to the Subsidy, a dividing line must be drawn about the middle of the sixteenth century. Prior to that date, persons earning wages of 20s. a year and upwards were taxed on several occasions.[4] Thus in 1523[5] any person over 16 taking daily, weekly, or yearly wages to the yearly value of 20s. or above was to pay 4d. ; and it is clear from the North Erpingham records,[6] that this provision was carried out, and that it affected large numbers of labourers, whose wages were probably then well over

---

[1] The limits in 1322 (see Dowell, i. 262) and 1332 (*Parl. Rolls*, ii.).
[2] See 1463 grant (*Parl. Rolls*, v. 497) attempting to enforce a new limit of exemption at 10s. yearly value of lands and £3, 6s. 8d. of goods.
[3] Dowell, i. 102 *seq.*   [4] See note 5, p. 18.
[5] 14 & 15 H. VIII. c. 16.
[6] Walter Rye, *op. cit.*, see *e.g.* Beeston Parish, pp. 435–6.

that amount.[1] In 1544 the limit of exemption was raised to 40s. in yearly service,[2] which would still include many labourers. But from 1552–53 wages were explicitly exempted from subsidy.[3] Thereafter it may be said that the poor were exempted, for in addition to wage-earners, persons having land or offices up to 20s. yearly value, moveables up to £3, or church livings up to £6, 13s. 4d. a year, were specially exempted by the Acts,[4] and it is probable that the limit of exemption was much higher in practice. Apart from occasional underhand attempts to include the poor,[5] the subsidy became a tax on the middle sort and the gentry.[6]

Over a course of centuries, therefore, there was no uniform tradition regarding the taxation of the poor man ; but for the century immediately preceding the Long Parliament, the tradition was exemption.[7]

[1] See Cunningham, i. 534–5 (4th edition).
[2] See note 5 above, p. 18.   [3] 7 Ed. VI., c. 12.
[4] e.g. 1570, 13 Eliz. c. 27. The figures given do not all apply from 1552, and the exemptions for the clergy are somewhat complicated (see e.g. 18 Eliz. c. 22).
[5] e.g. Acts of the Privy Council, 26th July 1598, 28. 625–7.
[6] Cf. ship-money instructions, Miss Gordon, loc. cit. p. 148.
[7] This tradition is not substantially affected by the extent to which the poor may be considered to have paid an unofficial tax involved in the salt and soap monopolies of Charles I. See W. Hyde Price, English Patents of Monopoly, pp. 112–28.

III

1640–1713—CUSTOMS AND DIRECT TAXES

THE period between the meeting of the Long Parliament and the Treaty of Utrecht is of great importance in English financial history. It marks the transition between two very different systems of finance, those of the early seventeenth and of the eighteenth centuries, and it is one of the few formative periods in English tax policy and opinion.

The financial setting of the tax problems of the time was the need for an enormously increased revenue. The resources of the first Stuarts were absurdly inadequate for the heavy and continuous demands of the Civil War and the Commonwealth ; and while financial pressure between the Restoration and the Revolution was less severe as well as less adequately met, from 1689 to 1713 the strain of the French wars led to an annual budget which would have been inconceivable in 1640. The total revenue and expenditure of Charles I. were both under one million a year.[1] The total expenditure after 1701 was never under five millions a year, and in one year (1710–11) it was fifteen millions ; while the total revenue fluctuated round five millions and a half,[2] and the accumulated debt amounted in 1713 to about thirty-five millions.[3]

The result was to break down the sectional form in

[1] Gardiner, *op. cit.* viii. 81–2, x. 222 ; Miss Gordon, *op. cit.* ; Dowell, ii. 17.
[2] *Return of Public Income and Expenditure,* 1869, i. 27–49.
[3] *Ibid.* ii. 298.

which tax questions presented themselves in the centuries preceding the Civil War. The Customs, which, although treated by the King as part of the ordinary revenue, had been considered by Parliament as set aside for the support of the Navy, lost this destination, even in theory, and the Navy came to be regarded as merely one of the objects of national expenditure. Thus, for instance, the constitutional proposals of 1653[1] provided for a constant yearly revenue to be raised by Customs and other ways and means, for the maintenance of a standing army, a navy and the ordinary administrative establish- ments; and the sum of £1,200,000 voted to Charles II. and William and Mary as ordinary annual supply was provided in the first place by the Customs revenue.[2] But even the distinction of ordinary and extraordinary revenue gradually disappeared in any but a formal sense. Extraordinary supply, as we have seen, was occasional, prior to the Civil War, and was provided by occasional direct taxes. But during the Interregnum, the direct tax became annual in face of increased annual expenditure, indirect taxes in the form of Excise duties on commodities were imposed for war-revenue, and in fact, though not in the schemes of constitution-mongers, expenditure of all kinds had to be treated as a whole, and a general revenue provided to meet it. Between 1660 and 1689, a return to the old distinction was attempted, and occasional extraordinary revenue voted for special occasions; but temporary Customs[3] and Excise[4] duties were imposed along with direct taxes to provide this revenue, and in 1685[5] Customs duties on imports of wine,

[1] Gardiner, *Constitutional Documents of the Puritan Revolution,* ' The Instrument of Government,' § 27, p. 414.

[2] Dowell, ii. 17, 29, 42–4. Attempts during Charles II.'s time to appropriate Customs revenue to the Navy had only a constitutional meaning, as a device of Parliamentary control. See Anchitell Gray, *Debates of the House of Commons,* iii. 317 (762. d. 3–12).

[3] 1668, 'An Act for raising £310,000 by an imposition on wines and other liquors,' 19 & 20 Chas. II. c. 6 ; also 22 Chas. II. c. 3 and 30 Chas. II. c. 2.

[4] 1671, 22 & 23 Chas. II. c. 5, continued by 29 Chas. II. c. 2 till 1680.   [5] 1 Jas. II. c. 3, c. 4, c. 5.

sugar, tobacco, etc., were used alone for the purpose. Under William III. the need for money was so great that every source of revenue was strained and no distinction between ordinary and extraordinary possible. The distinction came to mean nothing more than the difference between the revenue sufficient for one year and the increase required in the next, for which taxes had then to be found. But not only did direct taxes thus cease to be treated as simply occasional taxes for emergencies[1]; indirect taxes came to be regularly used to obtain the annual increase of revenue. What was required, after the adoption of Montague's scheme for borrowing for the annual deficit, was only the interest of the new loan, but it had to be provided by taxes imposed for a long period so as to give proper security to the lenders.[2] Now when this system came into operation, the direct tax was already at the highest rate considered feasible,[3] and produced a large revenue; the tradition that direct taxes should not be perpetual, both on financial and constitutional grounds, would have prevented an attempt to mortgage it to secure loans; and, on the other hand, duties on particular commodities or objects of expenditure were financially well-suited for this purpose.

In this way financial need and the adoption of the funding system broke down the old distinction of ordinary and extraordinary revenue and the treatment of direct taxes as occasional levies. But the same causes had another important result in regard to the future. They stereotyped the tax system, in some of its main features, for the ensuing century.[4] A great mass

---

[1] They did not completely lose this character. They were reduced at the close of one war and increased again at the beginning of the next. But in the eighteenth century the real objection to the Land Tax was not that it should be reserved for war, but that it was in itself an inequitable tax.

[2] Lodge, *History of England*, 1660–1702, p. 381; Cunningham (1903), ii. 419 *seq.*; and see *e.g.* 4 Will. and Mary, c. 3, and 8 & 9 Will. c. 20.   [3] Nominally at 4s. per £ of income.

[4] The stereotyped condition of the Land Tax during the eighteenth century was due to other causes, discussed below.

of indirect taxes which by 1713 were mortgaged for the interest of the debt could not be repealed when peace was concluded; and the remaining taxes, including the direct tax, were required to defray the annual expenditure of the State other than the debt charge.

But within the changing form of the financial system developments of much greater moment were taking place in the taxes which had to be imposed to meet the need for increased revenue. These developments are sometimes regarded as summed up in the adoption of Excise duties on necessaries. That was without doubt their most important aspect, but they were in reality much wider in scope, and it is impossible to understand the state of opinion on tax questions in this period without discussing them more generally. It will be convenient to trace first the changes in policy and opinion regarding the taxes which were taken over from the preceding period, and then to deal with the new Excise duties.[1]

The first of these changes was the gradual disappearance of the old attitude towards Customs duties, which regarded them as a special charge on merchandise for the protection of trade. The unreality of this theory now became as apparent to Parliament as it had long been to the Crown. Customs revenue, as we have noticed, was treated simply as part of the general revenue of the State, and the protection of trade was a subsidiary service required of the Navy compared with its employment in the Dutch and French wars which stretched across the period. The change in attitude was both illustrated and furthered by alterations in the duties. On the one hand, additional duties on imports were imposed, avowedly for general revenue, and as taxes on the consumer; such were those of the Interregnum

---

[1] Revenue obtained from more or less compulsory loans and from special levies on Royalists during the Interregnum is of no importance from the point of view of taxation, and will not be dealt with.

known as the Foreign Excise,[1] the impositions on wine under Charles II., the special Customs of 1685,[2] and the numerous additions made during the French wars.[3]   On the other hand, under the influence of Mercantile ideas, duties on exports were gradually reduced and repealed [4]—a result quite inconsistent with levying a charge on merchandise for its own protection.

The traditional theory, however, did not disappear at once, and traces are to be found all through this period.   The statutes of 1660 and 1689,[5] continuing and amending the ordinary duties, both set out the old formula of guarding the seas against the disturbance of trade and the invasion of the realm.   Harrington, in constructing his ideal commonwealth, without any discussion reserved the Customs revenue for the support of the Navy [6]; and Thomas Sheridan,[7] who wrote a short treatise on the origin of law and institutions, deduced Customs duties from the need for the protection of trade by sea.   But these were survivals of a past state of opinion, as Petty's discussion of the question in 1662 indicates.   One paragraph of his *Treatise of Taxes and Contributions* [8] is indexed thus : ' A conjecture that Customs at first were a kind of premium of insurance against pirates.'   But the ' natural reasons '

[1] See ordinances of 22nd July 1643, 8th September 1643 and 17th March 1654, Firth and Rait, i. 202, 274, ii. 845.   The technical difference between Foreign Excise and Customs duties was that the former was ordered to be levied on the first buyer from the importer. In practice, however, this was usually ignored, see *Trades Destruction* . . . 1659, E. 984 (6), p. 6.   [2] See notes 3 and 5 of p. 24.
[3] *e.g.* 6 & 7 Will. III. c. 7.   [4] See note 3 of p. 35.
[5] 12 Chas. II. c. 4 ; 2 Will. and Mary, c. 4.   In 1689 the needs of the French war and the reduction of Ireland are added to the guarding of the sea as reasons for the grant.
[6] Harrington, *The Commonwealth of Oceana*, 1656 (ed. 1887, Hy. Morley, p. 277).
[7] Thomas Sheridan, *A Discourse on the Rise and Power of Parliaments, of Laws* . . . 1677, reprinted by Saxe Bannister in *Some Revelations in Irish History*, 1870, p. 14.
[8] In *Economic Writings*, ed. C. H. Hull, i. 54.   Petty even suggested that, as a reform, Customs should be reduced into the nature of an insurance-premium, p. 57.

why Customs duties should be paid did not seem to him obvious, and he did not suggest that those of his own time could properly be regarded as a charge for the protection of trade.

Customs duties thus came gradually to be looked upon as ordinary taxes levied upon the consumers of imported commodities.[1] And parallel with this development there grew up a view of the nature and effect of Customs duties regarded simply as taxes on the subject. They were looked upon as taxes on people's consumption of luxuries or superfluities, and justified on this ground as both expedient and equitable. Prior to the Civil War, taxes had been levied according to some standard of means—the possession of income or property; but a new standard of taxation now appeared—that of expenditure or consumption—and was embodied in the new conception of Customs duties, as well as in the Excise. Excise duties, moreover, were levied on English commodities, and for the most part on necessaries; whereas Customs fell gradually more and more on foreign imports, and for the most part on luxuries. Customs, in consequence, came not only to be approved as taxes on consumption, but came to be considered the ideal form of taxation. This result, however, was only fully reached in the eighteenth century, and it is the process of change which is typical of the present period.

The new tax view of the Customs was clearly expressed at first only in connection with special duties on particular imports. The Foreign Excise or New Impost[2] of the Long Parliament fell at first on such commodities as wine, tobacco, spices and silks, and when extended to imports in general, corn and victual were exempted. Pym, it is reported, attempted to placate the opposition which was aroused by his suggestion of a general Excise,

---

[1] The process of change which led to this view of the Customs may be said to have been formally completed by Walpole's repeal in 1721 of practically all the remaining duties on exports except those on raw materials, 8 Geo. I. c. 15.

[2] See note 1, p. 27.

by proposing that it should be confined to superfluous commodities imported into the kingdom.[1] The Foreign Excise was justified as an equitable tax which would compel Royalists and neutrals to contribute their proportionable share to the cost of the war,[2] and later it shared in the general approval of the Excise as the most easy and equal levy.[3] Two pamphlets of the Restoration time show the grounds on which it was defended. The equitableness of the levy, according to one,[4] consisted in its being laid chiefly on foreign commodities of vast and profuse expense, such as wine, silks and tobacco; it had also the great incidental virtue of allowing the subject to make his contribution gradually and insensibly at his own occasions. According to another,[5] it fell on all sorts and ranks of people, it was forced upon no man, " but every one is voluntary in it," it was paid insensibly by the ultimate taxpayer, and it fell in no wise on commodities of absolute necessity. There can be no doubt, although records are scanty,[6] that the special impositions of the succeeding forty years were defended on the same grounds. The doctrine that taxes should fall on superfluities rather than necessaries was widely accepted. In the Parliament of 1668,[7] for instance, Sir John Cotton was for raising the supply

[1] D'Ewes' Diary, 28th March 1643, in *Harleian MSS.* 164. f. 346. b.
[2] See preamble of ordinances, *e.g.* 22nd July 1643.
[3] *e.g.* ordinances of 28th August 1647 and 28th February 1655, Firth and Rait, i. 1004, ii. 1035.
[4] *Considerations touching the Excise of native and foreign commodities* . . . (undated c. 1661), 712. m. 1 (3), p. 2.
[5] *The Foreign Excise considered* . . . by W. S., 1663, 518. h. 1 (7), p. 5 *seq.*
[6] About the most interesting of the impositions, those of 1685, I can find only Roger North's brief record of the policy of his brother Dudley who carried them through. He considered that tobacco and sugar could bear small additions which would yield the required sum and 'would scarce be any burden sensible to the people.' *Lives of the Norths* (Bohn, ii. 210). The MS. records for 1685 deal with the short and fruitless second session in November, and only show a continued approval of Customs duties as the best means of raising extraordinary supply. *Harleian MSS.* 6801 (37), 7187 and 1236.
[7] J. Milward's Diary, 27th February 1668 (*Add. MSS.* 33413, f. 63).

by laying duties on the luxuries of eating and drinking, on wine and excess of apparel ; in 1674, Carew Reynall[1] defined the best taxes as those which fell on the vices of the people, including their consumption of foreign needless commodities ; and in 1694 the House of Commons agreed to a proposal to impose a wine duty rather than a suggested leather tax, on the principle, which it had embodied in a resolution, that it is better to impose taxes which fall on superfluities rather than necessaries, and on the rich rather than the common people.[2]

Special impositions for revenue could not, however, be isolated from the mass of Customs duties. The Foreign Excise became simply another set of general import duties,[3] and after 1689 the general duties were increased several times. Consequently we find the doctrines just noticed beginning to be applied to the whole of the Customs revenue. An able anonymous pamphlet of 1690,[4] dealing with the question how best to raise the necessary supply, argued in favour of Customs duties and against Excise. It was a general rule ' that taxes ought first rather to be laid upon luxury than necessity ; and, secondly, rather on things of foreign than domestic growth.' ' And since it is the happiness of this island that all those wares which are imported from abroad conduce only for our ease, not our support ; and all our domestic commodities are necessary to our being or well-being ; it follows that the two rules laid down before do in this nation fall into one, and carry only a double reason with them for one and the same action.'

---

[1] *The True English Interest* . . . 1674, 291. d. 42, pp. 10, 69. Cf. *Taxes no Charge* . . . 1690, in *Harleian Miscellany*, viii. 519–20.

[2] Bonnet Reports, 23rd February, 16th and 20th March, in Ranke, *History of England* (Engl. tr., vi. 243, 245). The proposal was not carried out, but the debate is none the less significant of the principles which were in conflict.

[3] *e.g.* Act of 26th June 1657, Firth and Rait, ii. 1186 *seq.*

[4] *A Letter from N. J. to E. T., Esq., his representative in Parliament*, 1690, pp. 3–4 (Lincoln's Inn Library, Brydall Collection, 33, f. 407).

But, while Customs duties came to be justified as taxes on men's consumption of superfluities, it is easy to exaggerate the extent to which this amounted to a distributive justification. In the first place, two entirely non-distributive ideas were involved—the gradual and insensible payment which is a feature of most taxes on commodities, and the avoidance of disturbance and repression of home industry, secured by placing the duties on imported goods. In the second place, one of the doctrines of seventeenth-century trade policy was the mischief of importing commodities merely for consumption, and the principle that taxes should be on superfluities no doubt gained much of its support on this ground. Similarly it found favour with advocates of a sumptuary policy.[1] In the third place, regarded simply as a doctrine of tax distribution, it included two ideas which, although widely accepted, were not very frequently insisted on, in reference to Customs, in this period. The first was the doctrine, taken over from old Customs policy, that the necessaries of the poor man should be exempted from taxation ; the second was the theory that a tax on articles of consumption (here superfluities) makes men pay roughly in proportion to their ability, since they are their own assessors, and the richer they are, the more they consume and therefore pay. The significance of these theories will be discussed in connection with the Excise. Here it is sufficient to notice that the elimination of the question of taxing the poor man tended to keep distributive questions relatively in the background, so far as Customs duties were concerned.[2] This effect was reinforced by the absence of a traditional distributive attitude towards them, and by the degree of attention which was given to their manipulation for purposes of trade policy.

[1] *e.g.* Petty, *Treatise of Taxes and Contributions* (Hull, i. 55, 6), Reynall and 1690 *Taxes no Charge*.
[2] The way in which distributive issues were sometimes ignored in connection with Customs is very striking. Petty's discussion in his *Treatise* (chap. vi.) is a good case.

The result of these developments in opinion was to mark out Customs duties as the first resort of Parliaments hard pressed for additional revenue. So much was this the case that at last only the grossest smuggling [1] set limits to their increase. The total Customs revenue increased from under £400,000 a year in the time of Charles I.[2] to about a million and a half in 1713.[3] The increase in rates was even greater. Portuguese wine, for instance, paid a duty of £4, 10s. per tun in 1642, if imported into London by an English merchant; in 1713 it paid £28, 10s., and the rise probably implied a real *ad valorem* increase from roughly 15 per cent. to roughly 45 per cent. on the price to the consumer of large quantities.[4] The duties on French wine were still higher. The duty on Colonial tobacco increased from 1d. per lb. in 1660 to 6d. per lb. in 1713, at which date the *ad valorem* rate amounted, on retail prices, to about 25 per cent.[5] What the general *ad valorem* rate on imports amounted to at the Peace of Utrecht could only be discovered by an exhaustive and very difficult inquiry, but the formal rate [6] for a great mass of

---

[1] Dowell, ii. 97; Atton and Holland, *The King's Customs*, pp. 144, 148, 171, 172, 179 *seq.*; *Journals of the House of Commons*, xvii. 368, Report of a discussion between a Committee and the Tobacco merchants in 1713 Smuggling in the eighteenth century is sometimes regarded as a result of Mercantile policy. But it is clear that in the case of great staples of the smuggling trade like wine, tea and tobacco, the excessive rates of duty which made smuggling profitable were motived as much by the purpose of obtaining revenue as by that of trade policy. See Report of 1733 in *Reports of Committees of the House of Commons*, i. 610, etc., and Acts of 1745 and 1784 reducing the duties on tea, 18 Geo. II. c. 26, and 24 Geo. III. c. 38.

[2] Gardiner, *op. cit.*, x. 222.

[3] *Return of Public Income and Expenditure*, 1869, i. 46-8.

[4] Thorold Rogers, *History of Agriculture and Prices*, v. 448-9, notes purchases of sack in 1624 at £7 and in 1631 at £8 per hogshead (¼ tun), and of red and white Lisbon in 1704 at £16 and £18 per hogshead (vii. 353), which are confirmed by Hervey's purchase in 1711 and 1714 of red port at £16 and £16, 5s., *Diary of John Hervey, First Earl of Bristol*, pp. 172-3.

[5] Thorold Rogers, vi. 447-8, vii. 372 *seq.*, retail price c. 1s. 6d. to 2s. per lb. of Virginia.

[6] No general revision of the 1660 Book of Rates took place during this period, in spite of much discussion. See *Treasury Papers*

goods had risen to 15 per cent., against 5 per cent. in 1660.[1]

During this period a development of another kind was also taking place in the Customs. We have seen that trade policy, as well as revenue, was a purpose of the duties in force prior to 1640. That purpose now became steadily more important, and had a considerable influence in moulding the kind and extent of the eighteenth-century duties.

The connection between trade policy and Customs duties at the beginning of this period is clearly set out

(Record Office), xx. 31 and xxvi. 20, Reports of the Commissioners of Customs of 22nd November 1692 and 26th January 1693¾, and a Representation to the King by the Commissioners of Trade of 20th November 1697 (copy in *Harleian MSS.*, 1324, f. 37 *seq.*). The Book of Rates defines the prices to be assumed for different imports (apart from a small number charged with specific duties), and the duty in 1660 was 5 per cent. on these values (12 Chas. II. c. 4). In 1697 an additional 5 per cent. was added (8 & 9 Will. III. c. 24) and another in 1703 and 1704 (2 & 3 Anne, c. 18, and 3 & 4 Anne, c. 3), and by various Acts these additions were continued indefinitely. Further, a very large number of imports paid further duties under 4 Will. and Mary, c. 5, and continuing Acts.

[1] It may be useful to add a note of some sources for this question. The actual duties can, of course, be discovered by a very laborious search through the Statutes, and no other plan is available, so far as I know, for those of any year between 1642 and 1714. Before that, the duties can be discovered comparatively easily from the Books of Rates of 1604, 1610, 1635 and 1642 (Goldsmith's Library). A compendium of the duties was issued in 1714 by Wm. Edgar, Inspector-General of the Ports in Scotland (*Vectigalium Systema*, 1129. f. 1 MS. copy, *Harleian MSS.*, 4309), and simplifies the question for the subsequent period. It was re-issued in 1718 and in 1724. Later handbooks of the same kind are those of Henry Saxby, *The British Customs . . . digested*, 1757 (517. e. 5), and Samuel Baldwin, *A Survey of the British Customs*, 1770 (514. k. 18). For yields of duties, see *Add. MSS.*, 36,785 (note Davenant's caution) and the Inspector-General's accounts of exports and imports, after the Revolution (Record Office). For the prices of imported commodities, see Thorold Rogers, *History of Agriculture and Prices* ; Jas. O. Halliwell, *Some account of a collection . . . illustrating the history of prices . . .* 1650–1750 (in Guildhall Library) ; Ordinances of the Interregnum and John Hervey's *Diary* (1689–1740), for wine prices ; Broad Sheets of 25th March 1674 and 3rd January 1682, ' the prizes of merchandise in London ' (at end of vol. cxii. of Burney collection of newspapers) for a large number of imported goods ; John Houghton, *A Collection for the Improvement of Husbandry and Trade*, 1692–1702 (a few im-

in a pamphlet by Giles Greene, Chairman of the Long Parliament's Committee on the Navy and Customs.[1] Greene's object was to vindicate the work of the Committee, and to explain *inter alia* the principles which had guided it in framing the new Book of Rates of 1642 'in relation to the support of the trade of the kingdom on the one side, and the revenue of the kingdom for the support of the Navy . . . on the other side.'   Exports of domestic commodities were divided into those totally to be prohibited, those of woollen manufacture which were eased on account of the danger of competition, and other staple commodities, such as tin and lead, not so subject, which were raised.   Imports were divided into necessaries including victual and raw materials, which were eased, and superfluities which might be spared and were incentives to prodigality, which had their full load, unless, being bulky, they were advantageous in the employment of shipping and mariners.   The influence of trade policy upon the Customs in 1642 was thus comparatively mild.[2]   But it gradually became more dominant through the stricter application of the same ideas.   John Cary[3] was typical of opinion at the end of the seventeenth century in recommending, as means to improve our manufactures, the repeal of all Customs on manufactured exports and on imports of raw material, the better enforcement of the prohibition of wool exportation, and the discouragement of importation of manufactured commodities.   Indeed, so far as opinion went, trade policy became for many people the chief

ports), and *The Weekly Packet*, 1712–14 (Goldsmith's Library). Mr. W. R. Scott informs me that the Court Books of the East India Company give full particulars of wholesale prices.   It is to be wished that a series of periodical broadsheets of prices could be discovered for the seventeenth century.

[1] Giles Greene, *Declaration in Vindication of . . . Parliament . . .* 1647, E 405 (8) pp. 3–5.

[2] This was typical also in the realm of opinion, see Petty, *Treatise*, in Hull, i. 54–6.

[3] John Cary (Bristol merchant), *An Essay on the state of England in relation to its Trade, its Poor and its Taxes . . .*, 1695, 1029, a. 5 (1), pp. 23–5, 37.

consideration.   A letter [1] of 1702, for instance, recommended a review of the Book of Rates, 'respect being
had not so much what commodities will raise the greatest
revenue to the Crown, as what is the true interest of
the nation.'

The most striking effect of the influence of trade
policy was the gradual reduction and abolition of export
duties on manufactured goods, the relation of which to
the changing view of Customs duties has been already
noticed.   The motive of the process was, of course, the
promotion of home industry and the maintenance of a
favourable balance of trade.[2]   In 1656 it was applied
to agricultural products such as grains, meat and butter,
and to candles, beer, lead, etc.   Portions of this policy
were adopted between the Restoration and the Revolution.   Thereafter we come upon cases of total repeal of
export duties—in 1691 those on beef, pork, butter,
cheese and candles (for the encouragement of the
breeding and feeding of cattle), in 1699 those on woollen
manufactures and on corn, bread, meal, etc., and in
1709 those on coal exported in British ships.   Finally in
1721 Walpole made a wholesale repeal of the remaining
duties on exports other than raw material.[3]   The result
of this process, from the point of view of the purposes
of Customs duties, was, by abolishing so many duties,
pro tanto to abolish the purpose of trade policy from
the Customs ; but at the same time it involved the
sacrifice of revenue on grounds of trade policy.

Two other cases in which the interest of revenue
was entirely sacrificed to that of trade policy were the

---

[1] *A Letter written to a member of Parliament relating to Trade,*
by Mr. John Egleton, 1st January 1702 (in *Somers' Tracts,* xi. 614).
   [2] See, for instances, preambles of Acts of 1656, 1699 and 1721,
and the King's speech in 1721 (given in Coxe's *Memoirs of Walpole,*
i. 163).
   [3] Act of 1656, 27th November, in Firth and Rait, ii. 1043 *seq.* ;
1663, 15 Chas. II. c. 7 (grains) ; 1671, 22 & 23 Chas. II. c. 13 (beer) ;
1672, 25 Chas. II. c. 6 (repeal of alien duties) ; 1691, 3 Will. and Mary,
c. 8 ; 1699, 11 Will. III. c. 20 ; 1709, 8 Anne, c. 14 ; 1721, 8 Geo. I.
c. 15.

prohibition of the export of wool[1] and the prohibitions at various times of trade with France (directly or by means of prohibitory duties).[2]

But in the case of the bulk of the import duties trade policy co-operated with the need for revenue to produce that condition of high rates which has been noticed. Superfluous imports, such as tea, tobacco, and wine, although they did not directly compete with English industry, were regarded as competing indirectly, in the sense that tea, for instance, tended to displace the use of English-made beer. They diminished the proportion of expenditure on English commodities and influenced the balance of trade adversely.[3] Consequently it was considered wise policy to discourage them, and this could be done by the same means which raised revenue on superfluous consumption. This policy, on the other hand, was in some cases pushed so far that revenue was again sacrificed. Thus in 1690 an additional duty of 20 per cent. *ad val.* was placed on Indian textiles to raise revenue for the war ; further duties were imposed in 1699 ; but before they came into force an " Act for the more effectual employing the poor by encouraging the manufactures of this kingdom " was passed, prohibiting their import for English consumption, on the ground that they exhausted the treasure of the kingdom and took away the labour of the people.[4] Indian

---

[1] Ordinance of 19th January 1648 (Firth and Rait, i. 1059) ; 1660, 12 Chas. II. c. 32 ; 1662, 14 Chas. II. c. 18, etc.

[2] *e.g.* ordinance of 28th August 1649 (Firth and Rait, ii. 239), repealed 1657, ii. 1129 ; 1678, 29 & 30 Chas. II. c. 1, § 70 ; 1689, 1 Will. and Mary, c. 34 ; 1696, 7 & 8 Will. III. c. 20 (additional £25 per tun on French wine, etc.), and see L'Hermitage's ' Secret Despatches to the Hague ' (transcripts, *Add. MSS.* 17,677, A–YY), February 1696, vol. QQ. p. 251.

[3] See *e.g.* Samuel Fortrey, *England's Interest and Improvement*, 1663, T. 1816 (1), pp. 28–9 ; *The Grand Concern of England explained*, 1673 (*Harl. Miscl.* viii. 559) ; Preamble of 1 Will. and Mary, c. 34, prohibiting trade with France ; Report of the Commissioners of Trade and Plantations to the House of Commons in 1700, regarding the woollen industry (copy in *Sloane MSS.* 2902) ; *General Maxims of Trade*, 1713, T. 807 (2).

[4] 2 Will. and Mary, sess. 2, c. 4 ; 11 Will. III. c. 3 and c. 10.

textiles competed directly with the English silk and
cotton manufactures and indirectly with linen and
woollen goods. Similarly French brandy,[1] when not
prohibited, was subjected, in the interest of the home
manufacture, to prohibitive duties which made the
commodity one of the staples of the smuggling trade.[2]

Customs duties in the eighteenth century thus
became taxes almost entirely on imported commodities,
levied at high rates, regarded for the most part as
falling on superfluities, and imposed for two purposes,
both of which were important, revenue and trade
policy. This result, of course, was not attained without
opposition. The increasing rates were condemned
throughout the period as restricting the merchant's
trade, locking up his capital merely in taxes, imposing
'impossible oaths,' leading to frauds and smuggling,
decreasing instead of increasing the yield, and generally
injuring the welfare of the whole nation which was
dependent chiefly on the operations of that 'best and
most profitable member of the commonwealth,' the
merchant.[3] But in spite of the considerable truth
contained in these arguments, they did not represent
the dominant ideas of the time, and had little influence
on policy. The seventeenth century was indeed very
critical of what it considered the mere interest of

[1] 7 & 8 Will. III. c. 20.
[2] This sketch is very far from a complete account, even in outline,
of the relations between revenue and trade policy in the Customs
duties.   It neglects, for instance, the whole question of colonial and
shipping policy.   What I have attempted to do is merely to show the
kind of connection which some of the important duties illustrate.
[3] *Excise anatomized and Trade epitomized* . . ., by Z. G., 1659,
E. 999 (1), and *Trades Destruction is England's Ruin, or Excise
decried* . . ., by W. C., 1659, E. 984 (6), dealing, *inter alia*, with the
Foreign Excise ; Andrew Marvell's *Correspondence* (brief reports
of Parliament to his constituents in Hull), in *Works*, ed. Grosart,
ii. 296–7 (17th December 1669) ; Anchitell Gray, *Debates*, 6th March
1668 (i. 107) ; Charles Davenant, *Essay upon Ways and Means* . . .,
1695, pp. 29, 58–60 ; Abraham Hill, *Considerations on Taxes*, 1701
(*Sloane MSS.* 2902, f. 43) ; Jo. of H. of C., 1713, xvii. 368–70, on
tobacco duties.   For the opposition to certain sides of trade policy,
see W. J. Ashley, *The Tory Origin of Free Trade Policy*, in *Surveys
Historic and Economic*.

'private merchants,'[1] and no doubt relished Petty's quiet reflection on their assertiveness, that all men pay Customs 'though merchants chiefly talk of it.'[2]

The second great branch of the tax system of this period was the development of the direct taxes which we discussed in last chapter. As we saw, these were taxes in the full sense of the word and raised the problem of distribution in the most direct form. Not only so, but they constituted the only properly tax source of revenue before 1640. It was therefore natural that in this period of great financial pressure attempts should be made once more to achieve an equitable direct tax with a yield proportionate to the real wealth of the country. The attempts failed and the Land Tax of the eighteenth century was their legacy; but from the point of view of opinion and policy on distribution they are none the less interesting on that account. What we want chiefly to do is to understand the distributive scheme which was intended to be enforced, and at the same time to note in outline the methods employed and the difficulties which they were inadequate to overcome.

The period from the fourteenth to the sixteenth century witnessed a development in the intended standard of direct taxes from that of moveable property to that of income for the majority of taxpayers and moveable property for the remainder. The most important aspect of the development of the seventeenth century was the adoption of income as the standard for all who paid direct taxes. The taxes by which it was attempted to get an

---

[1] See, e.g., Shaftesbury's statement of the reasons for setting up a Council of Trade, 1670 (in B. Martyn's *Life*, 10,816, f. 9, pp. 209–12, and quoted in Christie's *Life*, ii. app. i.).

[2] *Treatise of Taxes and Contributions*, p. 95. It is unnecessary to bring together the evidence for the acceptance of the ordinary view of the incidence of Customs duties on the consumer. Reference should be made to an able short pamphlet (undated, but prior to 1685), *The Case of His Majesty's Sugar Plantations* (in Somers' *Tracts*, viii. 480), which argues partly against the ordinary view. The question is similarly discussed in *The Groans of the Plantations*, 1689, 1391. d. 3.

equitable direct assessment on means were, in intention, income taxes.

The case of an emergency tax at the beginning of this period will show how common the idea of taxation in proportion to income had already become. In 1641 a graduated Poll Tax [1] was imposed to raise means for the speedy disbanding of the Army, and as the object was speedy assessment, men were rated at fixed sums according to their ranks, offices, and occupations—a duke, for instance, paying £100, and an esquire £10. But as some could not be taxed even approximately fairly in this way, general clauses were provided for taxing according to their incomes those not rated specifically. Thus it was provided that every person ' who can dispend one hundred pounds per annum of his or her own, either in lands, leases, money, stock, or otherwise,' should pay £5, if £50 then £2, and so on. A similar tax was imposed in 1660, providing an income tax of 2 per cent., both above and below £100, on those not rated by rank or calling.[2] No provisions were, of course, made for getting returns of income, but the clauses afford a conclusive test of what constituted the standard which assessors were to have in mind in considering a man's ability to pay.

It is the more important to notice this, because, in the attempts of the Long Parliament to reform the system of the direct tax, the actual standard of assessment was left to the local assessors to decide. In the £400,000 assessments of 1642, and the Weekly Assessment of 1643,[3] all Parliament did was to fix the sum which each district was to pay, and the limits of exemption ; it was then left to the localities ' to enquire of the substance after the the usual manner ' of every inhabitant, and thence to charge evey one his ' proportionable part and proportion ' of the assessment. No relation therefore was defined

[1] 16 Chas. I. c. 9.
[2] 12 Chas. II. c. 9, and amending Act, 12 Chas. II. c. 28.
[3] 16 Chas. I. c. 32 ; ordinance of 24th February 1643 (Firth and Rait, i. 85).

between people of landed and personal estates ; but an interesting provision enacting that the tenant of lands let at an ' easy rent ' should pay tax on the annual value of his beneficial interest, shows what the ' usual manner ' of taxation meant as regards lands.[1] The more lasting Monthly Assessment which began in 1645,[2] had the same essential features, and its elaboration only brings out more clearly the delegation to the local assessors of principles of assessment. The rating committees had power ' to assess and levy the several sums . . . upon the lands, goods, annuities, rents, offices, or other estate, real or personal, in such manner and form, and according to the most equal and usual rates for levying of money . . . or by a certain rate upon the true yearly values of lands, rents, annuities, offices and hereditaments, and according to the true value of goods, chattels, debts, or other estate real or personal . . . '

This state of affairs continued till 1649. By an Act of 7th April of that year, imposing an assessment of £90,000 per month for six months, it was ordered[3] that as regards the second half of the assessment, the fixed contribution of each county was to be raised by an equal pound rate upon all lands, goods, offices, etc., within it, ' wherein every twenty pounds in money stock or other personal estate shall bear the like charge as shall be laid upon every twenty shillings yearly rent or yearly value of land.' Men of personal property, in other words, were to be taxed on the same basis as landed men, and to secure this their annual means, which in the case of landed men were easily known from their rents, were calculated at an assumed percentage (here 5 per cent.) of the capital value of their stock. This system of assessment was adopted again in 1650 and 1652. In 1653 the whole question was considered by a Grand Committee

---

[1] *e.g.* § 13 of 16 Chas. I. c. 32.

[2] Ordinance of 21st February 1645 (Firth and Rait, i. 630). The Monthly Assessment was not levied monthly.

[3] Act of 7th April 1649, Firth and Rait, ii. 26, 54 ; 26th November 1650, *ibid.* p. 484 ; 10th December 1652, p. 681.

of the Little Parliament, which reported on 14th October [1] in favour of retaining the system of fixing the total contribution of each county, but recommended the principle of levying the fixed sums ' by a pound rate upon estates real and personal ' within the county. The resulting Act [2] permitted the local commissioners, if necessary, to adopt the ordinary way of rating for the first half of the assessment, but required that the second half should be levied by a pound rate in which, again, £20 of personalty was to be taxed equally with £1 of rent.

But even the prescription of local income taxes in this form was too much for the tax system of the time. In February 1654 an ordinance [3] was issued waiving the rating provisions of the Act as regards the second half also, ' in case the way or manner of assessing the said later three months' assessment by a pound rate in such sort as is prescribed by the said Act shall prove prejudicial and obstructive to the bringing in the said . . . assessment . . . by the time . . . limited,' and authorizing the commissioners of the different districts in such cases ' to proceed according to the most just and equal way of rates held in such places.' The Monthly Assessment continued to be levied regularly under the Commonwealth, and at intervals thereafter till 1692 ; rating was to be by a pound rate as formerly, but it was always left to the local authorities to use ' the most just and usual rates ' if they thought fit.[4]

It is clear what kind of tax Parliament desired the Monthly Assessment to be. But central control over the local taxing authorities was so weak that it had to permit concessions to practicability which left its view of equitable distribution little more than a statement of

---

[1] Jo. of H. of C. vii. 334.
[2] Act of Little Parliament, 24th November 1653, E. 1062 (32), pp. 331-2.
[3] Ord. of 17th February 165¾ (Firth and Rait, ii. 842). The marginal analysis is erroneous.
[4] *e.g.* 16 & 17 Chas. II. c. 1, § 25, and 3 Will. and Mary, c. 5, § 21.

opinion. These concessions were two. First, to secure that the State received a definite and not a steadily declining revenue, the total contribution of each district was fixed and had to be made up by the district at whatever rate of tax it found necessary. It followed, of course, that different parts of the country came to pay very different rates of tax. This was well recognized,[1] and proposals were several times made before the Revolution to impose a true national pound rate, with oaths and penalties. A debate on the subject in 1657 is fairly well reported.[2] The answer given was that the revenue under such a scheme would come to nothing; 'instead of giving my Lord Protector a substance, we shall be giving him a shadow.' Gentlemen would labour to keep it down as much as they could. The thing was impracticable. 'If you appoint strangers to survey, I doubt you will raise greater disturbance than ever was in England. If assessors are appointed to assess their neighbours, there will be great partiality.' The whole idea of strict assessment was resented by some. 'As to this plan of surveying and searching into men's estates, it is that which your ancestors would never endure. That the chief magistrates should know men's estates was always avoided.' Sir Wm. Strickland said that 'the way that is propounded looks like a Court project.' 'Our ancestors have always declined such courses.' Parliament's view of the local taxing Commissioners is also well illustrated by a dispute with the Lords[3] in 1666, over a proposal by the latter to make additions to those named by the Commons. The Lower House refused on the ground that it was always

---

[1] See next note ; also debate of 12th to 14th December 1670, in A. Gray, *Debates*, i. 321 *seq.*, sp. Sir Richard Temple and John Swynfen ; and debates of 8th November 1675, iii. 427 (Boscawen).

[2] Burton's *Diary*, ed. J. J. Rutt, 12th June 1657, ii. 229 *seq.* Note that the £ rate proposed was again to charge £20 on goods as £1 in lands (West).

[3] Cobbett's *Parliamentary History*, iv. 354-5. Cf. L'Hermitage, 11th February 1698, on the same difficulty then, Transcripts, vol. SS, p. 152b-153.

observed that ' the greater the number of commissioners, the less money hath been raised ; for many commissioners encumber one another and rather procure the ease of themselves and their many friends than the advance of the king's service and the public benefit.' The second concession, as we have seen, was the permission granted to the local authorities to settle the principles of assessment to be applied in their respective districts.

The result was that the Monthly Assessment became for the most part a stereotyped land tax, levied on an old and not the real valuation of landed estates, and omitting or grossly under-assessing men with personal property or income from offices.[1]

One attempt was made under Charles II. to break this stereotyped system. It failed completely, but it is of importance as again witnessing to opinion regarding the distribution which ought to prevail. On 15th December 1670, Marvel wrote to his constituents : ' I suppose you have heard the vote of the Committee, that the sum about and not exceeding £800,000 should be raised by way of subsidy according to the present rent, with respect also to money, goods and offices.' The statute,[2] after providing a special tax on bankers, imposed 1s. per £ on the clear yearly value of lands and tenements, 1s. per £ on mortgages and rent charges on land (to be levied at the source by allowing the landowner to deduct the tax in paying the interest, etc.), 6s. per £100 on net personal estate, including stock on the land, money and debts, and under deduction of debts due by the taxpayer—i.e. 1s. per £ on an assumed income of £6 per £100 of capital—and 2s. per £ on the income from public offices, calculated at $\frac{2}{3}$ of the gross

---

[1] See § 9 of 14 Chas. II. c. 8 (a special tax on income from offices), and 18 & 19 Chas. II. c. 1 and 29 & 30 Chas. II. c. 1, imposing special taxes on bankers, moneyed men, lawyers, men with offices, etc., besides a graduated Poll Tax ; also recital in 22 & 23 Chas. II. c. 3.

[2] 22 & 23 Chas. II. c. 3 ; according to Dr. Shaw's table in Introduction to *Calendar of Treasury Books*, 1669–72, i. x, the yield was £59,000 in 1670–1, and £152,000 in 1671.

receipt. Bankers and men in offices paid a heavier rate, no doubt to make up for ordinary under-assessment.[1]

But after the Revolution the stereotyped Monthly Assessment was finally superseded by a new direct tax, the General Aid of the time of William III. This tax, in its essential features, was a revival of the subsidy of 1670–1. It gave up the system of fixing the contribution of each district, and imposed a pound rate over England, at first of 1s., and in 1692 of 4s. per £ of income.[2] To take the 1s. rate of 1689. All persons with property in goods, merchandise, money, debts, etc.,[3] were to pay 1s. per £ 'according to the true yearly profit thereof,' that is to say, the clause continues, 'for every hundred pounds worth of such goods . . . the sum of six shillings and so after that rate. . . .' The yearly profit was thus assumed again to be 6 per cent. of the value of the property, which was to be the net capital, debts owing being deducted. Next, persons in offices, other than naval and military, were to pay 1s. per £ of their salaries or profits.[4] Thirdly, 1s. per £ was to be levied on the true yearly value of all lands, tenements, tithes, mines, etc., 'without any respect had to present rents' or former rates and taxes. Lastly, in order to tax the landowner on his real net income, and to bring in the moneyed man, rent charges and interest on mortgages on land were to be taxed at 1s. per £ by deduction at the source.

As things went in the seventeenth century, the Aids were comparatively successful in yield. A 1s. Aid raised nearly half a million,[5] and there is no doubt that

---

[1] A debate on the subject is reported on 15th December in Gray, i. 324–6, but it is not full enough to show clearly what chiefly influenced the decision.

[2] *e.g.*, 1689, 1 Will. and Mary, c. 20; 1692, 4 Will. and Mary, c. 1.

[3] Including stock upon lands and household stuff.

[4] So called Poll Taxes of 1689 and 1690, also taxed professional men, such as judges, advocates and doctors, on their annual gains : and servants (1689) at 1s. per £ on their wages if over £3 a year, and 6d. per £ if under. 1 Will. and Mary, c. 13, and 2 Will. and Mary, c. 2.

[5] Cobbett's *Parliamentary History*, v., app. xix.

in very many cases it was strictly assessed. But from the beginning the old difficulties of assessment were involved, with the result that personal property was much under-assessed, and lands paid very different rates in different districts.[1] Supplemental taxes,[2] which went by the inaccurate name of Poll Taxes, were granted almost yearly. The yield also began to decline. A 4s. aid produced £1,922,712 in 1693, and £1,736,248 in 1696. In the winter of that year an elaborate attempt was made to reach men's real ability more fully by a tax which was a combination of the Aids and the supplemental Poll Taxes.[3] The rate on land and mortgages was reduced from 4s. to 3s. in the £. Regularly employed servants, State pensioners, public officers and lawyers were taxed at various rates per £ on their wages, pensions, salaries, fees and profits. Moneyed men, wholesale and retail traders, and farmers and graziers, were taxed, under this classification, at various rates per £100 of their money or debts, wares or stock, and great or small cattle on the land. And, lastly, a simple Poll Tax was imposed. But the yield did not improve, and in 1698 the system of a national pound rate was abandoned. The quota of each district was fixed on the basis, L'Hermitage reports,[4] of the returns of 1692; personal estate was to pay 3s. per £ of the true yearly value calculated at 6 per cent. of the capital value, and public officers 3s. per £ on their salaries or profits; and the

---

[1] *e.g. Autobiography of Sir John Bramston* (Camden Socy.), pp. 372–3; Oldmixon's *History of England*, p. 11; *A Proposal for an Equal Land Tax*, 1691 (*Harl. Miscel.* ii. 506 *seq.*); Davenant, *Essay upon Ways and Means*, 1695, pp. 103–4, 111; L'Hermitage, 18th December 1694, 15th December 1696, and 11th February 1698 (Transcripts, vols. PP, p. 99, QQ, pp. 639–40, and SS, pp. 152–3); [Defoe] *An Essay upon Projects*, 1697 (1029. b. 24), preface vii–xi.

[2] ' I propose a Poll Bill because of the great inequality of the tax when it falls wholly upon the landed man,' Sir Ed. Seymour, 11th January 1692, in Gray, *Debates*, x. p. 227; also *Proposal* of 1691, pp. 511–2.

[3] 8 & 9 Will. III. c. 6. See L'Hermitage's reports of debates, 15th December and 26th January.

[4] Transcripts, vol. SS, p. 752. b.

balance of the sum fixed for each district was to be
raised by a pound rate on lands, tenements, tithes,
mines, mortgages, etc., within it. This was the form
of the famous Land Tax Act which remained substantially
unchanged for the next century. It marks the final
surrender of the seventeenth century attempt at an
equitably distributed direct tax, and merely secured to
the State so much revenue—about half a million for
every nominal shilling of tax. All the defects of the
aids were stereotyped in its allocation among the different districts, and personal property more and more
escaped altogether. It became for the most part a mere
tax on land rent.[1]

The substance of the story was briefly summed up
by Abraham Hill, one of the Commissioners of Trade
and Plantations, in a letter[2] of 1701, entitled ' Considerations on Taxes.' The Government, he held,
should depend chiefly on Land Tax and Excise, but the
former ' should be a tax on every one in proportion to
his revenue,'[3] whereas in fact, ' besides the inequality
as it lies on some counties and afterward on some
hundreds, the profit arising from personal estates and
professions is rated so little that in London the landlords
of houses pay about seven times as much as the tenants,
though the latter acquire much the greater gains.'

The essential difference between the direct taxes of
this period and the Income Tax of the nineteenth
century is not one of intention but of execution. The

[1] Dowell, ii. 53 ; Bourdin, *Exposition of the Land Tax*, 3rd ed.,
by Shirley Bunbury, 1885, p. 10. A judgment of Lord Loughborough on a Land Tax case is quoted in note K. ' This Tax,
although commonly called a Land Tax, is not in its nature a charge
upon land. It is a charge upon the faculties of men, estimated
first according to their personal estate, secondly by the offices they
hold, and lastly by the land in their occupation. The land is but
the measure by which the faculties of the persons taxed are estimated.'

[2] Hill's papers, *Sloane MSS.* 2902, f. 43–4.

[3] Hill's attempt to explain the reason why revenue should be
the standard of taxation was ' because the richer receives most
benefit by protection from the government.'

former failed, while the latter succeeded, in devising tolerably efficient methods of enforcing the provisions of the Acts ; and a very careful study of this aspect of the question will be found in Professor Seligman's history of the Income Tax.[1] But Professor Seligman also regards the taxes of the two periods as essentially different in intention. The later he calls an income tax ; the earlier, property taxes, or produce and property taxes, meaning thereby, I take it, taxes on property and on income from property.[2] I would suggest that this exaggerates a real but relatively minor difference, and gives a misleading idea of the relationship.

The above account does not leave it in question that the intention of the seventeenth century Acts was a tax on income ; the only question open is what sort of income. Was it only property incomes which were intended to be taxed ? It is clear that it was not. Income from offices, the earned though tithe-found income of clergy, and the endowed incomes of teachers and the like were taxed regularly, and the earnings of doctors, advocates, etc., and the wages of servants at intervals. Nevertheless it is true that the income subject to direct taxation in the seventeenth century was more predominantly property income than it was in the nineteenth century. The income of the landed gentry was, of course, taxed similarly in both periods ; but while, in the nineteenth century, the incomes of working landowners (yeomen, etc.), merchants, manufacturers and retailers were taxed according to direct returns and as a whole, in the seventeenth these classes were to pay only on the rental value of their holdings,[3]

---

[1] *The Income Tax*, 1911, pp. 80–2, and part i. book i. *passim*.

[2] See note 44 of Chap. II. An interesting criticism on lines similar to those developed here appeared in an anonymous review of *The Income Tax*, in *The Spectator* of 16th September 1911, p. 421.

[3] Working landowners were to pay on both the annual rental value of their land, and on their stock in the Monthly Assessment and the special subsidy of 1670–1 (and according to a Colchester paper which I happen to have noticed—*Stowe MSS.* 325, p. 142 *seq.*, sp. St. Martin's parish—they did pay on both in 1644); but in the

or on a percentage on their capital which was taken at
the rate of interest on loans. It was thus not their
total income, but that portion of it which might be
supposed to constitute their property income which
the Acts in effect ordered to be taxed. It does not
follow that this was clearly understood and intended
by Parliament;[1] it is not improbable, for instance,
that 6 per cent. was taken as a rough and perhaps
minimum estimate, necessarily inaccurate in a multitude
of cases, of the true yearly profit which a merchant
earned with his stock. The use of an assumed rate is,
of course, of no significance in itself; the same device
was repeated in the nineteenth century tax in estimating
the profits of the farmer at a proportion of the rent
he paid. So far as intention was concerned, therefore,
we may properly say that Pitt in 1799 applied the
standard of income more strictly than was the case in
the seventeenth century enactments;[2] but it is
equally correct and important to say that taxation
according to income was a seventeenth century
conception.

The result of the development of the direct tax
during the seventeenth century was to fix in opinion
the doctrine of income as the standard of equitable
distribution. But this doctrine was accepted in a
general form only, and many of the finer problems within
the principle of income taxation were ignored. Should
the earned income pay at the same rate as the income
of the landed gentleman, and the small income at the
same rate as the large? Attention was too fully
engrossed with the difficulty of getting in practice
any approach to equitable distribution to be able to

Aids, stock upon land was not to be taxed. This, no doubt, had the
further result of exempting tenant farmers; but they were taxed
in the special Act of 1696-7, 8 & 9 Will. III. c. 6.

[1] I am unaware of any direct evidence.

[2] It must not be forgotten that in economic development and
differentiation, England advanced enormously between 1689 and
1799.

spare such questions serious consideration. Evasion was such a danger that even the proposal to exempt the rental value of empty houses was frowned upon.[1] Simple proportionality to income [2] was consequently the vague tradition which, in an undiscussed way, the seventeenth century imposed on subsequent opinion. On the other hand, an important theoretical qualification of this principle was very generally admitted. This was the repudiation of a rigid standard like income as the complete test of a man's ability to pay taxation. It was contended now,[3] as in the sixteenth century, that allowances should be made for expenses of family and port; and it is probable that in the actual assessment of taxes such considerations were taken into account,[4] although to what extent it is impossible to say.

Finally, to what extent did the direct taxes of this period carry on the Elizabethan and Stuart tradition of exempting the poor man from taxation? In effect they departed from it, and returned for half a century to the practice of the first half of the sixteenth century; for while the regular direct taxes exempted

[1] Bonnet reports (in Ranke), 12th and 19th January 1694, p. 232. To prevent former abuses, the Commissioners were to be put on oath to make no allowances on any consideration whatever. A discussion of the rate as between offices and lands in the special subsidy of 1670–1 is reported in Gray, *Debates*, i. 326 (15th December 1670).

[2] Exceptions to this rule were very rare in the Statutes. Poll Taxes sometimes included an income clause graduated up to a low figure of income ; see 16 Chas. I. 9, § 4 ; 1 Will. and Mary, c. 13, and 8 & 9 Will. III. c. 6.

[3] A member argued on 10th March 1668 that the Monthly Assessment should be made like the subsidy, which was on ' the sparable part of a man's estate, debts and charge of children considered ' (Waller, in Gray, *Debates*, i. 109). On 21st January 1671, Sir Thomas Meres moved for a deduction of one-third part for men's expenses, hospitality and debts, in levying the special subsidy (i. 362). See also Marquis of Halifax, *An Essay upon Taxes . . .*, 1693 (in *Somers' Tracts*, xi. 79–80).

[4] Halifax, and Fabian Philipps, *Restauranda*, 1662, E. 1957 (8), p. 4. Cf. Gray, *Debates*, i. 359–60 (Swynfen, 20th January, 1761).

him,[1] the poor man was taxed by occasional Poll Taxes, which, between the Revolution and the settlement of the Land Tax, became fairly frequent. There was a Poll Tax of 6d. per head in 1641, 1s. in 1660, 1666, 1678, 1689 and 1690, and 4s. in 1691, 1694, 1697 (4s. 4d.) and 1698 ; in addition servants paid 1s. per £ on their wages in 1666 and 1678, 1s. per £ in 1689 if over £3, and 6d. per £ if under, and at rates varying from 1s. 1d. to 4s. 4d. per £ in 1697 on wages of over £4 a year.[2] The Poll Taxes exempted paupers and the children of the labouring poor.[3] In the eighteenth century, the direct taxation of the poor was discontinued.[4]

But the direct taxes were the less important form of the taxation of the poor in this period, and the discussion of the question which took place had reference almost entirely to the more important form. For opinion, therefore, we must wait on the history of the Excise.

[1] This is to some extent a deduction. The £400,000 assessment exempted servants under £10 a year wages, land up to £1 a year, and personalty up to £3, and the Weekly Assessment exempted all servants ; but the Monthly Assessment made no provisions about exemptions, doubtless leaving this with other questions of rating to the usual custom of the district. The poor were therefore exempted in all probability. The special subsidy of 1670–1, and the Aids exempted lands up to £1 a year, and no doubt wages, by lack of mention of them ; while the exemption of household stuff under personalty would free the poor from assessment in that direction. It should be noticed that Customs officers with salaries up to £60 a year, and Excise officers up to £100 a year, were exempted from the Aids, on the ground of poverty, by having their tax paid as a departmental charge ; e.g. *Treasury Papers*, vii. 74 (1690), x. 39, and xiii. 60 (1691); and iv. 10 (1689), xiv. 34 (1691), and xxxvii. 44 (1696). The practice was continued in the eighteenth century as regards Land Tax, *e.g.* xciv. 87 (1705).

[2] 16 Chas. I. c. 9 ; 12 Chas. II. c. 9 ; 18 & 19 Chas. II. c. 1 ; 29 & 30 Chas. II. c. 1 ; 1 Will. and Mary, c. 13 ; 2 Will. and Mary, c. 2 ; 3 Will. and Mary, c. 6 ; 5 & 6 Will. and Mary, c. 14 ; 8 & 9 Will. III. c. 6 ; 9 Will. III. c. 38.

[3] The exemption for children is complicated in form, but it comes roughly to this ; see, *e.g.*, 1 Will. and Mary, c. 13, § 4.

[4] I do not include house taxes and the like in the term direct tax.

IV

1640–1713—EXCISE

In the seventeenth century, discussion of the theory of taxation centred chiefly round the question of Excise duties. This was a natural result of the financial tradition of the time. Excise not only raised very fundamental problems, but its way of dealing with them constituted an innovation on the opinion and practice of centuries. Customs duties and direct taxes, although undergoing important changes during this period, were yet gradual developments of long established policy. But the Excise was a new departure of the most striking kind. Properly speaking, it had no antecedents in England. Excise duties had, of course, been long known from the practice of continental States, but they were regarded with great antipathy as foreign oppressions, from which we were happily free.[1] It was only extreme financial pressure which induced Parliament

[1] Dowell, ii. 8–9 ; Parl. Rolls, iii. 89–90, Suggestions by the Lords for taxes in 1380 ; Fortescue, *Governance of England*, ed. Plummer, pp. 132–3 ; Bodin (Eng. tr., 1606, p. 669 ; 1593, French ed. p. 887) ; 1627–8, Gardiner, vi. 222, 225, 227 ; *Hargrave MSS.* 321, pp. 300–1 ; and Cobbett's *Parliamentary History*, ii. 416. It is true that under certain industrial patents of monopoly, Charles I. obtained a revenue which was in effect an Excise revenue (W. Hyde Price, *The English Patents of Monopoly*, p. 42) ; but to regard these as means by which ' the people became accustomed to Excise taxation ' (pp. 131–2) seems to me to misunderstand the situation. In 1628, Parliament denounced the Commission, which it suspected was set up to discuss Excise duties ; in October 1642 it described the rumour that such duties were under consideration as false and scandalous (*A Declaration of the Commons* . . ., 8th October 1642, E. 121 (27), and see E. 699 (17), *The Judicial Arraignment* . . ., 1653, and E. 813 (16), Prynne, *A Declaration and Protestation*, p. 8 *seq.*) ; and the history to which we proceed shows how little the way was prepared

to adopt and develop this third means of providing for increasing expenditure; and opposition to it was just as determined in the time of William III. as during the Civil War. Nevertheless, from the first, reasons were not lacking to prove that Excise duties were equitable, as well as easy and productive taxes; and the joint influence of favourable opinion and the need for money gradually made them one of the chief portions of the English tax system. Before we attempt to analyse opinion on the subject, let us sketch in outline the more obvious aspects of this process as they appear in the rather meagre Parliamentary records.

On 28th March 1643, about a month after the first ordinance for a general Weekly Assessment had been passed, Pym proposed 'another way for the speedie raising of money,' by laying an Excise on commodities bought and sold.[1] Two years earlier, as D'Ewes says, such a motion would have been thought 'to have tended no less than to the ruin of the kingdom,' and it met with strong opposition. Pym then 'thought to have amended the matter somewhat by saying that he only intended to have this Excise laid upon superfluous commodities that were imported into the kingdom'; but the 'unjust, scandalous and destructive' proposal was apparently rejected. Nevertheless, the project was ultimately accepted, and on 22nd July an ordinance[2] was issued, laying a tax on beer, ale, cider and perry, in addition to duties on imports. The money was stated to be raised for the better securing of trade, the maintenance of the forces, and the payment of the debts of the Commonwealth; and it was explained that, since the malignants had evaded the levies already imposed, the Lords and Commons held it fit to establish a constant and equal way for the levying of moneys, 'whereby the

---

for Excise. Any connection between the monopolies and the Excise could, indeed, only have prejudiced opinion still more against the latter.

[1] D'Ewes' Diary, *Harleian MSS.* 164, f. 346 b., and Gardiner.
[2] Ordinance of 22nd July 1643 (Firth and Rait, i. 202).

said malignants and neutrals may be brought to and compelled to pay their proportionable parts of the aforesaid charge, and that the levies . . . may be borne with as much indifference to the subject in general as may be.' An amended ordinance was issued on 8th September,[1] which added soap, cloth and spirits. The duties on beer were 2s. per barrel of strong beer (over 8s., later 6s., a barrel in price), and 6d. per barrel of small beer (under 8s.), and were payable by the brewer, but were to be allowed him in the price.[2]

On 9th January 1644 the Excise was extended to flesh and salt,[3] butchers' meat to pay 1s. per £ (on the value of the animal alive), and salt ½d. per gallon, payable by the maker. The money was for the Navy, and the way of raising it described as ' equal and indifferent,' and ' most easy to the well-affected subjects of this kingdom.' We learn from news letters that a proposal to include a duty on oatmeal was dropped, and that a tax on poultry was restricted to rabbits and pigeons.[4] In July of the same year further articles were brought in, including hats, starch and copper,[5] and in November 1645 a large number of additional duties was imposed.[6]

We know almost nothing of the early reception of the Excise by the public, but it is clear that by 1647 feeling was strongly roused against it. On 15th February a riot at Smithfield resulted from a refusal to pay duty upon the purchase of an ox,[7] and on 22nd February, Parliament issued a Declaration concerning the Excise,[8] taking notice of the tumults in different parts of the kingdom

[1] Firth and Rait, i. 274.

[2] Cf. Ordinances of 17th March 1654, and Act of 26th June 1657, Firth and Rait, ii. 846, 1189. By an order of the General Quarter Sessions of the City of London in 1655, the price of beer was fixed at 10s., 8s., 6s., and 4s. per barrel for the four grades, from the best to the smallest, 669, f. 19 (76).

[3] Firth and Rait, i. 364. Salt used in the fishing trades was to be exempt; cp. Act of 1657, ii. 1196.

[4] *The Perfect Diurnal*, E. 252 (14), see 1st and 10th January, p. 198.

[5] Ordinance of 8th July 1644, Firth and Rait, i. 466.

[6] Ordinance of 24th November 1645, *ibid.* i. 806.

[7] Gardiner, iii. 216.   [8] Firth and Rait, i. 916 *seq.*

against its collection, and setting forth the grounds of
their policy and their intentions as regards the future.
Nothing, it was declared, could have drawn the Lords
and Commons to resolve upon this imposition but the
preservation of religion, law and liberty from utter ruin
and destruction ; it was the only means available to
draw in the malignants and neutrals to bear their proportionable parts of the charge ; its continuance was
required to pay debt and permit the settlement of the
kingdom ; but when these objects were by God's mercy
accomplished, they would then make it appear how much
more ready they were to ease the people of this charge
than they had been willing at first to impose it. In
the meantime, in order to remedy grievances, they
prohibited a system, which seems to have grown up, of
compelling people to pay an assessment of the nature
of a poll tax for their home-brewed beer, and ordered
that poor people in receipt of alms should not be charged
for beer brewed and used in their own houses.

Discontent continued, however, and on 11th June
it was ordered that the Excise of flesh and salt should
cease within a fortnight.[1]   " A good piece of news,"
was the brief comment of a news letter.[2]   But this did
not bring satisfaction. The Army, in the Heads of
Proposals of 1st August,[3] demanded that the Excise
should be taken off ' from such commodities whereon
the poor people of the land do ordinarily live,' and that
a certain time should be fixed within which it should
cease on other commodities also. Three weeks later,
Parliament replied with a second Declaration,[4] calling
to witness the repeal of the duties on flesh and salt as a
proof of their readiness to ease the people as far as
circumstances would allow, referring to the continued
opposition, and asserting that the Excise was ' the most

---

[1] *Ibid.* iii. lii., and *Ordinances of Excise*, 506, c. 17 (1), p. 79.
[2] *The Perfect Weekly Account*, E. 392 (28), see 12th June.
[3] Gardiner, *Constitutional Documents*, p. 324.
[4] Ordinances of 28th August 1647, Firth and Rait, i. 1044.

easy and equal way' of raising money, both in relation to the people and to the public, and that they were resolved 'through all opposition whatever' to insist upon its due collection until it should be possible to do without it.

It is clear from an ordinance of July 1648 that obstruction continued,[1] but it must have been gradually worn down by the determination of Parliament. In December 1649 the Excise on salt was re-established [2] and a long-continued [3] but unsuccessful [4] attempt was made to devise a practicable system of levying the most vexatious duty on home-brewed beer. No objection was made in the Constitutional proposals of 1653 and 1657 to the Excise, which was impliedly treated as a source of ordinary revenue,[5] and in the ordinances [6] it was regularly described as 'the most easy and indifferent levy that can be laid upon the people.'

The Commonwealth thus depended on an annual revenue from Excise duties, levied chiefly on beer brewed for sale, but also at low rates on other necessaries like salt and soap, as well as on luxuries such as spirits, and industrial commodities like iron and lead.

Unfortunately we have no helpful records of the debates [7] on the Restoration tax settlement.[8] The

---

[1] 11th July 1648, *ibid.* i. 1168.

[2] Ordinance of 21st Deeember 1649, *Ordinances of Excise*, pp. 133, 139–40. Note that the suspending ordinance of 26th January 1650 (p. 144) did not apply to salt.

[3] On this subject, see ordinances of 8th September 1643, 22nd February 1647, 14th August 1649 (§ 38), 28th March 1650 (and rules of 30th April 1650), Frith and Raith ii. 227, 368 , and for rules, *Ordinances*, p. 149.

[4] 12th December 1651, see 506, c. 17 (1), p. 173 beyond paging.

[5] Gardiner, *Constitutional Documents*, pp. 414, 453.

[6] *e.g.* 26th June 1657.

[7] See Cobbett's *Parliamentary History*, iv. 118 *seq.*, and Marvell's *Correspondence* (ed. Grosart) for November to December 1660, p. 37, etc. A MS. paper, *Some Considerations about an Excise*, written by an M.P. since the Revolution (*Harleian*, 1243, f. 166 *seq.*), asserts that the Excise was continued in 1660 through the machinations of the Court and against the opinion of the wise men of the Parliament. The paper is probably a draft of part of John Hampden's *Considerations* of 1692 (*State Tracts*, 1705–6, ii. 314–5), *q.v.* The assertion stands alone, so far as I know.

[8] Dowell, ii. 17–29, gives a very good account.

result,[1] however, was that the chief source of Excise
revenue, the duty on beer, was continued at the same
rates as before,[2] and the other duties, except that on
spirits, abolished. A new duty, called the Hearth Tax,[3]
was added in 1662, by which the occupier of every
dwelling-house was charged 2s. per hearth per annum.
Exemptions were provided which probably amounted
to the exemption of a large proportion of the labouring
poor.[4] The duties on beer and hearths thus constituted
a portion of the regular revenue of the second Stuarts.
An additional temporary duty on beer was also levied,
for extraordinary revenue, between 1671 and 1680.[5]
In a debate on the subject in 1677, Williamson, Danby's
Secretary of State, said that 'when all things shall be
considered, there is nothing more easy for the people

[1] 12 Chas. II. c. 23 and 24. Tea, coffee, etc., were also included.
Strange as it may seem, they paid on the beverage by the gallon,
not on the dry commodity; see 22 & 23 Chas. II. c. 5, and 1 Will. and
Mary, sess. 2, c. 6, by which Act of 1689 they were transferred to
the Customs.

[2] One-half of the Excise was technically granted in lieu of the
Crown's rights to the revenue of the Court of Wards, to purveyance,
etc. (12 Chas. II. c. 24), and much misdirected indignation has been
expressed against the landed classes for the exchange (*e.g.* H. O.
Meredith, *Economic History*, p. 217, and Hammond, *The Village
Labourer*, p. 22). In reality the abolition of the feudal incidents and
the imposition of excises are two separate questions. As regards
the first, which really took place during the Interregnum, Dowell's
statement of the case seems to me difficult to controvert (ii. 20–23);
the second is part of the general question of the distribution of
taxation in this period, and it is impossible to discuss it by itself.
It should be remembered, too, that the question at issue was only
one of £100,000 a year.

[3] 14 Chas. II. c. 10, 15 Chas. II. c. 13, and 16 Chas. II. c. 3. The
Hearth Tax, as Petty properly treated it (*Treatise*, p. 94), was in its
nature an Excise duty on an object of expenditure or consumption,
although it differed from the usual Excise duties in being levied on
the ultimate tax-payer and in a lump sum.

[4] The Act of 1662 provided for the exemption (1) of those who
were exempted, by reason of poverty or smallness of estate, from
Church and poor rates, and (2) of those occupying houses and land
not over 20s. a year in value, provided they did not possess lands
or goods worth £10. The Act of 1664 provided that only people with
fewer than three hearths should be exempted.

[5] 22 & 23 Chas. II. c. 5, and 29 Chas. II. c. 2. The other usual
liquors were also included.

than this of excise, though it is not without its troubles ';
but interest centred round its effect on land and on the
brewing trade.[1]

With the Revolution, acute financial pressure returned, and the Excise was rapidly increased and extended. By the end of our period the beer duty had
been increased from 2s. 6d. and 6d. per barrel (strong
and small beer) to 5s. and 1s. 4d.,[2] and beer was taxed
in addition through malt and hops; while new duties
were in force on salt, candles, leather, soap and coal, on
windows, paper, spirits, etc.[3]—all granted for long
periods as security for the interest of the debt.

During a part of this time we can follow the course
of Parliamentary debates in a general way from the
reports of Bonnet and L'Hermitage to the Court of
Brandenburg and the States General of the Netherlands
respectively.[4] Both reporters, however, had a marked
bias, and it is necessary to keep it in mind in reading
their accounts. They were the agents of governments
whose interest lay in having William well supplied with
funds for the war against France, and they were inclined
to consider proposed taxes simply from the standpoint
of productivity and financial convenience.[5] Their

---

[1] Gray, *Debates*, 12th March 1677, iv. 225 *seq.*, and cf. MS
report, fuller in some ways, in *Add. MSS.* 28,091, p. 41 *seq.*

[2] The Acts are complicated. I take it that the additions in
force in 1713 were 4 Will. and Mary, c. 3, 9d. and 3d.; 5 Will. and
Mary, c. 7, 9d. and 3d. (contd. by 4 & 5 Anne, c. 18); 5 & 6 Will. and
Mary, c. 20, 9d. and 3d.; 8 Anne, c. 12, 3d. and 1d During 1691
the rates were higher, and they fluctuated considerably during
William's time.

[3] See Dowell, ii. 84.

[4] The Gray *Debates* are of little value after the Revolution.
The Bonnet reports I have used are the excerpts given by Ranke in
his *History* (Engl. tr. vi. 144, *seq.*), which extend from 1690 to 1695,
and the much less interesting later reports by Bonnet and his brother
of which transcripts are in *Add. MSS.* 30,000 A–E (1696 onwards,
practically valueless after 1698). The L'Hermitage Secret Despatches are valuable from 1694 to 1698; transcripts are in *Add.
MSS.* 17,677, vols. OO–SS.

[5] On 7th December 1694 Bonnet reports a grant of five millions
for supply for the war, and adds that nothing of much interest
need be expected during the remainder of the session, 'important

familiarity with continental excises no doubt also made them unsympathetic to opposition to Excise duties in England.[1]

Curiously enough, the period opens with the repeal of a duty, the Hearth Tax of 1662, on the direct intercession of the new King.[2] Parliament decided that the popular grievances against it could not be removed by regulation, and gave it up as 'in itself not only a great oppression to the poorer sort, but a badge of slavery upon the whole people, exposing every man's house to be entered into and searched at pleasure by persons unknown to him.' But at the same time the other Excise duties in force were continued and temporary increases in rate voted.[3] In the winter of 1690, many suggestions were put forward for new taxes, including duties on windows and an excise on victuals; but the House rejected a tax on corn and some other commodities, and decided on another addition to the beer tax.[4] In 1691–92 the same conditions were repeated. Bonnet reports on 13th November : 'Nothing would be more productive or less oppressive to the people than a duty on the consumption of victuals and especially of meat, and yet nothing is so much opposed by the majority of members, who fear either that if once established they would not have the power to repeal it when they desired to do

peu de quelle manière on lévera cette somme pourveu qu'on la fournisse effectivement,' pp. 253–4.

[1] To understand these reports, it is also necessary to bear in mind that Parliament was still without ministerial or Cabinet direction in regard to proposals for taxes. Substantially the King's ministers did no more than get Parliament to grant sums of money desired ; they had little influence on the taxes by which these sums would be raised, although their influence was increasing in this period. The result was extraordinary vacillation and delay. The system probably also gave undue weight to individual and temporary feelings and interests. See Gray, *Debates* of Charles II.'s time ; W. A. Shaw, Introduction to *Calendar of Treasury Books*, 1667–8, p. xxxix; Bonnet, pp. 149, 150, 153, etc. ; *S. P. Dom.*, 16th August 1692, Memorandum by Lord Rochester (*Calendar*, pp. 410–1).

[2] 1 Will. and Mary, c. 10.

[3] For the Acts here and below, see Dowell.

[4] Bonnet, pp. 149, 151, 153 ; 2 Will. and Mary, c. 10.

so, or that it would cause disturbances in places, as has happened before.' Members would even prefer to reimpose the Hearth Tax.[1] The beer Excise was alone increased. Next year, duties were again suggested on hearths, salt and candles, but without result ; ' as for a general excise on victuals, the majority will not hear of it.' [2]

The critical struggle took place in the winter of 1693–94.[3] As security for a loan, a salt tax was resolved upon in December, in spite of the protests of those who said, *inter alia*, that the liberty of the nation was destroyed if the House would permit a tax on food. Similar opposition was made to resolutions for leather and soap taxes, and the final decision was delayed. At last a day in March was fixed when all members were ordered to attend so as the more solemnly to repre-sent the nation, and resolve finally whether new Excise duties were to be adopted. On the one side, Sir Edward Seymour, a Tory member of the Council, made as moving (*pathétique*) an appeal as he could against their adoption ; and, on the other, Sir John Lowther, who had been head of the Treasury in 1690, maintained the view that no more efficacious means of raising money was available. But, although the Court was for excises, the question dragged on. Salt tax was accepted, but when the leather and soap proposals came up the opposition was united and prepared with equivalents first a chimney tax and a poll tax, which were rejected, and then an additional duty on wine, which was accepted by the House, the principle having been previously adopted that superfluities should be taxed rather than necessaries and commodities which affected the rich rather than the people. Soap and leather were finally rejected, partly on the ground of injury to the woollen industry and to cattle rearing. The proposed equivalent

<hr/>

[1] Bonnet, pp. 165–6.   [2] *Ibid*. p. 194.
[3] *Ibid*. pp. 227–8, 240, 243, 245, 247, 248, and L'Hermitage, vol. OO, pp. 180–1, 194b–195, 200, 210, 213, 214, 216.

was also changed, but necessaries were avoided. The result, therefore, was a duty on salt of 1½d. per gallon, together with duties on legal deeds, hackney coaches and ships. L'Hermitage considered that the real motive of the opposition to excises was disaffection and dislike of the war, and that its strength lay in the prejudice that they would be injurious to liberty—an obviously one-sided explanation.

Next year the struggle over the leather tax was renewed.[1] It was adopted by a majority of five votes, shortly afterwards rejected, then again adopted and again rejected. The Court was for it, but did not think it worth while to waste the time necessary to force it through. In its place a glass duty and a tax on births, deaths and marriages were granted. Bonnet remarks that the hatred of excises is made very obvious by the resort to such an extraordinary means of supply.

So the fight went on,[2] some duties being dropped as unsuccessful, some continued and increased, and others added. In 1696 a window tax was imposed; malt, leather and paper duties were in force for a few years from 1697; in 1698 the coal tax was revived and the salt duty increased; in 1701 the malt tax was revived, and between 1710 and 1712 candles, leather, paper, hops and soap became permanent sources of Excise revenue.

Opinion regarding Excise duties may be divided into

---

[1] Bonnet, pp. 265, 268, 272, and L'Hermitage, vol. PP, pp. 116b, 118, 123, 154, 166, 169, 186.

[2] The records are still interesting for sessions 1695–6, 1696–7 and 1697–8, but they do not add much that is new. The opposition to Excises still continued to be vigorous. In the last-mentioned session a proposal to revive the coal duty was carried. It was objected that it involved administrative difficulties, that it was oppressive to the poor, who paid as much as the rich and in whose interest it had lately been abolished, and that it injured manufactures using coal. It was answered that all taxes are onerous, financial needs required the new duty, and manufactures would not suffer since the price of coal had fallen since the war. Bonnet Transcripts, vol. B, pp. 90, 110, and L'Hermitage, vol. SS, pp. 218–9 and 246.

two classes, according as it referred to their administrative features or their distributive effect. It is with the second class that we are chiefly concerned, but opinion on administrative questions had an equal influence in determining policy. With this caution, we may summarise it briefly.

The outstanding administrative advantage of Excise duties, in the view of the seventeenth century, was that they were 'easy' levies.[1] Like Customs duties, they were directly imposed only on a comparatively small number of producers or traders, they took the form of any other expense of production, and were paid by the real taxpayers, the great multitude of consumers, gradually and insensibly, as part of the price of commodities. When once set going, therefore, they avoided the widespread disturbance and vexation which a direct tax always involves. Even a nation 'so zealous of liberty' as the Dutch adopted them. They respected English ideas of freedom from interference. The flesh Excise and the hearth tax failed in this respect, and we have consequently the Smithfield Riot, followed by the abolition of the former, in 1647, and the repeal of the latter as a 'badge of slavery' in 1689.

The second advantage was that Excise duties were comparatively 'sure' levies. Because they were collected from a small number of individuals, they could be efficiently supervised, provided the rates were not excessive, and the yield, instead of declining like that of the Subsidy and the Aids, would probably increase with time. The advantage became important from a new point of view in William's reign, when a regular system of funding began. Excise duties formed good security for the interest of loans.[2] Hence the approval of Bonnet and L'Hermitage.

---

[1] The history just outlined supplies examples. See also *The Standard of Equality* . . . 1647, par. 11 (in *Harleian Miscl.* ix. p. 115); Harrington, *Oceana*, 1656 (Morley's ed. p. 273); *Letter from a gentleman* . . . *touching* . . . *Petty's* . . . *Verbum Sapienti*, 1691, 518. h. 1 (18), p. 14.   [2] Bonnet, p. 268; L'Hermitage, vol. PP, p. 116b.

Opponents of Excise duties, on the other hand, denounced them as dangerous to constitutional liberty, an invasion of personal liberty, and injurious to trade and industry. Just because they were paid so insensibly, they easily became perpetual, and so, it was feared, the control of Parliament over taxation, and hence its power as a whole, would be destroyed.[1] And even if arbitrary government did not come to its own again in this way, the same result might be achieved through the influence of Excise officers, under the control of the Crown, on elections.[2] But this constitutional objection, though still capable of rousing strong feeling, was essentially the relic of a past political problem, and towards the close of this period tended to appear merely factious.[3] The search and general control exercised by Excise officers, sometimes no doubt oppressively, was also resented as an invasion of the liberty of manufacturers and traders.[4] Finally, numerous industrial objections were urged. It was sometimes contended even that the duties were really borne by the producers [5] (or in the case of beer and malt, by the land), and more generally that they restricted industry and employment, involved disturbance and vexation, and affected home instead of foreign commodities.[6] When not exaggerated, these

[1] 12th March 1677, Gray, *Debates*, iv. 227–8 (Garroway), and *Add. MS.* 28,091, p. 41 (Sir Thomas Meres); 2nd March 1694, L'Hermitage, vol. OO, p. 194b–195; Halifax, *An Essay upon Taxes*, 1693 (*Somers' Tracts*, xi. 77).

[2] See recital in 3 Will. and Mary, c. 1, § 11 (1691), and cf. *Letter* of 1691, pp. 14–5.

[3] The Malt Tax in Anne's reign was granted yearly, along with the Land Tax, as a sign of Parliamentary control of finance.

[4] *Second Remonstrance of James Ibeson* . . . 1652, E. 678 (9); Wm. Prynne, *Declaration and Protestation* . . . 1654, E. 813 (16); *Excise anatomised* . . . 1659, E. 999 (1), §§ 2, 5 8; *A Letter from N. J.* . . . 1690 (Lincoln's Inn Library, Brydall Coll. 33, f. 407), p. 3; John Hampden, *Some Considerations about the most proper way of raising money in the present Conjuncture* (*State Tracts*, 1705–6, ii. 309 *seq.*); John Cary, *An Essay on the State of England*, 1695, p. 170 *seq.*

[5] Debates of 12th March 1677, and pamphlets of Hampden, 1692, p. 317, and Halifax, 1693, p. 76.

[6] *Reasons against the Excise of native commodities other than Ale and Beer*, 1660 (*Add. MSS.* 33,051, f. 188, § 3); Petition of Brewers, 1660

objections were of the kind apt to be considered by practical financiers as unfortunate but far from intolerable incidents of this species of taxation.

Excise duties gained support on distributive grounds from the development of favourable opinion on two connected but more general questions. The first was the question of the standard of distribution; the second, the question of the taxation of the poor.

Customs duties, when they came to be looked upon as ordinary national taxes, and Excise duties which were considered in this light from the beginning, were alike in this, that they made men pay taxation not according to an estimate of their income or means, but according to their expenditure on certain commodities. What a man ' *can* dispend ' was the intended standard of the direct taxes; what a man does spend was the standard of commodity taxation. Now in support of Excise duties it was commonly contended in this period that expenditure is an equitable standard of the distribution of taxation, and indeed that it is strictly more equitable than that of means or income. The argument, in effect, was that a man's total expenditure is a good test of his ability; taxation distributed on this basis would make him share equitably in national charges according to his proportion. The idea is put forward by Hobbes (1651), Petty (1662), Thomas Sheridan (1677), and Abraham Hill (1701).[1] It tended to be mixed up with the erroneous theory, which was never accepted in an effective or influential way by

(*S. P. Dom.* Ch. II. vol. i. 146); Gray, *Debates*, i. 272 (Meres, 1670); L'Hermitage, vol. OO, p. 210, and Bonnet, p. 243 (Soap and Leather, 1694); 1690, *Letter*, p. 3. The industrial objection to Excises, based on the theory that they are shifted by the poor consumers in higher wages, was only developing towards the end of this period and was not yet influential, so far as I can judge. See note 1, p. 80.

[1] Hobbes, *Leviathan*, 1651, ed. Waller, p. 251; Petty, *Treatise of Taxes and Contributions*, 1662 (ed. Hull, p. 91); Thomas Sheridan, *A Discourse on the rise and power of Parliaments . . . taxes, trade . . .* 1677, reprinted by Saxe Bannister, pp. 172, 174; Abraham Hill *Considerations on Taxes*, 1701 (in *Sloane MSS.* 2902, f. 43–4).

any one, that people ought to pay in proportion to the
benefit they derive from the State[1]; but in reality it
remained an interpretation of the undefined idea that
people should pay according to their ability. It was
an interpretation, it must be noted, substantially the
same as that of means or income, for in a general way
the amount men spend varies with the amount of their
incomes; and the easy acceptance of the idea of taxation according to expenditure was due, without doubt,
to its close relation to the traditional standard of income.

In some cases, of course, the two standards differ
considerably; some men spend only a small part of their
incomes. It was from such cases that our theorists
attempted to prove the superiority of the standard of
expenditure. Petty put the case thus : ‘ It is generally

---

[1] Insistence, in connection with tax-theory, on the benefit which
the individual derives from the State was a feature of the view of
the State as simply a means of protecting people's rights. Its
real result was to support the theory, discussed below, that everyone should pay taxation. The further attempted deduction that
people should pay taxation *according to the amount of protection
they receive* was impossible to work with, because the protection,
much more the general services, of the State do not come to individuals
in definable or divisible proportions at all. Attempts in the seventeenth and eighteenth century to proceed from such a theory to an
actual standard of distribution break down regularly ; and in the
result the standard adopted is based on ideas of ability, whether
avowed or not, and not on benefit. Hobbes, for instance, in trying
to define how much benefit men get by the sovereign power, says
that ‘ the benefit that each one receiveth thereby is the enjoyment
of life, which is equally dear to poor and rich ’ ; but then, instead
of saying that all men should therefore pay the same amount of
taxation, he attempts inconsistently and unsuccessfully to introduce
qualifications which will lead to the conclusion which he really
wanted to establish, viz. that men should pay in proportion to
their expenditure. Petty says that men should pay according to the
interest they have in the public peace, and merely asserts that that
is according to their riches and estates. Walpole in 1732 (Cobbett's
Parliamentary History, viii. pp. 943–4) set out with the principle
that everyone should contribute his share in proportion to the
benefit he receives, but he justified his actual proposals on the
ground of taxation according to circumstances and condition in life.
Adam Smith's standard is ability ; he only attempts indecisively and
certainly unsatisfactorily to deduce taxation according to revenue
from a conception of society as made up of independent individuals
receiving protection from the State. See below.

allowed by all that men should contribute to the public charge but according to the share and interest they have in the public peace; that is, according to their estates or riches; now there are two sorts of riches, one actual and the other potential. A man is actually and truly rich according to what he eateth, drinketh, weareth, or any other way really and actually enjoyeth; others are but potentially or imaginatively rich, who, though they have power over much, make little use of it; these being rather stewards and exchangers for the other sort, than owners for themselves.' Hence he concluded 'every man ought to contribute according to what he taketh to himself and actually enjoyeth.' So Sheridan approved of taxation on general expenditure, since 'no man pays but according to his enjoyment or actual riches, of which none can be said to have more than what he spends.' But it was just in this contention that these theorists failed to carry general opinion with them. It was a standing objection to the system of assessing men according to their apparent means, as judged from their way of living, that the miser, or the man who lived below his rank or means, thus evaded his fair share of taxation;[1] and in the eighteenth century, when taxes on consumption were predominant, it was often allowed, as an unfortunate but unavoidable qualification of their equitable character, that the miser or the parsimonious rich man who lived in a small way paid less than his just proportion.[2] Taxation according

---

[1] e.g. Gibbon, The Order of Equality, 1604, 8226. a. 14, p. 24 ; Halifax, An Essay upon Taxes, 1693 (Somers' Tracts, xi. 74–5).

[2] e.g. Francis Hutcheson, A System of Moral Philosophy, 1755, ii. 342 ; Fauquier, An Essay on ways and means . . . 1756, T. 1627 (3), p. 39; Adam Smith, Wealth of Nations, Everyman ed., ii. 376–7. Cf. Letter of 1691, p. 14—'Excise, you know, hath obtained a current repute of perfect equality : Now though I by no means admit of that ; not only niggards but all those whose condition obliges them not to live honourably upon their demesnes, at pleasure avoiding it ; yet I must allow, 't is, singly considered, perhaps the most equal and innocent of any particular way of taxing commonly proposed or discoursed of ; excepting imposts on some foreign hurtful superfluities for the due regulating of trade.'

to expenditure was, in fact, simply another roughly satisfactory expression of taxation according to income.

The second and more important general characteristic of the Excise duties of this period was that they made the poor man regularly pay taxation. As contrasted with traditional tax policy, this was perhaps their chief distinguishing feature; and it was supported by the most influential intellectual opinion of the time. The argument, in brief, was that it is an obligation on every citizen, rich and poor, to pay taxation. Impositions, said Hobbes,[1] are but the wages of them that hold the public sword to defend private men in the exercise of several trades and callings, and the poor man benefits thereby, and owes a debt for the benefit just as much as the rich man. *All* men, Petty held, should pay taxation, according to their interest in the public peace; and he had no sympathy with what he believed to be one of the causes of the ill-management of taxation in his time [2]— ' a fallacious tenderness towards the poor (who now pay scarce 1s. per head per annum towards all manner of charges) interwoven with the cruelty of not providing them work. . . . ' ' All subjects,' said Sheridan,[3] ' as well the meanest as the greatest, are alike concerned in the common safety, and therefore should, according to their respective interests of riches or enjoyments, bear the charge in equal proportions.' Petty and Sheridan not only approved of taxing the poor man, but, as we shall see below, were careful to define precisely how he was and was not to be made to pay his equitable share. But the idea found its most complete expression and justification in Locke's political theory, from which it was a direct deduction, that ' everyone who enjoys his share of the protection should pay out of his estate his proportion for the maintenance of it.' [4] By the end of the

---

[1] *Leviathan, loc. cit.*

[2] *Verbum Sapienti* (written *c.* 1665), in Works, ed. Hull, i. 114, and see p. 112.   [3] *Discourse*, p. 146.

[4] *Two Treatises of Civil Government*, ed. Hy. Morley, p. 266, *et passim.*

seventeenth century this may be said to have become a
commonplace. Even those who objected to the taxation of the poor were unable directly to controvert it ;
and an opponent of the Excise was familiar enough
with the argument to describe excise,[1] in the words
of its supporters, as a tax 'which makes the burden as
extensive and universal as the benefit that arises
from it.'

The acceptance in the sevententh century of the
doctrine that the poor man should pay taxation is one
of the landmarks in English political opinion, and we
shall make an attempt below to understand its significance more fully. Meantime, we have to notice that
this doctrine was an essential element in the distributive
approval of Excise duties in this period.

But it did not necessarily follow that particular Excise
duties were equitable, because it was considered just to
impose taxation in proportion to expenditure, and to
make the poor man contribute. Excise duties fell not on
a man's total expenditure, but on his expenditure on the
particular commodities subject to duty ; and the poor
man was not only taxed by them, but taxed in a certain
proportion, relatively to other men, which might or
might not be equitable. What, then, was considered
to be the distributive justification of the actual Excise
duties in force ?

The justification was that a duty on a particular
object of expenditure, like taxation in proportion to
general expenditure, taxed different people, in a rough
but tolerably accurate way, according to their ability.
It made every one pay his proportionable share, measured
by the extent of his consumption. This was the meaning of the declarations during the Interregnum that the
Excise was the 'most equal' way of raising money.
Every one, including Royalists, paid their fair share of

[1] *Letter* of 1690, p. 2 ; cf. *A Proposal for an equal Land Tax*,
1691 (*Harl. Miscl.* ii. 511–2).

the charge.[1]   At the Restoration it was argued, in connection with a proposal to exchange the beer excise for
a malt tax, that the tax would thus be made more equal,
for while all users of publicly-brewed beer were equally
charged by the existing duties, home-brewing escaped.[2]
In the time of William III., as a result, no doubt, of the
Parliamentary controversy, a more precise statement
of the contention appears in the pamphlet literature.[3]
In 1695, various tax proposals, including one for an
excise on flesh and hides, were put forward in a pamphlet
entitled *A Book of Funds* by Thomas Houghton [4]; he
contended that ' in these duties every person will be
taxed, and pay more or less according to the quantity
he or she useth ; if poor, they use little and therefore
pay the less ; if rich, they pay the more in proportion
to what their expense and consumptions are ; so that
nothing can be more equally laid and charged upon the
people than the taxes aforesaid.'[5] Davenant's *Essay*
of the same year was also in favour of Excises for the
war ; usurers, lawyers, tradesmen and retailers, who
usually paid very little taxation, would so be brought
' to bear their proportions of the common burden,' and
' the disproportion between what the rich and what
the poor consume would make this fall easily upon the
poor and not very heavily upon the richer sort.' A
proposal next year for a malt tax [6] was similarly defended ; it would ' affect every person though not

---

[1] *e.g.* Ordinances of 22nd July 1643, 22nd February 1647, and
28th February 1655.

[2] *The Representation of Francis Rockley, Esq.* (*Somers' Tracts*,
vii. 508).

[3] Vaguer statements of the equitableness of Excise duties appear,
e.g. in *Letter* of 1691, p. 14.

[4] 1138. *a.* 10 (p. 13, and see p. 20); cf. Broadsheet project (? 1696)
for Excise on butchers' meat and skins—' It will be most equal, for
tradesmen and foreigners will pay as much as gentlemen, proportionable to what they spend,' 816. m. 6 (47–8).

[5] *Essay on ways and means of supplying the war,* 1695, 1028. h. 1
(1), pp. 120, 122, 123.

[6] A. Burnaby, *An Essay upon the excising of malt* . . . 1696.
T. 1814 (4), pp. 11, 22–3.

with the like sum but proportioned to every person's circumstances.' 'Men of great estates and figure are for the most part attended with a family and a numerous train of all kinds of servants proportionable; men of less figure with less, and so of the meanest person.' Therefore, the writer held, every man would stand on an equal foot with his neighbour, and he that consumed little would have little to pay. A pamphleteer of 1713, suggesting a duty on various kinds of cloth,[1] even went so far as to show in detail that all would pay according to their ability; a gentleman of £1000 a year, with his family and establishment, would, he calculated, pay £9, 11s. per annum; while a poor man, with his wife and four small children, would only pay 3s. or less.

This view of the distributive effect of Excise duties on articles of ordinary consumption seems to us at the present day strange and perhaps even insincere. It has come to be accepted as almost axiomatic that such duties lay a larger tax on the poor man, proportionately to his income, than on the rich man; for while it is true that the rich man uses more of the articles and so pays more tax, he does not use and pay more in proportion to his larger income. But, in reality, that is not a quite simple or obvious truth, and not more than two or three men in the seventeenth and eighteenth centuries seem to have realised it. Even Adam Smith, as we shall see, failed to discover it. The distributive justification of Excise duties given in this period was, therefore, although incorrect, not so absurd as we might at first suppose. It based itself upon the general fact that the richer man normally used more of the taxed commodity than the poorer, and then made the false, but not patently false, assumption that he used proportionately more, relatively to his means.

This becomes clearer when we consider the objections made to the view that the Excise duties were equitable

[1] Ephraim Parker, *Proposals for a very easy tax* . . . 1713, E. 1997 (13), pp. 6–7.

between rich and poor. What we may call the official opposition—the opposition which objected to Excise duties on necessaries altogether—was unable to meet the argument directly at all, just as it failed to meet the argument that the poor should, as citizens, pay taxation.[1] Indeed, as we shall see, from its own point of view it was almost uninterested in meeting it ; by implication it said that this was not the way to approach the subject. In any case, it did not meet it, and as a natural consequence the argument became a common doctrine. Direct criticism came chiefly from men who were in different degrees favourable to Excise duties. The commoner and not very important criticism was that some particular duty, because of a special feature, was unfair to the poor. Thus, for instance, it was argued by some that the exemption of home-brewed beer allowed the rich to escape the beer duty, since they were the persons who brewed beer at home.[2] It is doubtful if the facts supported this contention,[3] but in any case it was admitted that the exemption of home-brewed beer was a distributive anomaly only justified because of administrative difficulties. Similarly it was argued at a later time that the poor man used as much salt as the rich ;[4] the fact was denied, but if such were the case, it was admittedly unjust and did not invalidate the argument for other Excise duties. The fundamental weakness of that argument—to come to the second and more important line of criticism—was exposed fully only by Sir William Petty. Petty was a man of acute mind, and in 1662 he gave a very careful analysis of the question.[5] But his very precision made him

---

[1] The only exception was John Cary, who had a direct answer to both arguments. But he was not typical. See below.

[2] Sheridan, *op. cit.* p. 172, and Rockley, *loc. cit.*

[3] *e.g.* exemption of people in receipt of alms from tax on home-brewed beer, Ordinance of 22nd February 1647.

[4] In 1732 debates—see Chap. VI.

[5] *Treatise of Taxes and Contributions*, in Hull, i. 91–4. Petty was a man of wide interests and of great practical as well as speculative ability. He was physician to the Commonwealth army in Ireland,

difficult to follow, and it is not wonderful that his view did not obtain general recognition. He set out with the position, which we have already discussed, that taxation in proportion to total expenditure is equitable. But, taxation of all objects of expenditure being impracticable, it was necessary, if a tax on a particular object of expenditure were to be equitable, that this object should be 'nearest the common standard of all expense.' A tax on such a commodity would be an 'accumulative excise'; a man's total expenditure would be accumulated upon and represented by this one commodity; and so this particular excise would fall in proportion to total expenditure. But no ordinary commodity that could be suggested would satisfy this condition. 'Some propounded beer to be the only exciseable commodity, supposing that in the proportion that men drink they make all other expenses.' This, Petty showed, was not the case. Apart from the fact that some poor men drank twice as much strong beer as gentlemen drank small, he pointed out that 'upon the artisan's beer is accumulated only a little bread and cheeze, leathern cloths, neck beef and inwards twice a week, stale fish, old pease without butter, etc.; whereas on the other is accumulated as many more things as nature and art can produce.' The same criticism would apply to other commodities, salt, fuel, bread, etc. Particular Excise duties, therefore, were not distributively equitable, but imposed a heavier proportionate tax on the poor man than on the rich. It is possible that Thomas Sheridan[1] also realised this position, but apart from him it only appears in one

made a survey of lands there which yielded him a large profit, became himself a proprietor, and died in 1687 worth perhaps £100,000. He was in touch with the political and philosophical ideas of his day. In taxation he is the most important English writer before Adam Smith, and taking into account the transitional character of his period compared with Adam Smith's, he showed equal and in some respects greater acuteness. See Hull's *Introduction* and *Life* by Fitzmaurice.

[1] Sheridan, *op. cit.* pp. 173–4.

other writer, John Cary,[1] who disliked Excises and the
taxation of the poor as a whole. A general excise,
he said in 1695, makes the poor 'pay more than
the wealthiest of their neighbours, suitable to what
they have; for though a rich man spends more in
excisable things than a poor man doth, yet it is not his
all, whereas the other's poverty gives him leave to lay
up nothing, but it is as much as he can do to provide
necessaries for his family, out of all which he pays his
proportion.' This was not such an accurate statement
as Petty's, but it contained the essential idea that the
poor man spent a larger proportion of his income on
ordinary excised commodities (beer, salt, leather, candles,
soap, coal) than the rich man did.

Of these unrepresentative condemnations of Excise
duties, Petty's was much the more important, both
because of his personal repute and because he wrote
at a time when opinion was less settled. Four causes
may be suggested for his failure to influence it on this
point. First, his position was not a simple or obvious
one, and his terminology accentuated rather than
reduced the resulting difficulty. Second, he did not
attempt to make a distributive use of the traditional
feeling against taxes on necessaries,[2] and, since he dis-
approved of the exemption of the poor from taxation,
he could not accept it in the ordinary form, which
amounted practically to a demand for such exemption.[3]
Third, the condemnation was practically weakened,
though intellectually strengthened and completed, by
his approval of excises as part of a compensatory system
of taxation.[4] Fourth, Excise duties had none of the
gross and palpable injustice which was prevalent in
France, where the rich were in many cases exempted
from certain taxes; excises at least made the rich man
pay more than the poor man.

---

[1] *An Essay on the state of England in relation to its Trade, its
Poor and its Taxes for carrying on the present war against France,*
1695, 1029. a. 5 (I), p. 174 *seq.*
    [2] Discussed below.   [3] *Ibid.*   [4] *Ibid.*

The approval of Excise duties in the seventeenth century as distributively equitable is not more striking to modern eyes than a second characteristic of distributive opinion at that time. As we saw, in noticing the tax system of the Gladstonian epoch, we do not now think of each tax as equitable by itself, but of an equitable compensatory system of taxation, in which the inequality of one tax is balanced by that of another. But in the seventeenth and eighteenth centuries, hardly anyone realised such a conception. Each tax was looked at by itself, and required to be equitable in itself. This was both a cause and a consequence of the acceptance of Excise duties as distributively just. The tradition which the Long Parliament inherited was of a single national tax, the direct tax, which necessarily had to be made equitable in itself. Consequently when a new species of tax, the Excise duty, was proposed, it was inevitable that it also should be looked at alone, and required to be also equitable in itself. There was, so to say, no intellectual framework into which Excise duties could be fitted and be at the same time recognised as inequitable between rich and poor. And, on the other hand, unusual insight being needed to discern that such an inequality was fundamentally involved in Excise duties, no insufficiency was generally discovered in the tacitly accepted non-compensatory view of tax questions. The result was the attempt throughout this period to get an equitable direct tax on one plan, equitable Excise duties on another and equitable Customs duties on a third. Consequently, we may note in passing, if we want to sit in judgment on the mere facts of Excise policy in the seventeenth century, we must distinguish at least three separate standards by which they may be tried—first, the standard which condemns any taxation of the poor man ; second, the standard, common in the seventeenth century, which requires that rich and poor shall, in Excise duties, pay proportionately to income ; and third, the standard, common in the later nineteenth century, requiring that rich and poor shall, in taxation as a whole, pay proportionately to income. Sentence would be very different in the three cases, and most favourable in the third.

Again it is Petty who by contrast emphasises the predominant attitude. Recognising that Excise duties were inequitable in themselves, he also came to see that they could be made part of an equitable system of taxation. The essay known as *Verbum Sapienti*, which was probably written in 1665, but was not published till 1691,[1] gives the outline of such a scheme. Petty proposed in it to show the remedy for the disproportion which defaced the taxes of the time, and which, he said, was 'the true and proper grievance of taxes.' What was wanted was a tax in proportion to every man's income; it was to be obtained by imposing taxes on the actual or assumed income received from property of all kinds, and by adding a poll tax, or better a poll tax and an excise, so as to get at the income of labouring people.[2] The scheme is rough, for it does not go in detail into the question of the Excise duty or duties to be imposed; but its central idea is clear and modern. The poor were to pay by Excise and a poll tax, the rich by direct taxes on income.

But Petty stood alone. An echo may possibly be detected in a pamphlet of 1691,[3] which suggested that when a land tax was granted, a poll tax (or even a general Excise) should go along with it, and in the vague argument in favour of a malt tax in 1697 that hitherto the taxes had fallen mostly on people of means.[4]

---

[1] It was known before that, however (see Hull's note). A pamphlet of 1689, entitled *A Discourse of the growth of England . . .*, 712. m. 1 (13), p. 192, gives the substance of the scheme, in the form of a letter dated 27th January 1680.

[2] In Hull, i. 104, 111, 112 *et passim*.

[3] *A Proposal for an equal Land-tax . . .* 1691 (*Harl. Miscl.* ii. 511).

[4] L'Hermitage, 12th March 1697, vol. RR, p. 244. A vague, compensatory position is taken up in *Short Reflections upon the present state of affairs . . .* 1691, T. 1707 (7), p. 18, which argues that since for ten years before the Revolution no direct tax was in force, there is now no ground for complaint at the Land Tax.

But the real point of such contentions was the desire to enforce the doctrine that the poor should share the burden of taxation—' that so,' as the pamphleteer said, ' the whole kingdom being concerned, every man in it may contribute something '—and not the recognition of equitable taxation of the poor by means of a compensatory system. And it was easy for the capable writer of another pamphlet of 1691 to set out to discuss Excises with Petty's essay in his hand, and yet to miss its whole point.[1]

Excise duties were thus defended as equitable by themselves, between rich and poor. One other advantage, of a quasi-distributive kind, was also claimed for them. It was based on the supposed optional character of duties on consumption, which, it was held, made such taxes equitable, or at least had an influence in that direction. The idea was put forward somewhat doubtfully at first, and it was not until the eighteenth century that it blossomed out into one of the foremost tax virtues. Petty in 1662 gave as one of the chief reasons for Excise that it is ' scarce forced upon any and is very light to those who please to be content with natural necessaries.' Sheridan thought that a general Excise put it into the power of every man to pay more or less as he resolved to live loosely or thriftily. The *Letter* of 1691 allowed that Excise had at first sight ' a notable air and aspect of freedom, every one being indeed his own assessor.' Davenant thought that Excise duties must be very easy, since ' everyone, in a manner, taxes himself, making consumption according to his will or ability '; and the defender of a malt tax in 1696 said that ' as it is in every person's power to charge himself with this tax as it pleaseth himself, so it is undeniably

---

[1] *A Letter . . . touching Sir Wm. Petty's posthumous treatise entitled 'Verbum Sapienti,'* 1691, 518. h. 1 (18), *passim*, and sp. pp. 14–15. It was, in fact, not until after the middle of the nineteenth century that the conception of a compensatory system of taxation became general. See Fawcett's preaching on the subject, *Manual*, 2nd ed. pp. 525–7.

equal.'[1] The contention, however, was somewhat thin as applied to Excise duties, which were imposed so largely on necessaries; it was more applicable to Customs duties, and in the eighteenth century was chiefly connected with them and with other taxes on luxuries. Even the seventeenth century, however, was inclined to rhapsodise about the freedom of the individual to tax himself; it was partly an aspect of the view that a rigid standard of distribution is necessarily inequitable.

The one objection of a distributive kind which opponents of Excise duties always urged against them [2] was that they were taxes on the necessaries of the poor. As we have seen, the Army in 1647 demanded the immediate removal of Excise duties on 'such commodities whereon the poor people of the land do ordinarily live.' The soap makers of London petitioned in 1650 against the duty on their product, on this among other grounds: 'soap is most necessary for all sorts of people next to victuals, and must be used by the poorest people.'[3] Even those who supported the Excise were influenced by the idea. The writer of *The Standard of Equality* proposed in 1647 that, when peace was restored, 'a tender care be had of the fundamentals, as I may term them, of man's life, namely, bread, flesh, salt, small beer, etc.—that in all matters of taxes the state lay her finger on things necessary for men's sustenance and her loins on such things as are merely superfluous. Otherwise it would be lamentable that the poor labourer who hath threshed all day for a livelihood should himself

---

[1] Petty, i. 94; Sheridan, p. 172; *Letter* of 1691, p. 14; Davenant, *Essay*, 1695, 1028. h. 1 (1), p. 124; Burnaby, T. 1814 (4), pp. 22-3.

[2] To be quite correct, it should be pointed out that the objection was made against such Excise duties as fell on necessaries. Most, however, did so, although a few, of which the spirit duty is important and will be discussed later, did not. 'Necessaries' was, of course, not a sharply defined term. It stood broadly for the staples of the poor man's subsistence.

[3] 669. f. 15 (62). See also *Exclamatio pauperum . . .* 1648, E. 452 (26).

be threshed at night with unconscionable payment for things tending to the bare support of nature.'[1]   The Brewers Company of London petitioned against the continuation of the beer Excise at the Restoration, on two grounds : the burden on themselves and the fact that 'being only upon victuals ' — 'beer and ale, next to bread, are the stay and staff of the poor '—it was ' an imposition most unequal and unreasonable,' and fell chiefly on poor people in and about London.[2]   The Parliamentary opposition, after the Revolution, urged the same doctrine, and as we have seen got the House of Commons to pass a resolution that taxes should be imposed on superfluities rather than on necessaries. Pamphlets illustrate it more fully.   To the writer of the *Letter* of 1690 an Excise on victuals was ' scandalous,' as falling on the common indispensable necessaries of life.[3] Halifax[4] said that in granting taxes ' our ancestors have observed these rules : First, they must not consist of things of common necessity or livelihood, but rather superfluity.'   The author of a pamphlet entitled *Taxes no Charge* held the Excise to be a most proper tax, but laying it upon the food of the poor ' might be thought a grievance' and was to be avoided.[5]   Davenant[6] approved Excises, but thought that necessaries should

---

[1] *Harl. Miscl.* ix. 116, par. 14.   See also *A Mite to the Treasury* . . ., by J. W., 1653 (in Goldsmith's Library).   'If excise may not be removed, can it not be reduced and principally lean upon the richest and most superfluous commodities, as silver, silks, wine, tobacco, sauces, coaches, sedans, beavers, scarlets, fine cloths, etc,' p. 15.

[2] *S. P. Dom.*, Chas. II., vol. i. 146, and see Minutes of a Committee on Revenue, June–July 1661 (in Shaftesbury Papers, Bunde 34, No. 20), rejecting the petition since it asked not for the improvement of the tax, but for its abolition as oppressive.   (Record Office.)

[3] P. 3.   See also *Considerations . . . against passing the Bill for laying a further duty on coals*, 816. m. 12 (90).   ' Coals is a thing of so absolute necessity that it is impossible to preserve the poor from perishing without having the same at a moderate price.'

[4] *Op. cit.* p. 74.

[5] *Taxes no Charge* . . . 1690 (*Harl. Miscl.* viii. 526).

[6] *Essay upon Ways and Means*, 1695, p. 123.   In 1699, during the peace, Davenant wrote against keeping on Excise duties, *Balance of Trade* Essay, 1029. c. 4, pp. 41–9.

be taxed low, and various projectors of taxes were careful
to provide for the exemption of the poor.[1]

It is only in a limited sense that this doctrine can
be called distributive in character. In its strict form
it amounted practically to a demand for the complete
exemption of the poor from taxation; and yet its
supporters had no direct answer to the theory that the
poor, as citizens, should pay taxation. Still less did
the doctrine say how taxation should be distributed,
or answer the contention that an Excise duty on an
article of ordinary consumption is in itself equitably
distributed between rich and poor. It was, in fact,
non-distributive in origin — the application to tax
theory of a principle of Customs policy when Customs
were not yet looked upon in the light of general taxes.
To exempt necessaries was not so much a tax doctrine
as a doctrine of general social policy in the interest of
the poor. And so it remained in essence—the assertion
against the theory of tax-paying citizenship of a not
well defined feeling that the poor man did not properly
fit into that conception of society. We may perhaps
call it a plea for compassion upon the poor man. In
the great debate on Excises which took place on
14th March 1694,[2] Sir Edward Seymour, the spokesman
of the opposition, employed his time, as we learn from
the unsympathetic account of Bonnet, *'pour haranguer
le plus pathétiquement qu'il pût contre l'introduction des
accises.'* As we shall see, the description was equally
applicable to opposition against taxes on necessaries in
the eighteenth century.

Now, a compassionate plea of this kind is necessarily
weak in some respects. Nobody knows precisely upon
what it is based or to what it may lead. It lacks an
intellectual defence. And this weakness was very

---

[1] Proposal for a House Tax, in *Harleian MSS.* 1243 f. 214 b.
Edward Henning's *Proposal* (for a tax on beds, discussed fairly
fully), Bodleian Library, B. 8. 22 Jur. (No. 4).
[2] Bonnet, p. 243.

pertinent in the seventeenth century; for a much
better defined and defended doctrine was set up against
it. The result was that while it gave a basis for
opposing Excise duties, it did not give a basis for
answering the arguments by which Excise duties were
supported. In truth, it had such a basis up to a certain
point, but it was in the political philosophy of a by-
gone age; while the basis of the supporters of Excises
was in the philosophy of their own time. This is an
aspect of the problem to which it is necessary now to
proceed. But in the meantime we may note one
exception to the prevailing indefiniteness of the plea
for the exemption of the necessaries of the poor. In
the late seventeenth century John Cary[1] not only
saw that Excises were distributively unfair to the poor,
but argued that in laying taxes the poor should bear
little or none of the burden—'their province being
more properly to labour and fight than pay.' And
having thus given his answer—though few, perhaps,
recognised it as such—to the doctrine that it is an
obligation on the poor man to pay taxation, he went
on to point out political reasons which made it inex-
pedient to tax them. 'He that gets his money by
the sweat of his brows parts not from it without much
remorse and discontent, and when all is done, 'tis but
a little they pay; therefore taxes that light heavy on
them (such as chimney-money and oftentimes a poll)
tend rather to unhinge than assist the government. . . .'

To sum up. Excise duties, mostly on necessaries,
were the third source to which resort was had, for the
first time, in this period, to meet increasing expenditure.
They were approved as being paid gradually, insensibly

[1] *An Essay on the state of England* . . . 1695, pp. 173, 175–6.
Cary was a leading Bristol merchant. He became acquainted with
Locke in 1696 and met him frequently in London thereafter
(R. H. Fox Bourne, *Life of John Locke*, 1876, ii. 342–3). He was
interested in the founding and work of the Council of Trade. *Add.
MS.* 5540 is a volume of his letters and papers, bound in 1696.

and surely, as making the poor man contributary to the
cost of a benefit which he shared, as distributing the
burden of taxation equitably between rich and poor
on the basis of a rough test of ability approaching that
of expenditure or income, and as in a measure making
the individual his own assessor. They were looked
upon as equitable in themselves, and not as part of a
compensatory system of taxation. They were opposed
with great persistence on the grounds that it was
grievous to tax the necessaries of the poor, and that
Excises were destructive of personal or constitutional
liberty and injurious to industry.[1]

[1] In the course of the discussion of Customs, Land Tax and
Excise, we have, without paying specific attention to it, established
a proposition of some importance in the history of economic theories
of the incidence of taxes. The proposition is that the ordinary
doctrines, that Land Tax falls on the landlord and Customs and
Excise duties on the consumers, rich and poor, of the dutied commodities, were for practical purposes accepted universally in this
period, and that various, as we may call them, fancy doctrines
of incidence which were sometimes put forward had no practical
influence. This period, in other words, simply carried on the
traditional views of the incidence of taxes on commodities and of
the subsidy. At the same time, economic speculation was beginning
here and there to throw up new and strange theories, some of which
were put forward even by important men, and one of which—
the doctrine that the poor man does not pay taxes on necessaries
but shifts them in higher wages—came to have important practical
influence, both on general opinion and on policy, in the eighteenth
century. It must be observed that in many cases the authors
themselves repudiated their theories, by implication, in dealing
with tax policy.
    It is sufficient to notice the various fancy theories in this period
briefly, as they are discussed at length, but from the point of view
rather of their meaning as economic theories than of their practical
influence, in Professor Seligman's *Incidence of Taxation*, 3rd ed.
pt. i. bk. i. chaps. 1 and 5. (1) Petty argued in 1662 (Hull, i. 39–40)
that a land tax resolved itself into an irregular excise upon consumptions, except during the term of a long lease within which it was
imposed. In the *Verbum Sapienti*, however, he tacitly repudiated
the theory. (2) Several writers argued that an Excise on necessaries
does not really fall on the poor consumer, but is shifted by him
through an increase of wages. Mun asserts this (*England's Treasure*,
1664, written c. 1630, ed. Ashley, p. 85). It was elaborately argued
by Locke in 1691 (*Considerations of the lowering of interest*, in *Works*,
1823, v. 55–60), repeating a line of thought he had developed as early
as 1672 (Letter of John Strachey in Fox Bourne's *Life*, i. 312–3).

His conclusion was that, along with all other taxes, it fell ultimately on land. As Locke states it, the argument includes a piece of mere faulty logic, but its essence is that the labourer lives on the margin of subsistence and so cannot bear taxation and remain independent. The merchant will not bear it, the labourer cannot, and therefore the landlord must. From slightly different premises, the *Letter* of 1690, Hampden (*Some Considerations*, 1692, *State Tracts*, ii. 317–8) and Halifax (1693, *Somers' Tracts*, xi. 76–7) also argued that excises, which they opposed on many grounds, fall on land. Cary (*Essay*, 1695, p. 143 *seq.*) and Davenant (*Essay*, 1699, pp. 44–6) both agreed that high prices of necessaries—a cause not identical, we should say, with increased price due to a tax—resulted in higher wages ; but while Davenant regarded such a result as ' utterly destructive to that principal part of England's wealth,' manufactures and specially exporting manufactures, Cary held that our manufactures ' may be carried on to advantage without running down the labour of the poor.' Davenant's writings are full of indefiniteness and often inconsistency on the subject of incidence ; and Cary does not reconcile his view about prices and wages (if indeed he held it to bear on taxes) with his view about the exemption of the poor from taxation. (3) It was sometimes argued that all taxes fall on or injure the poor, by reducing expenditure and so employment—a fallacy regarding the country as a whole, since taxes are expended, but having a measure of local truth. Davenant, 1699 *Essay*, p. 44, and *The Humble Petition of the Common People of England*, against the Land Tax (t. Will. III., Lincoln's Inn Library, Brydall Coll., 33. f. 1). (4) It was suggested by John Houghton (*Collection for improvement of Husbandry and Trade*, 522. m. 11 (2), under date 16th April 1698) that a tax on necessaries should be imposed so as to make the generality of the poor, who are ' very lazy and expensive,' work harder and so make manufactures cheaper and more plentiful. I do not think that this idea had any influence on taxation, but cf. second half of eighteenth century below. It seems a strained interpretation of Petty (Seligman, p. 49) to attribute Houghton's policy to him (i. 274–5).

V

POLITICAL PHILOSOPHY AND THE TAXATION OF THE POOR

THE problem of the distribution of taxation in England has always been one of distribution among individuals of widely different economic and social status. It was usual in the seventeenth century to divide men into three grades or classes, known as the richer sort (chiefly the governing landed class), the middle sort (including yeomen and shopkeepers), and the poorer sort (wage-earning labourers, artificers and tradesmen, with the smallest yeomen and cottagers) ; and this division, while not precise, was tolerably accurate at the time. The first of these classes was a propertied aristocracy, living on an income from land and freed from economic activity ; the third was dependent wholly or chiefly on the earnings of its labour. The contrast between these two classes is the most striking fact of English social history, and the largest question in taxation arose out of this contrast. Should the members of all these very different classes all pay taxes ? In England (unlike France) this question was in practice considered in the less general form, should the poor man (*i.e.* the member of our third class) pay taxation ?

Before the meeting of the Long Parliament the practice of taxation in relation to the poor had varied. As we have seen, they were charged to the national taxes on moveables of the thirteenth and fourteenth centuries, and to the subsidy of the first half of the sixteenth century. But, on the other hand, from the middle of the sixteenth century down to 1640, the poor were very nearly exempt from taxation, both in intention and practice. Policy therefore varied ; the poor were sometimes made to bear a share of the burden of taxation and sometimes were exempted. It is probable also that there was no consistent opinion on the problem involved ; certainly the literature of the first half of the sixteenth century, which was much occupied with the poor, does not give evidence of any doctrine that the poor either should or should not pay taxes.[1]

From the time of the Civil War onwards the poor always paid taxation—regularly in Excise duties and at intervals during half a century in direct taxes—and a consistent and widely accepted opinion grew up that the poor man ought to pay taxation. The practice of this doctrine was vigorously opposed, but almost without exception the opposition was unable to answer the case for taxing the poor. Briefly, this case, as we have seen, was that since every one shared in the common benefits secured by the state, every one should share in the cost involved in providing them. This idea was the achievement, in the realm of tax theory, of the Parliamentary and religious struggle of the seventeenth century.

There is an apparent simplicity about the idea which gives it support. But, in reality, it is less simple than it seems. No doubt everyone shares in the benefits secured by the state, and none the less because these benefits, like those of sunlight, do not reach the individual in separate measurable portions. There was no general desire, either before or after 1640, to deny this portion of the argument. But does it follow that therefore everyone should contribute to the cost of maintaining state services ? In reality that depends on the conception of society and of the state which is accepted. It did not follow on the basis of the English political

[1] For references see note 1, p. 85.

theory of the first half of the sixteenth century; it did follow, inevitably, on the basis of the political theory of the seventeenth century, which attained its clearest expression in Locke. The difference may be put in a word. The sixteenth century theory conceived of society as made up of individuals (and classes) who ought to and did perform functions in their society; the provisions of the means for certain services (*i.e.* taxation) was one out of many functions; and it might or might not be the place of a particular class to perform that particular function. The seventeenth century theory, on the other hand, conceived of society as made up of independent individuals, who did not perform functions, but each of whom had rights which only required to be recognised and protected; the state was an institution formed for this purpose,—personified in the Crown, it was the one member of society which had a function to perform; and consequently every individual, receiving the benefit of this unique service, was bound in fairness to others to share in the cost of its provision.

Opinion on taxation in the seventeenth and eighteenth centuries was dominated by the second of these political philosophies—which may be termed the ' freeholder ' view of society. But to understand it aright, we must first try to sketch in outline the main features of the earlier philosophy which it supplanted. That philosophy accepted, as did Locke, the class organisation of society which was the legacy of feudalism; but, unlike him, it tried to moralise it by identifying classes with functions. It developed in the Middle Ages and was essentially the work of the Church. It pictured society on the analogy of the human body, recognised the necessity for differences of classes as for differences of organs, and preached their interdependence, and the duty or function of each in the service of the whole society.[1]

[1] Giercke, *Political Theories of the Middle Age,* tr. Maitland, pp.

The social and economic disturbance of the first half of the sixteenth century in England led to a vigorous and detailed exposition of the view.[1] The keynote is that every man has an office in the community. The office of the commonalty is to labour for the sustaining of the whole body; that of the gentlemen of landed estates to govern, help and defend the people—" to keep society in good order and civility," as Starkey says. It is for this that they receive their rents and are maintained without labour by the labour of others. Their rights, in other words, implied duties. The king, as the head of the society, is in the same position, and his duties are often set out at length.

This ethical and political philosophy both defended and criticised the actual class organisation of society. When the landed class was condemned as unproductive, living like drones on the labour of others,[2] it pointed out that while no one should be idle or unprofitable to the state, economic labour was not the only form of service which the state required, and that the gentry performed the service of governing and defending it. On the other hand, when the landed men made use of their property rights to advantage themselves at the expense of the poor (*e.g.* in some forms of enclosures) it insisted that their rights were not given them for

7, 8, 22, 27, 28, 33, 34, and § ix.; Thomas Starkey, *England in the Reign of King Henry the Eighth* (Dialogue), ed. Cowper, pp. 45–6, 48, 78.

[1] Wm. Tyndale, *The Obedience of a Christian Man*, 1528 (ed. Christian Classics Series, pp. 86, 124–6); Starkey, pp. 55, 78, 110–11; Select Works of Robert Crowley, E.E.T.S. (*The Voice of the Last Trumpet*, 1550, *passim*, and sp. pp. 86, 90–2, and *An Information and petition against the oppressors of the poor Commons of this Realm*, pp. 157, 163); King Edward VI., *A Discourse about the Reformation of many abuses*, c. 1550 (in Gilbert Burnet, *History of the Reformation*, v. 97–102); [John Hales], *A Discourse of the Commonweal of this Realm of England*, ed. Lamond, pp. 14, 22. Also the less definite Hugh Latimer, *Sermons* (Everyman ed. pp. 84, 185, 292–4) and Thomas Becon, *The Catechism* (ed. Ayre, p. 302 *seq.*).

[2] Sir Thomas More, *Utopia*, c. 1515 (Scott Library ed., pp. 87, 113, but cf. p. 127 for his use of idea of unproductive); and Starkey's discussion, pp. 77–8.

merely self-interested ends, but in order to enable them to perform duties in society. They might not do as they liked with their own.[1]

The Church in the sixteenth century had thus a generally accepted doctrine with which it could preach to the powerful propertied aristocracy of that time, and although the doctrine was not embodied in a precise way in law or economic institution, it was not without importance on that account. There are some kinds of duties of which it is specially true that they cannot be enforced fully or well by mere law or self-interest, but must depend for their support largely on opinion or doctrine ; such are the duties of a Church, or of a governing body or class, or of a self-governing people. The priests' office was one of rights (e.g. tithe) and duties ; in conception it was and remained an office. The landed man, in the doctrine we have been discussing, also had an office with rights and duties ; but the conception of office was to a large extent superseded by the absolutely antagonistic one of mere rights. It was one of the signs and forms of this change that the Church in the eighteenth century preached very little to the landed aristocracy of that time.[2]

The weakness or limitation of this sixteenth century functional view of society was that, like all political philosophies, it was never made concrete enough[3] to supply detailed rules of social and economic life. The

[1] Starkey, pp. 77, 110–12 ; Crowley, The Way to Wealth, p. 139 seq. and Information, p. 157, 163 ; and other works referred to. See also A. F. Pollard, Factors in Modern History, p. 147 seq. Since this chapter was written, I have read Mr. R. H. Tawney's recently published book, The Agrarian Problem in the Sixteenth Century, which brings out, with a knowledge of the question to which I have no claim, the place which this doctrine held in the opinion and policy of the time, and throws many suggestive lights on the general subject of this chapter. See sp. Introduction and pp. 188–191, 347–351.

[2] The Church never gave up the idea that every man has duties towards his society, e.g. Swift, Sermons (in Prose Works, ed. Temple Scott, iv. 112 seq.).

[3] This is not the place to discuss the question to what extent and in what way such concretization is possible.

duties of defence and government which it laid on the
propertied classes were relatively ill-defined ; this, however, was the less important aspect of the limitation,
for these classes did govern the country in a very real
way for centuries, although a particular landed man
might take no part in the work. The more important
defect was the lack of a definition of the rights which
should belong to the governing class. In law their
rights consisted in various forms of property in land.
But the Church's political theory gave absolutely no
suggestion whether these rights were excessive, or liable
to dangerous abuse, or to excessive augmentation in
the future, or, on the other hand, were inadequate or
liable to future inadequacy. Consequently it could do
very little more than denounce change. To put the
matter briefly, the moralist did not know how to allow for
and control economic self-interest in a time when that
motive was increasing and destined to increase in power.
The ideas of function and duty were inadequate to
regulate the practical affairs of the world of economic
motive, and it was inevitable that that world should tend
to be viewed as being independent and self-contained,
and ideas of function dispensed with. Already an acute
man like John Hales was feeling in 1549 towards the
political theory of the economists, that, for getting
work or service performed, rewards to self-interest are
to be relied on, and for preventing injury and wrong
the penalties of punitive law.[1]

Both the strength and the weakness of this functional
view of society are illustrated by its lack of a doctrine
on the question whether the poor should pay taxation.
The fundamental fact which it recognised was that the
poor did perform a function in the state—that of providing for its sustenance. Consequently Locke's argument that, since the poor benefit by the State, they
should contribute towards its maintenance, could have

---

[1] *Discourse*, pp. 50, 53, 54, 57–9, 121–2. See a most illuminating
appreciation of John Hales in Cunningham, i. 561 *seq.* (4th ed.),

no influence; they contribute in labouring. It was therefore left open to consider all kinds of circumstances bearing on the 'function' of paying taxation. It could be argued with John Cary that it is the business of the poor to work and fight, but not to pay; it could be pointed out that it is difficult to tax the poor, and that they feel the burden acutely. Or, on the other hand, it might be argued that the poor should pay taxation with other classes, and that in some or all circumstances no other mode of taxation was possible.

In this lay the strength and truth of the functional view, in its relation to taxation. Its weakness was that, while providing an opening for considering the various problems connected with the function of paying taxation, it did not in practice go on to consider them, and consequently left no rule or even fruitful discussion on the subject.

The transition from ideas of office and function in the sixteenth century to the widespread acceptance of the Lockean theory of society in the seventeenth and eighteenth, may be attributed to two main causes.[1] The less apparent was the dominance, in the actual legal and economic organisation of society, of ideas of unrelated rights and the motive of self-interest. The obvious fact was that the landed man had property and that the merchant traded for his own advantage; the functions which they fulfilled or should have fulfilled lay beneath the surface. Locke therefore, accepting the obvious fact and treating it as the whole truth, naturally appealed in his time, as the Roman Law had in earlier centuries, to the motive of individual self-interest in every man. The more apparent and better understood cause of the transition was the struggle of the landed and middle classes for freedom from the control of the

[1] For the earlier history of the theory, see Giercke, *op. cit.*; Figgis, *From Gerson to Grotius*, sp. lecture vii.; *Camb. Mod. Hist.* iii. 747 *seq.*; Vinogradoff, *Roman Law in Medieval Europe*, pp. 97–101 *et passim.*

Crown, primarily in religious matters and thence more generally, and among other things, in taxation.[1] It was one of the chief duties of the King, in sixteenth-century theory, to provide for religion and to put down schism ; but from the Reformation this duty came to clash with the demand of considerable classes for changes in the established forms or for freedom to exercise their religion as they deemed proper. To enforce this demand, the dominance of Parliament over the King was asserted, and to justify it appeal was made to the indefeasible rights of the individual and to the traditional English idea of individual freedom. In the struggle the office of the Crown was limited and the rights of the dominant classes asserted. The state, instead of being conceived, as the Crown was in the sixteenth century, as an instrument for the general regulation and defence of the whole community, came to be thought of rather as an instrument for protecting the rights of the members ; and their duty to the state came to be limited in theory to the payment of their share of the cost of maintaining this protecting instrument.

The political theory which came to power in this way is sometimes called individualistic, sometimes a theory of natural rights. Both epithets mark certain of its characteristics.[2] It was individualistic in its conception of society as made up of independent individuals, each essentially self-interested, and, as Blackstone[3] put it, without any absolute duties. The individual's duties were of a negative character ultimately—the

---

[1] Acton, *Lectures on Modern History*, chaps. xi.–xiii. For the history of the doctrine by which this control was asserted, and for the transition generally, see Figgis, *Theory of the Divine Right of Kings*. For democratic political doctrine, see Gooch, *History of English Democratic Ideas in the Seventeenth Century*.

[2] The analysis here is of Locke's *Two Treatises of Government*, 1689 (Book ii.). See *Camb. Mod. Hist.* vi. chap. 23 for the general course of political theory.

[3] Wm. Blackstone, *Commentaries on the laws of England*, 1765, i. 119–121.

duty not to infringe the rights of others. It was also a theory of natural rights in that it endowed the independent individuals with rights (of life, liberty and property) which it conceived as unrelated to duties, as prior to the existence of the state, and as the end which the state existed to secure and protect.

But both these descriptions tend to give an inaccurate account of the conception of society which was involved. It is both more accurate and more suggestive to term it a ' freeholder ' view—a conception of society as made up of men who are freeholders.[1] To call it individualistic tends to slur the fact that the individual was not simply thought of as independent and self-sufficient—there was the qualification that he was dependent on his society as a whole for the protection of his rights and that he had at least negative duties, if no functions. To call it a theory of natural rights tends to slur the fact that while it accepted property rights of the nature and extent of those of English law, it only managed to do so by the most fantastic proof that these were derivatives from original natural rights.[2] In fact, it simply accepted the existing organisation of society, as the sixteenth-century functional theory had, without any real explanation or justification of it.[3] The whole conception, with these qualifications, is better expressed by the term ' society of freeholders.' Had England been ruled by a merchant instead of a landed aristocracy, the term would have been ' free merchant adventurers.'[4]

This description has the merit of indicating at once

[1] This description was suggested to me by a phrase in some political history, which I cannot now locate, that the theory of the divine right of kings was succeeded by the theory of the divine right of freeholders.

[2] Locke, chap. v. and sp. §§ 44–50.

[3] Indeed, with less justification than the sixteenth century theory, which explained rights as conditions of duties.

[4] *The Standard of Equality*, 1647, par. 4 (*Harl. Miscl.* ix. 114). ' Our state is no galley wherein any slaves are bound to row at the oars, but it is a ship wherein all the passengers are free merchant adventurers, though according to their different proportions.'

the truth and falsity of the conception, regarded as
an account of English society. In its strict form, such
as is found in Locke, every Englishman was supposed
to be an individual of the freeholder type; but in fact,
nothing was more untrue. English society was not
made up of similar individuals each with similar property
and other rights; a large part of it consisted of people
whose property rights were very small or non-existent.
This inconsistency of theory and fact led to an indefiniteness of feeling which appears in the seventeenth
but was more typical of the eighteenth century. The
freeholder view of taxation required that every one
should pay taxation; but men often felt that in some
way the theory did not satisfy them when applied
in practice; whence a sentimental and philanthropic
pity for the poor,[1] very different from the more robust
attitude of the sixteenth century moralist. Many other
results were also connected with this inconsistency;
as an instance take the *laisser faire* attitude—dominant
long before the day of the Philosophic Radicals—
which assumed both that cotton operatives were
independent individuals in the same essential conditions
as mill-owners, and that small yeomen and wage-earning
cottagers could be treated, in enclosing village lands,
in the same way as lords of manors. It would probably
not be incorrect to say that the whole range of social
opinion in the eighteenth century was warped by this
falsity in the Lockean conception of society.

On the other hand, the freeholder conception of
society might be taken to mean a society of independent
landed proprietors who did not labour, but were
maintained by the labour of a class, outside that
society, which cultivated their lands. So understood
it is possible to say that English society, in a narrow
sense, was one of freeholders; for the propertied
landed class practically monopolised political power.[2]

---

[1] *e.g. ibid.* par. 14.
[2] Edward Porritt, *The Unreformed House of Commons.*

It was not in this sense, of course, that Locke or general opinion justified the political system of the day ; but neither was this idea of society either unfamiliar or undefended. By far the most striking instance occurs in the debates of the Council of the Parliamentary Army in 1647.[1] Ireton was the spokesman of the officers in their opposition to a proposal of the Levellers for manhood suffrage. No person, he contended, had a right to an interest or share in the disposing or determining the affairs of the kingdom unless he had a permanent fixed interest in it ; such were men of landed estates and members of trading corporations ; these were the freemen of the state ; other men, tenants, tradesmen, labourers and people of personal property, had no fixed interest in the country, nothing more than the interest of breathing ; and no doubt, like aliens settling in England, they were to be given the right to live and work here, but also, like aliens, they were to accept the laws which those who had the real interest in the country thought proper to make. No doubt, Ireton's was an extreme statement of an attitude which in a milder form was concerned simply to secure rights of property ; but it is obvious that, in the comparative absence of a functional view of society, there must have been a strong tendency to regard the non-propertied classes as merely subordinate. Sir Thomas Smith, in Elizabeth's reign, said of the labouring sort, that no account is made of them, but only to be ruled.[2] The author of *The Standard of Equality*[3] described the poor as ' necessitous persons, un-interested in the state, as obliged thereto by no con-siderable fortune.' And Harrington, whose *Oceana* contains a scheme for limiting the size of estates in land,[4] nevertheless divides the people into two classes—

[1] *The Clarke Papers*, ed. Firth, i. 299–333 and lxvii. *seq.*
[2] *De Republica Anglorum*, bk. i. chap. 24 (ed. Alston, p. 46). He adds, ' and yet they be not altogether neglected ' ; they form juries, are made churchwardens, etc.
[3] Par. 37. [4] Ed. Hy. Morley, pp. 78, 104.

first, freemen or citizens, and second, servants who are neither freemen nor citizens, ' in regard of the nature of servitude, which is inconsistent with freedom or participation of government in a commonwealth.' [1]

From the point of view of the governing landed class, this conception of society had two lamentable weaknesses. In the first place, it ignored the fundamental fact about a propertied class, namely, that it is maintained by the labour of others. Such a class might be necessary, but nothing could be more injurious than the failure to take account of the economic basis on which it rested. As an extreme result we even find the idea that the man of property is performing a service by spending his income.[2] In the second place, it required of them the fulfilment of no duties or functions in their society ; it merely gave them rights, and their rights, like those of other men, were their own, to be enjoyed for their own particular advantage or pleasure.

In fact, of course, the landed gentry did perform very important functions in their society ; they governed it both locally and nationally ; and it is scarcely doubtful that they considered it their office

[1] The political philosophy of the seventeenth century which Locke represents is sometimes regarded as an assertion of the rights and citizenship of the poor man.   Three points need to be noticed in regard to this statement.   First, the strict form of the Locke theory did not endow the poor man with human worth and citizenship, in the ethical sense, more fully than the sixteenth century functional theory, which made the poor man the equal of princes in the sight of God.   Second, the Locke theory in its practical form, as accepted by the officers of the army or the statesmen of the Revolution, and as tacitly supported by Locke, did not give the poor man citizenship in the political sense of a share in political control of the state ; and it fostered a hard individualistic attitude to the poor, alien to the spirit of the sixteenth century philosophy.   Third, the Locke theory in its strict form gave to *future* democratic speculation (of the late eighteenth century), familiar with the philosophy of individual rights, the opening to argue that the poor man should have political power on Locke's principles.   The truth in the first statement is thus not large.

[2] *e.g.* Lord Kames, *Sketches of the History of Man*, 1774, p. 464.

to do so. But it is equally unquestionable that the political theory had great influence both on their opinion and practice.[1] At best, it failed to give any theoretical or systematised intellectual support for their performance of functions ; if they did their duty, it was without the support of the view of society which dominated political thought. At worst, it made of government itself a mere means to secure the legal rights or the private advantage of their class. And if doctrine was not to demand of them duties, what was ? The controlling power of the sixteenth century Crown had for most purposes been overthrown even more completely than the functional philosophy of that time.

This, then, was the political philosophy one of the results of which was the tax doctrine of the seventeenth century, that all men should pay taxation. We shall also find that it dominated all thinking on fundamental tax questions in the eighteenth century.

[1] The influence of political theory on taxation in the seventeenth century has already been noticed, and, as regards the eighteenth, is discussed in the following chapters. On the general subject of this paragraph not much has yet been written ; but see the very suggestive sketches in Leslie Stephen, *The English Utilitarians*, vol. i. chap. i., and Temperley, *The Age of Walpole and the Pelhams* (*Camb. Mod. History*, vi. chap. ii. pp. 76–89) ; also S. and B. Webb, *English Local Government*, vol. i., The County, *passim*. *The Village Labourer*, by J. L. and B. Hammond, throws new and vivid light upon a most important side of the rule and social attitude of the landed class, but it seems to me difficult to accept many of the general descriptions of that attitude. An interesting discussion, which also brings out the limitation of our knowledge, occurs in J. H. Rose, *William Pitt and the National Revival*, pp. 13–15. See chap. ix. below.

VI

THE EIGHTEENTH CENTURY—WALPOLE

THE seventeenth century was occupied in reshaping an antiquated system of taxation in order to meet the financial needs of the changing political situation ; and in it policy and opinion developed *pari passu*. The eighteenth century inherited a system of taxation which for a long time was fairly satisfactory from the merely financial point of view ; and the developments of policy which were ultimately demanded by a succession of wars were preceded and prepared by a great development of opinion. The eighteenth century therefore divides itself naturally into two parts—first, a period ending in 1776 with the publication of Adam Smith's *Wealth of Nations*, during which comparatively few changes were made in a stereotyped tax system but during which tax doctrine was gradually welded into something approaching a new orthodox canon ; and second, a period beginning in 1776 with the finance of the American War of Independence, during which a large increase in taxation took place, culminating in the imposition of the Income Tax in 1799, and in which attempts were made to stand by the rules of this canon. In this and the following chapter we shall deal with the first of these periods.

In contrast with the seventeenth century, when what was done was at least as important and significant as what was thought and said on taxation, the interest of the period between 1713 and 1776 lies almost entirely in what was thought and said. This was due not only

to the fact that comparatively little was done beyond
maintaining the taxes which the seventeenth century
handed on, but also to the divergence which existed
between policy and opinion on some of the most important questions. Opinion had no doubt some effect
on policy,[1] but in the main it was critical of a system
whose real support lay in the difficulty and uncertainty
of change, and it must be treated chiefly for its own sake
and for the influence it exercised on subsequent opinion
and policy.

The facts of the legislation may therefore be summarized briefly.[2] The stereotyped Land Tax was in force
during the whole period at rates which averaged practically 3s. in the £ (nominal rating). Apart from an
unsuccessful attempt by Walpole to keep the rate down
to 1s.,[3] it fluctuated between 2s. in peace and 4s. in war.
As debt increased, however, it became more difficult to
reduce the tax at the conclusion of war, and it was not
for some years after the close of the Seven Years' War
that the 4s. rate was lowered, and then only to 3s.,[4]
below which it never afterwards fell. On the other
hand, the Excise duties on salt, candles, leather, soap
and coal were also in force during the whole period and
were neither increased nor reduced in rates. An
exception of little financial but much doctrinal importance was the disappearance of the Salt Tax during
two years between 1730 and 1732. Similarly the duties
on paper, printed calico and starch remained unchanged.
The only important reductions were reductions in
Customs duties [5]—Walpole's repeal of duties on manufactured exports and his reduction of those on imports of

[1] The two chief aspects of the influence of opinion on policy
during this period were the re-imposition of the Salt Tax in 1732 and
the use of superfluities as the chief source of additional revenue
during the War of the Austrian Succession and the Seven Years'
War.

[2] For the chronological record, and for references to the Statutes,
see Dowell, ii. 85–159.

[3] The rate was 1s. in 1732 and 1733. See below.

[4] 1767.   [5] Dowell, ii. 91–6, and 18 Geo. II. c. 26.

raw material, together with some reduction of excessive duties on East India goods, particularly of the duty on tea in 1745 in order to lessen smuggling in that commodity. Such additions to taxation as were made to provide for the interest of new war loans were of two sorts.[1] The first affected for the most part only the rich and middle classes; such were (1) increased duties on imports like wine, groceries, tobacco and sugar[2]; (2) new taxes, levied directly on the owner, in respect of pleasure carriages and plate[3]; and (3) increased deed stamps, increased duties on newspapers and advertisements, and a tax on offices.[4] The second sort fell on all classes—(1) additions to the house and window tax graduated against large houses,[5] and (2) additions to the beer and malt duties.[6] Finally, a new species of tax appeared in this period, a spirit duty aimed for a time entirely, and later partly, at the restriction of consumption.[7]

Opinion in this period falls into two well-marked groups. On the one side is the tax policy represented by Walpole, which was the culmination of the dominant doctrines of the seventeenth century; on the other side is the opposition which his policy encountered, and

---

[1] This classification neglects a few minor taxes, including a glass duty (1746) and licence duties (1757).

[2] Wine, 1745 and 1763; an additional 5 per cent. subsidy on imports, 1748; groceries, tobacco, sugar, East India goods, etc., additional 5 per cent., 1759.

[3] 1747, 1756.   [4] 1757 and 1758.

[5] 1747, 20 Geo. II. c. 3; 1758, 31 Geo. II. c. 22; 1761, 2 Geo. III. c. 8. The only increase affecting the poor was 1s. per dwelling house per annum, added in 1758 to the old 2s. The window tax did not begin until the house had ten windows, later eight (1761). The exemption of cottages from the house tax affected only cottages exempted by reason of poverty from poor and church rates (see also 7 & 8 Will. III. c. 18, § 28).

[6] Malt, 1760, 6¼d. to 9¼d. per bushel; strong beer, 1761, 5s. to 8s. per barrel. In 1763, cider was added to the liquor excise, against much opposition on administrative grounds; it was repealed in 1766.

[7] 1736, 9 Geo. II. c. 23; 1743, 16 Geo. II. c. 8; 1751, 24 Geo. II. c. 40; 1753, 26 Geo. II. c. 13. See below.

which defined the main lines on which opinion was developing in the eighteenth century. The time of Walpole marks the transition between seventeenth and eighteenth century views of taxation.

The seventeenth century discussed four main questions—direct taxation, taxes on necessaries, taxes on luxuries, and taxes in relation to trade policy. It approved a direct tax on income but failed to achieve it, and instead handed on a Land Tax ; it approved taxes on necessaries and obtained them in various Excise duties ; it approved taxes on luxuries, which it obtained chiefly in Customs duties ; and it approved certain kinds of taxes on foreign trade, to which it was occupied in making Customs duties conform. Walpole's policy touched all these questions, and attempted, in the tax situation of his day, to apply to them the essential ideas which had motived seventeenth century policy. In the first place, adopting the generally accepted principles of Mercantile trade policy in relation to Customs, he reduced import duties on raw material and carried to completion the abolition of all duties on the export of English manufactures.[1] In the second place, he treated Customs duties on imported superfluities as an approved and permanent part of the ordinary tax revenue ; he provided for the more efficient administration of the tea and coffee duties in 1723, and proposed but failed to carry similar improvements in 1733 as regards wine and tobacco [2] ; and he declared in answer to opposition from the merchants that a tax on a luxury so little essential to the support or real comfort of human life as tobacco was the most obvious of all forms of taxation.[3] In the third place, he regarded an Excise on a necessary such as salt as an equitably

---

[1] Dowell, ii. 92 seq. ; King's speech of 1721 (Coxe's Memoirs of Walpole, i. 163) ; 8 Geo. I. c. 15.
[2] Dowell, ii. 97 seq. ; Cobbett, Parl. Hist., viii. 1269 seq.
[3] Cobbett, p. 1270 ; cf. [Walpole] Some General Considerations concerning the Alteration and Improvement of Public Revenue, 1733, T. 1744 (5), pp. 16–17.

distributed tax, and in 1732 deliberately reimposed this tax, which had been taken off in 1730, in order to enable him to reduce the Land Tax.[1] Finally, basing himself on the admitted injustice of the Land Tax in falling entirely or almost entirely on one class, the landlords, he proposed that it should be reduced and perhaps abolished, and that the revenue so lost should be made up by this Salt Tax and by the increased revenue to be expected from changes in Customs administration. In 1732 he carried the first part of this plan of compensation and reduced the Land Tax to 1s.; but such an outcry was raised against the second part, known as the Excise scheme of 1733, that he was forced to drop it. The Land Tax plan, in consequence, also failed.[2]

It is significant of the neglect into which the history of the more fundamental aspects of taxation has fallen, that while Walpole's dealings with the Customs are well known to students, and while the spectacular history of his Excise scheme is even famous, the other portion of his policy, viz. the substitution of a Salt Tax for 1s. of Land Tax in 1732, is almost universally ignored.[3] In tax interest, nevertheless, it altogether dwarfs the other portions of his policy. In his tariff policy, Walpole merely adopted ideas about which there was practically no dispute; and in the Excise scheme he proposed a sensible administrative reform which was merely distorted, to a great extent by political partisanship, into an attack on the liberties of the subject in general and of the trading class in particular. But in 1732 there was no distortion of the issue; it raised all the most fundamental questions in taxation and was recognized on both sides to do so; and Walpole's policy was strenuously opposed on the real merits so far as opinion at that time

[1] Cobbett, pp. 943–5.   [2] Dowell, *loc. cit.*
[3] An exception is Brisco, *The Economic Policy of Robert Walpole*, pp. 98–106, 120–5. I am not in entire agreement with Mr. Brisco on all points, but my account is written from a somewhat different point of view.

understood them. The issue, moreover, was a distributive
issue and little more; it was not complicated, as tax
issues usually are, by the necessity to raise more money
in some way; it was simply a question of deliberately
altering the existing distribution of taxation. In the
relatively full records of the policy of 1732 we obtain an
unrivalled view of the chief elements of distributive
opinion in the seventeenth and eighteenth centuries.

Added point was given to the episope of 1732 by
the fact that two years earlier Parliament employed
a surplus on the budget to repeal the Salt Tax as the
most suitable way of relieving the poor. The King's
speech of 13th January 1730[1] recommended 'giving
ease where the duties are most grievous,' and added
that the King looked 'with compassion upon the
hardships of the poor artificers and manufacturers.'
It appears[2] that in pursuance of this recommendation
it was first proposed in the Commons that the tax on
candles should be taken off. A counter-proposal,
however, was made to repeal the Salt Tax. The debate
accepted the standpoint of the King's speech that the
poor were objects of compassion,[3] and the question
was whether the users of salt or the users of candles
were 'the greater objects of pity and compassion.'
It was pointed out that the Candle Tax was paid very
largely by people of condition as well as by poor
artificers; and that its repeal would be little or no
relief to country people, 'the poor labourer and the

---

[1] Cobbett, p. 766.
[2] A report of the debate of 1730 was published in *The Political
State of Great Britain* for February 1732, vol. 43, pp. 163-7 (PP.
3400). It gives a close, possibly a full, report of the speech of the
proposer of Salt Tax rather than Candle Tax, and a summary of
the ensuing discussion.
[3] That this standpoint was common after the Peace of Utrecht
is obvious from pamphlets. See *The State and Condition of our Taxes
considered, or a Proposal for a Tax upon Funds* . . . 1714, T. 1990
(20), p. 16; [A. Boyer] *Animadversions and Observations . . . to
which is added a new Proposition to raise Money for the Use of the
Public*, 1718, 8223. d. 22, p. 46; *An Essay on Ways and Means* . . .
1726, 8245 b. 37, p. 8.

poor farmer,' who scarcely used candles. Salt Tax, on the other hand, was paid by the poor everywhere; it materially affected the price; and whereas the gentleman used far more candles than any farmer, the poor husbandman, in salting his produce, used more salt than the gentleman. On these grounds, and as a benefit to the salt trade and to shipping, the House decided in favour of repealing the Salt Tax.

It was typical of the absence of any definitely distributive principle in the opposition to taxes on necessaries, that Walpole should have been prepared to propose a re-imposition of the Salt Tax[1] in 1732 in substitution of Land Tax, and to defend his proposal as equitable between rich and poor. His defence consisted in a restatement of a view of taxation with which we are now familiar, but of which this is the most complete expression which is preserved.[2] In the first place, he contended that every one should pay taxation since every one shared in the benefit of the public service provided by the money raised. Consequently the poor man should pay as well as the rich man. As one of the pamphlets which supported Walpole put it, 'if he (the labourer) has no estate, yet he owes the protection of his life and liberty to the Government and should consequently contribute his mite to its support.'[3] In the second place, Walpole defined the standard according to which all men should

[1] Mr. Brisco, pp. 99-100, has made an attempt to explain why Walpole should have abolished the Salt Tax in 1730 and revived it in 1732. But we do not know that the abolition of 1730 was Walpole's idea; it is more probable, from the terms of the King's speech and from the debates of 1730 and 1732, that he wished to abolish the Candle Tax.

[2] Cobbett, pp. 943 *seq.* and 959 *seq.* Reports of these debates are included in several collections, *e.g.* A Collection of the Parl. Debates in England, 1688-1741 (pubd. 1741), x. 143-273. The original report is in the *Gentleman's Magazine*, ii. 991 *seq.* I see no reason to doubt their substantial accuracy. They are, of course, not verbatim, except in one or two cases. Walpole's speeches as given in Cobbett are revised from MS. notes discovered by Coxe.

[3] *The Case of the Salt Duty and the Land Tax offered to the Consideration of Every Freeholder*, 1732, 103. i. 21, p. 13.

pay as being in proportion to the benefit each receives
by reason of the tax. He did not, however, consider
how the benefit was distributed among different people,
and the actual standard he had in mind and by which
he expressly justified the Salt Tax was means or, more
vaguely, 'circumstances and condition in life.'[1] He
was thinking of an ability standard, and it was not
necessary for his purpose to define it very exactly.
In the third place, coming to the problem of how to
get taxes conforming to these principles, he laid it
down as obvious that any tax which was to be just
must necessarily be general—otherwise how make every
one contribute ? He simply accepted unthinkingly the
non-compensatory view of the seventeenth century
which regarded each tax by itself and required it to
be equitable in itself. It never occurred to him that
an equitable system of taxation might be devised in
which every tax would be distributively unfair. Taxation was for Walpole a mere aggregate of separate
taxes. Two consequences at once followed. Although
he was proposing to alter the distribution of taxation,
he did not first set out to consider how taxation as a
whole was distributed; and the Land Tax, which fell
almost entirely on one class, was condemned as inequitable out of hand—it was a partial and not a general
tax.[2] Finally, he contended, the Salt Tax was equitably
distributed and the substitution he proposed was
therefore the substitution of a just for an unjust tax.
'The duty upon salt is a tax that every man in the
nation contributes to according to his circumstances
and condition in life ; every subject contributes something ; if he be a poor man he contributes so small a
trifle it will hardly bear a name ; if he be rich he lives
more luxuriously and consequently contributes more ;
and if he be a man of a great estate, he keeps a great
number of servants and must therefore contribute a
great deal.'[3] Walpole reiterated this in a second

<hr>

[1] Cobbett, pp. 944, 968.   [2] Pp. 944-5.   [3] P. 944.

speech, and summed up his proposal thus : ' It is, I may say, self-evident that it (the Salt Tax) is a more just, a more equal and a better proportioned tax than any that is raised or can be contrived to be raised upon the people of this nation. The Land Tax, upon the other hand, is the most unequal, the most grievous and the most oppressive tax that ever was raised in this country ; it is a tax which never ought to be raised but in times of the most extreme necessity.'[1]

Walpole's motion was carried in the House of Commons by 225 to 187 on 7th February, 205 to 176 on 10th, and 209 to 154 on 2nd March (second reading), and in the House of Lords by 40 to 25 on 27th March.[2] He was ably supported by his brother Horatio,[3] by the writers of two anonymous pamphlets [4] and by the Duke of Newcastle,[5] all of whom presented the same case.

In spite of the monstrous suggestion (as it seems to us) that a Salt Tax makes rich and poor pay proportionately to their means, there is no reason to suppose that Walpole was dishonest in his presentation of his case, or that he was merely juggling with ideas which did not set out his real view of his policy. Any such suggestion is quite inconsistent with his speeches and with the inability of the opposition to meet them directly. It receives colour, however, from a real inconsistency in the views of Walpole and of the seventeenth century which it is necessary to understand. While in 1732 he argued that the tax on salt was equitable, in 1733 he repudiated the suggestion that he had ever had any intention of imposing an excise on food and all the necessaries of life, and declared that taxes on luxuries such as wine and tobacco were the ideal form of taxa-

---

[1] Cobbett, pp. 968 and 969. [2] Pp. 987, 1025, 1056.
[3] P. 950 *seq.* and p. 1048.
[4] *The Case of the Salt Duty,* etc., 1732, and *The Letter to a Free-holder on the Late Reduction of the Land Tax to One Shilling in the Pound,* 1732, 104. d. 9.
[5] Cobbett, pp. 950, *seq.* and p. 1048.

tion.[1] Premising the fact that a similar repudiation
was clearly made in the debates of 1732,[2] we have to
notice that the seventeenth century view of taxation
which was taken over by Walpole accepted as equitable
both taxes on necessaries and taxes on luxuries. Taxes
on necessaries were approved because they made every one
pay in proportion, as it was supposed, to his ability.
Taxes on luxuries were approved on various non-distributive grounds and to some extent on the distributive
ground that the use of the taxed luxury was a test of
his ability which the payer himself provided; but the
real ground of distributive or quasi-distributive approval
was that they laid no or almost no burden on the poor
man. In other words, while in regard to taxes on
necessaries the taxation of the poor was defended, in
regard to taxes on luxuries men were quite willing to
accept the compassionate plea that the poor should be
exempted. There was in this a real if not a formal
inconsistency indicating a failure even on the part of
supporters of the taxation of the poor to reconcile
their theory and their sentiment, and it was one which
long subsisted; but it does not imply any dishonest
combination of positions. It is altogether a mistake,
therefore, to suppose that when Walpole praised taxes
on luxuries in 1733 he was recanting what he said on
the Salt Tax in 1732.[3]

The opposition to Walpole's proposal was represented
chiefly by Walter Plumer, Wyndham, and Pulteney in
the Commons, and by Winchelsea, Bathurst, and Carteret
in the Lords. Many objections to the reimposition of

[1] Cobbett, p. 1270, and [Walpole] *Some General Considerations*,
etc., 1733, pp. 6, 16–17.
[2] Cobbett, pp. 951, 960–1.
[3] Apart from the fact that he ignores the position set out here,
Mr. Brisco seems to take too cataclysmic a view of the change in
opinion on the subject of excises on necessaries (pp. 123–4).
Moreover, the change was not due to Walpole's position having
been answered, but to the insistence on different ideas which came
to have greater influence. See below.

the Salt Tax were urged,[1] but two stand out as important elements of opinion and as general grounds of opposition to excises on necessaries. The first was that the Salt duty was grievous to the poor ; the second that it was injurious to trade and manufactures. Both were used by the same men, and it was chiefly the conjunction of these two lines of opinion that determined the eighteenth century view of tax questions.

The objection to the Salt Tax in the interest of the poor was the plea for compassion which we have already discussed in the seventeenth century and in 1730. Plumer[2] described Walpole's proposal as one ' to grind the face of the poor in order to relieve a few of the rich.' But Pulteney's speech best defined the point of view.[3] He calculated that the duty would make a poor man with a wife and family pay 4s. 6d. a year (1s. a head). Then he appealed to the House : ' Such a thing as a shilling or a crown may be looked upon as a trifle by a gentleman of a large estate and easy circumstances, but a poor man feels sometimes severely the want of a shilling. . . . Let us but imagine ourselves in the condition of a poor labourer with a wife and three children, almost the whole of the wife's time taken up in looking after the children, and the husband working for a shilling a day, and we shall easily see how hard it is to make such a poor man pay a tax of four or five shillings a year for the salt he must make use of for the scanty support of himself and family.' ' How cruel,' he repeated later, ' is it to take four or five shillings a

---

[1] Grounds of opposition in addition to those discussed at length below are set out briefly in the Lords' Protest (Cobbett, pp. 1061–3). They were : prelude to a general excise ; danger to constitutional liberty ; unfavourable to development of land ; cost of collection ; frauds ; no real relief to landlords, since tenant's cost of production would be increased (e.g. Carteret, p. 1042) ; all taxes fall ultimately on land, and so no real relief (discussed in next chapter) ; unfair between England and Scotland. None of these contentions was of much importance, and most of them were easily answered by Walpole and his brother (pp. 950 seq., 959 seq.).

[2] Cobbett, p. 946. Also pp. 956, 1040, 1041.

[3] Pp. 981–2, 987.

year away from the support of such a poor family. . . . I hope every man that hears me will allow his pity and compassion to exert itself to its utmost weight. I hope every man will consider upon which side of the present question are the cries of the poor and the wretched and the blessings of those that are yet unborn.'

The answer of Walpole's side to this kind of argument was that experience of the old Salt Tax proved that it was not burdensome upon the people,[1] and indeed that the duty would be paid by such a multitude ' that no single man can any way feel what he pays thereto.'[2] But it was more to the point that whether the tax was or was not burdensome to the poor did not answer Walpole's contention that it was an equitable tax. It is interesting to notice the extent to which the opposition attempted to translate their feeling against taxes on the poor into direct answers to Walpole's reasoning. To the initial position that the poor man should pay taxation with other men they were unable to find any reply. They merely tried to ignore it. And the reason is well illustrated by an exception to this attitude. Lord Bathurst, who condemned the proposed tax as most unjust and oppressive, was prepared to admit that every one should pay according to the benefit he received.[3] But, he said, ' in all cases it is hard, it is cruel to tax the poor journeymen and day labourers, because it is not to be presumed that they can get anything more than bare subsistence by their daily labour ; the profits that may be made go all to the benefit of the master who employs them. He it is that has the whole benefit of their labour and therefore ought to pay the taxes.' This was an attempt to rebut the Lockean conclusion, not by denying that it follows that every one should pay taxation because every one benefits, but by denying that some benefit at all. It amounted practically to an assertion that the poor man is a beast of burden and hence cannot and should not pay taxation. But while, as we

---

[1] Cobbett, pp. 950, 1048.   [2] Pp. 950, 969.   [3] Pp. 1050-1.

shall see, this feeling had considerable influence in the eighteenth century, it was both too clearly false and too destructive of the current political theory of the governing class to find explicit acceptance in Parliament. To Walpole's second position that a just tax must be a general tax and equitable by itself, the opposition had similarly no answer, except that a tax on luxuries, which is not a general tax, is the best [1]; and they admitted the injustice of the Land Tax.[2] And to the third position, that the Salt Tax falls on different men in proportion to their ability, they failed to find any answer which applied to taxes on necessaries generally, but spent themselves in asserting that in the case of salt poor men used more than rich, on account of the salted fish and meat they were compelled to use.[3] This, of course, was not admitted by Walpole's side and is improbable; but what the facts were it is impossible to know and difficult to estimate.[4] Moreover, there was a tendency to reduce even the contention that the Salt Tax was in consequence grossly unfair, to a mere plea for compassion.[5]

Opposition to excises on necessaries in the interest of the poor thus remained in the eighteenth, as it had been in the seventeenth century, an emotional rather than a doctrinal opposition. It opposed a feeling to a political theory, and it was so much under the influence of that theory that it was unable to define the real point at issue.

The second important ground of opposition to the

---

[1] Plumer, p. 946.

[2] E.g. [Pulteney] *The Case of the Revival of the Salt Duty* . . . 1732, 884, k. 16, pp. 6, 46–7.

[3] Wyndham, p. 1020; Carteret, p. 1042; Bathurst, p. 1051. The argument was adduced late in the discussion, and we have no direct criticism of it by Walpole or his brother.

[4] In 1756 Joseph Massie calculated that a gentleman of £1000 a year paid 14s. 2d., a farmer spending £100 a year 6s. 8d., an agricultural labourer earning 5s. a week 3s. 4d., and an artisan earning from 7s. 6d. to 12s. a week 2s. 6d., to the salt tax in a year (*Calculation of Taxes* . . ., 8226, b. 15).

[5] Wyndham, p. 1020.

Salt Tax was as hard and abstractly theoretical as the first was vague and compassionate. It was the doctrine that trade and particularly export trade would be injured by the tax, because wages would rise ; and it was based on the theory that a tax on a necessary of life is not really paid by the poor workman but by his employer, who has to raise wages.[1] Instead of imposing a further tax on a necessary, all such taxes should on the contrary be removed. The wages of the labouring poor would thus be reduced without laying any hardship on them, and this would ' not only be a great ease to the landed man who employs them, but give new life to our trade and encourage the exportation of our manufactures on which it depends.'[2]

Commercial ideas had always influenced Customs duties, but now for the first time they emerge as a powerful, if indirect, influence on opinion concerning the central problems of the distribution of taxation. They were powerful because they had the backing of the trading class and because that class was vigorous in its expression of them. This is clear in 1732 from the speeches of its mouthpieces in Parliament. As we have noticed, the opposition could not deny that the Land Tax was unfair to the landed class and practically exempted traders and moneyed men. In this new doctrine these classes had their answer. They said in effect that Walpole's proposal was the substitution for an unjust tax on land of a ruinous tax on trade. But it was still clearer in 1733, in the clamour over the Excise scheme, which again seemed to them to be a sacrifice of the trading classes (this time in the matter of their liberty) for the benefit of the landed men. Apart from the mere partisan standpoint of the Parliamentary opposition,

---

[1] Cobbett ; Plumer, p. 947, Wyndham, p. 954-5, Pulteney, p. 982, Bathurst, p. 1051. The pamphlets of 1733 (for which see list in Seligman, *Incidence*, Bibliography) make incidental reference to the doctrine. See also *Gentleman's Magazine*, June 1732, ii. 813.

[2] [Pulteney] *The Case of the Revival of the Salt Duty*, 1732, p. 54.

this was the chief significance of the struggle of 1733.[1] It was a fight between the landed and the trading classes, in which circumstances enabled the latter to win. Class feeling, too, was stirred on both sides. To one writer the proposal appeared to amount to relieving the wealthy useless part of society by burdening the body of the people ' whose arts and labour alone support the kingdom.' [2]

The theory on which this commercial opposition was based—the theory, namely, that a tax on necessaries raises wages—is of no small importance in the history of social opinion. It was taken over from occasional speculation of the seventeenth century,[3] and was an important influence down to the repeal of the Corn Laws in 1846.[4] We shall have to deal with it in more detail in the next chapter, but two important points about it must be emphasized with reference to the debates of 1732. In the first place, it was wholly inconsistent with the former ground on which the Salt Tax was opposed—namely, the grievousness of the burden to the poor man. For it was now declared that not the poor man but his employer really paid the tax. And yet the same speakers in Parliament used both arguments —that the Salt Tax was cruel to the poor because they paid it, and was injurious to trade because they did not pay it.[5] This inconsistency runs right through the eighteenth century, and marks an important cleavage

---

[1] The third important issue was the fear of the landed men who were assessed at low rates to Land Tax that after removal the tax would be reformed and laid on real rents. See Dowell, ii. 102.

[2] *The Nature of the Present Excise* . . ., 1733, 104. d. 19, p. 28-9. Also *A Letter of Advice to the Rev. Mr. Scurlock* . . ., 1733, E. 2202 (5); *Englishmen's Eyes Opened* . . ., 1733, T. 1618 (4), p. 2 ; *An Argument against Excises* . . ., by Caleb Danvers, 1733, 518. h. 8 (1), pp. 12, 14, 71.

[3] See note 1, p. 80.

[4] Any one who is interested both in economic ideas and in party politics will find considerable interest in the part which this doctrine played on both sides of the Corn Law controversy from the time Cobden entered it till 1846. See chiefly Hansard's *Debates*.

[5] See references to note 1, p. 108,

of attitude towards the poor—perhaps in a very rough
way the attitude of the landed and the commercial
classes [1]—as well as a certain superficiality of thought
which was characteristic of that century. In the
second place, the view of the poor which was involved
or tended to be involved in this theory was significant.
The theory said that the poor man shifted a tax on
necessaries because, living normally at the margin of
subsistence, he could not pay it and be independent.
Lord Bathurst, for instance, declared that any scheme
for taxing the poor 'is not only cruel but it is impracticable, because if by such taxes we enhance the price of
the very necessaries of life, they cannot possibly subsist
upon the same wages they subsisted on formerly; they
must starve or otherwise their wages must be raised, and
thus at last the master that employs them must pay
the taxes that are laid upon the poor he employs.' [2]
Now impliedly this view of the poor approached very
near to that position which Bathurst, as we noticed
before, stated explicitly—namely, that the poor man
received no benefit from the State. He tended to be
conceived as a different kind of being from the taxable
citizen of means, and much more like a beast of burden
or a mere factor of production. This was the second
indirect answer of the eighteenth century to the theory
that every man should pay taxation, and the real
nemesis of the 'freeholder' conception of English
society. The purpose and therefore the test of citizenship was thought of as the enjoyment of rights; but
compared with men of property the poor man seemed
to live rather for the benefit of others than for the
enjoyment of rights of his own.

[1] It is, of course, impossible to attribute any doctrine to a class
as a whole. It will be clear from next chapter, however, that the
theory that wages rise with a tax on necessaries was widely held by
men who were interested in trading and later in economic questions.
The attribution of the compassionate dislike to taxes on the poor to
the landed class is suggested by the debates of William III., of 1730
and 1732, and specially by those of 1776–99, for which see Chap. VIII.

[2] Cobbett, p. 1051.

It is important to notice that this view of the poor and this theory of the incidence of taxes on necessaries, while influential with one side, were explicitly repudiated in 1732 by the other. For Walpole, the poor man was a taxable citizen as much as any other, and along with his brother he denied that taxes on necessaries raised wages or injured trade. They pointed out very properly that our trade never flourished more than in the thirty-four years during the existence of the old Salt Tax, and that wages did not diminish when it was removed in 1730.[1] Later on we shall come upon attempts to defend the theory more completely, but there is no doubt that in origin and always in essence it was a mere assumption or prejudice based on vague ideas of a margin of subsistence and fostered by the gulf between the life of the rich man and that of the labourer. But it seemed too natural to many people at that time for Walpole's criticism to overthrow it.

In 1732 the three ideas which had most influence on eighteenth century views on taxation were all represented. They were, first, that every one should pay taxation, including the poor man; second, that the poor man should, if possible, be exempted from taxation on compassionate grounds; and third, that the necessaries of his subsistence should be exempted to prevent high wages and for the benefit of trade.

The second and third of these ideas, although inconsistent, both led to the condemnation of taxes on necessaries, and this condemnation came gradually to be almost universally accepted and constituted the most important element of the eighteenth century view of the ideal tax, the tax on luxuries. This result was achieved, however, in spite of and not by overthrowing the doctrine that every man should pay taxation and that a just tax must be general. The new

[1] Cobbett, pp. 950, 969.

theory was therefore not directly the result of a view of distributive equity in taxation but rather of two ideas of non-tax policy, compassion for the poor and the advantage of low wages in the interest of trade.

VII

WALPOLE TO ADAM SMITH

THE mark of the tax literature of this period is the influence of commercial interests and ideas. This influence did not sum up the period ; it is clear, particularly from the subsequent history, that it was matched by an increase in the influence of compassionate or philanthropic ideas, and it did not in any way explain, for instance, the new policy regarding spirits. Nevertheless, this influence was the distinctive feature of the period ; it was the new influence of the time, and it affected doctrine on so many questions that it provides a clue to the meaning of a great mass of discussion which otherwise would seem both superficial and vacillating.

By far the most important effect of this influence was the condemnation of excises on necessaries on the the ground that they raise wages and are prejudicial to trade. Many striking statements of this doctrine are to be found subsequent to the debates of 1732. The burden of Jacob Vanderlint's long pamphlet of 1734 was the necessity for reducing the rates of labour which depended on the price of victuals and drink, in order to increase our foreign and domestic trade.[1] In 1737, Sir John Barnard, merchant and Lord Mayor of the City of London, whose reputation for financial capacity was second only to Walpole's, proposed in the

[1] Jacob Vanderlint, *Money answers all Things* . . . 1734, 104. g. 10, preface, pp. 6, 7, etc.

House of Commons [1] that the savings which would result from his scheme for the reduction of the interest on the debt, should be employed to take off taxes on necessaries, on the one ground of the 'increase or rather the revival of our trade.' The power and riches of a country, he held, depended on its ability to sell its manufactures cheaper than its neighbours, which in its turn depended on the price of labour (there being little difference in the cost of material), which again depended on the price of those provisions necessary for the convenient support of the labourers. Hence the necessity for abolishing taxes on necessaries. Only a few speeches in the ensuing debate are reported, but they all ignore the question of the poor paying such taxes. It was a question of trade, not of the poor. As one speaker [2] said, ' in all countries where the poor have any employment they are pretty near equally poor ; they neither get nor expect more than a comfortable subsistence by their labour, and if you enhance the means of that subsistence by taxes upon the necessaries or conveniences of life, their master must increase their wages.' The motion was defeated, apparently on grounds of procedure, by 200 to 142. In 1743, Sir Matthew Decker, a retired merchant, a director of the East India Company and a member of Parliament, published his well-known scheme for a single tax on houses. [3] His aim was to prevent smuggling and to free trade from the heavy load of duties which burdened and endangered it ; and for the advantage of trade he was careful to propose that the houses of some half a million of the poorest people should be exempted from his proposed taxes [4]—' that thereby

[1] Cobbett, *Parl. Hist.*, x. 155 *seq.* For short biographies of Barnard and those who follow, see *Dict. of Nat. Biography.*

[2] Cobbett, x. 173.

[3] [Sir Matthew Decker] *Serious Considerations* . . . 1743, 1093. d. 101. For the contemporary interest in the pamphlet see *Gentleman's Magazine*, 13. 653

[4] P 15.

their labour might become so much the cheaper, and the goods which are the product of their labour might by this means be sold at as low or even a lower rate than can be afforded by other nations.' One of the most absolute assertions of the doctrine was made by Francis Fauquier, the son of a director of the Bank of England, and himself a director of the South Sea Company, and later Lieutenant-Governor of Virginia. In 1756 he published an essay on the best ways of raising money for the war,[1] the whole burden of which was contained in the preliminary maxim that ' the poor do not, never have nor ever possibly can pay any tax whatever. A man that has nothing can pay nothing. . . . He that works for his living will and must live by his labour . . . and equally so whether provisions are dear or cheap.' Ultimately, therefore, it is the man of fortune who pays all the taxes, and it is a matter of great indifference by what particular taxes he is made to pay. Finally, to end the list of illustrations, Malachy Postlethwayt, as was natural, incorporated the doctrine in his *Dictionary of Trade and Commerce*.[2] Since ' people without property who work for their daily bread ' ' live but from hand to mouth, whatever is laid on them they must therefore shift off or they cannot subsist.'

Many other instances of this idea could be given,[3]

---

[1] F. F(auquier), *An Essay on Ways and Means for Raising Money for the Support of the Present War without Increasing the Public Debts*, 1756, E. 2213 (3), pp. 16, 17, 18, 20, 22, postscript to 2nd ed., T. 1627 (3), p. 37–8.

[2] *The Universal Dictionary of Trade and Commerce*, vol. ii. 1755, 14,000, e. 47, p. 3.

[3] See, *e.g.*, *Gentleman's Magazine*, 1732, ii. 813 ; *An Inquiry into the Causes of the Increase and Miseries of the Poor of England*, 1738, 104. n. 9, pp. 18, 79 ; *An Essay on the Inequality of our Present Taxes . . .*, 1746, 104, d. 8 (3), p. 78 ; [Josiah Tucker] *A Brief Essay . . . (with) an Appendix . . .*, 1750, 104, h. 10, pp. 38–9, 46–7—Tucker was rather indefinite on this question ; Debate on Linen duties, 1756, Cobbett, *Parl. Hist.*, 15, 674–5 (speech of Vyner) ; *Thoughts on the Pernicious Consequences of Borrowing Money . . .*, 1756, 104, c. 46, p. 12 ; *Thoughts on the Causes and Consequences of the Present High Price of Provisions*, 1767, 1027, b. 16 (2), pp. 4–5 ; Lord Kames, *Sketches of the History of Man*, 1774 (722, k. 18), viii., Finances (pp. 465–6, 470,

and it may be noted in passing that it was involved in the theory, to which occasional reference was made but which had little importance in England, that all taxes fall ultimately on the land.[1] But the best proof of its influence was the controversy about it which took place in the third quarter of the century. Up to about 1750 the doctrine that the poor man shifts a tax on necessaries was put forward without any serious explanation or understanding. It appeared self-evident. Vaguely, it seemed that the labourer and artisan lived at a subsistence minimum below which they could not or for some reason would not go.[2] But this assumption was now attacked in two forms. To take the shorter lived and less important first, it was maintained that, far from raising wages, a tax on necessaries really lowered them, by stimulating the lazy, careless manufacturing class to regular and strenuous exertion. It repudiated the doctrine that the poor lived at a subsistence margin ; on the contrary, wages were so high that they could afford to be both idle and riotous in living ; and obviously, it involved a low opinion of the labouring classes in manufactures—for it was to experience of these classes that appeal was made in proof. In 1750, Josiah Tucker, at that time Rector in Bristol, brought out the standpoint clearly without himself subscribing to it.[3] He explained how a great manufacturer in the clothing way, carefully attending to the facts, had observed ' that in exceeding

478 of vol. i.) ; *The Political Register* (J. A. Almon), x. 161–5, Letter to Lord North, *The Absurdity, Impolicy and Inutility of reducing the Taxes on Soap, Candles*, etc. (1772).

[1] See note 92 of Chap. IV. For the history of this theory in England, see Seligman, *Incidence*, pp. 62–5, 101–9, 114–20. The most interesting references to the doctrine are the refutations to it, which usually admit the theory that taxes on necessaries raise wages. See *Gentleman's Magazine* of 1732, *ibid.*, 1738 *Enquiry*, p. 78–9 ; Hume, *Political Discourses*, 1752, *Essay on Taxes*, at end ; Arthur Young, *Political Arithmetic*, 1774, 288, c. 13, pp. 209–13, and theories of Sir James Steuart and Adam Smith.

[2] A different attempt to explain the idea was made by Barnard in the debates of 1737. If the labourer did not get his convenient support he would emigrate. Cobbett, x. 158.

[3] 1750, *Brief Essay*, p. 54.

dear years when corn and provisions are at an extravagant price, then the work is best and cheapest done ; but that in cheap years the manufacturers are idle, wages high and work ill done.' And ' therefore he inferred that the high duties, taxes and excises upon the necessaries of life are so far from being a disadvantage to trade, as things are circumstanced amongst us, that they are eventually the chief support of it—and ought to be higher still in order to oblige the poor either to work or starve.' Tucker was not prepared directly to deny the facts stated, but as an humane and compassionate man he disliked the deduction, which involved the careful as well as the careless. Hume in his *Essay on Taxes* (1752) took up a similarly undogmatic position. The chief exponent of the attitude, however, admitted no doubts or qualifications. This was William Temple of Trowbridge, who discussed the subject in 1758 and 1765.[1] In his *Considerations on Taxes as they are supposed to affect the Price of Labour in our Manufactures* (1765), he laid it down, as a maxim proved by experience, ' first, that mankind in general are naturally inclined to ease and indolence, and that nothing but absolute necessity will enforce labour and industry ; secondly, that the poor in general work only for the bare necessaries of life and for the means of a low debauch, which when obtained they cease to labour till roused again by necessity.' He denied that the desire for marriage stimulated the young to energy and industry in order to provide for it. Those, he said, ' who are concerned in the manufactures of this kingdom know by experience that the poor do not labour, upon an average, above four days a week, unless provisions happen to be very dear.' Consequently taxes on necessaries were not only not to be condemned, they were necessary for

---

[1] *A Vindication of Commerce and the Arts . . .*, 1758, 1029. e. 9 (16), p. 36–7 ; *Considerations on Taxes . . .*, 1765, 2nd ed. corrected, 104, c. 64. His *Essay on Trade and Commerce of* 1770, 1139, i. 4, expands the 1765 pamphlet, which it is explained went through two editions quickly.

trade and industry, and should be the last taxes to be abolished.   Nor were they unkind to the poor ; on the contrary, they were really for their good.[1]

But this attitude, while discussed somewhat widely, does not appear to have been widely accepted or to have had any permanent influence.   It was probably based on experience of particular industries in which abnormally high wages were paid,[2] and it was overborne by the complaints against dearness of provisions in the sixties.   Nathaniel Forster,[3] an Oxford Fellow and a Rector in Essex, writing in 1767 on the causes of the high prices, which he attributed partly to taxes, protested against Temple's doctrine as false and inhuman, a proposal for oppression, coming generally from ' suspicious authorities,' and a ' shelter for avarice and rapacity in private life.'   That a sudden rise of wages might result in idleness and vice with a few worthless fellows he did not deny ; ' but the really industrious would never be less so from any extraordinary encouragement given to industry.'   These false doctrines, he said, ' were to be heard thrown out in conversation, but he had the most entire conviction that they had not the minutest influence on the counsels and measures of ministers.'   Adam Smith dismissed the whole idea without much consideration.[4]   He said that high wages in general encouraged the industry of the worker and that the case of those who, when they had earned enough in four days, idled the rest of the week, was not typical. This objection to the condemnation of taxes on necessaries did not become part of the tradition of English tax doctrine.

The more important and more moderate attack on

---

[1] Pp. 6-7, 8-9, 12-13, 27, 51-2.

[2] The plausibility of generalising it further lay probably in the outbreak of spirit-drinking which occurred in the second quarter of the century—discussed below.

[3] [N. Forster] *An Enquiry into the Causes of the present High Prices of Provisions*, T. 1466 (1), pp. 49, 56, 58, 59, 61, 63-4.

[4] *Wealth of Nations*, ed. Cannan, i. 83-4 ; Everyman ed. i. 73-4.

the theory that a tax on necessaries raises wages consisted in the appeal to experience as showing that wages did not rise when prices were high or fall when they were low. Walpole, as we have seen, pointed this out in 1732, and it was admitted by Hume.[1] Temple, of course, emphasised it strongly.[2] 'The nominal price of a day's labour in money,' he said, 'hardly ever varies with the price of provisions. Though from a bad harvest wheat should advance two shillings a bushel, which would affect the poor much more than all the taxes put together, yet the price of a day's labour would remain the same.' The origin of the fallacy, Temple thought, was this : 'Everyone clearly sees that if a populace can live cheap they can afford to live cheap ; from whence it is immediately concluded that they will do so '—a conclusion quite unwarranted and untrue. Thomas Mortimer, who published in 1772 a large *Treatise on the Elements of Commerce, Politics and Finances as a Supplement to the Education of British Youth*, also contended that experience showed that wages do not rise or fall with prices, and that the poor cannot thus be neglected in considering taxes on necessaries.[3]

Now, this criticism could not be ignored. Wages as a matter of experience do not rise and fall with the imposition or repeal of taxes on necessaries or with changes in prices due to several causes [4]; and we find Sir James Steuart [5] and Adam Smith [6] admitting this.

---

[1] *Loc. cit.*   [2] 1765, *Considerations*, pp. 15, 6.

[3] *The Elements of Commerce, Politics, and Finance* . . ., 1772, 29, d. 13, pp. 451–2.

[4] Changes in the value of money do, of course, affect wages as well as prices, though more slowly and with greater friction.

[5] *An Inquiry into the Principles of Political Economy*, 1767, 2 vols. 31. e. 5–6, ii. 505–7, 509. Steuart's theory of taxes and wages is complicated and not influential enough to demand discussion in detail here. For an account, see Seligman, *Incidence*, pp. 118–20. His general position was that taxes on commodities really affected only the idle and never the industrious (see pp. 488, 489, 493), but he did not approve of the consequent condemnation of them (p. 505).

[6] *Wealth of Nations*, ed. Cannan, i. 75–7 ; Everyman, ed. i. 65–7.

Nevertheless they continued to teach that a tax on wages or on the necessaries of the labourer must raise wages, but now on more carefully stated and more guarded premises. Resort was had to a distinction between the immediate and the medium or average effects of a tax on necessaries, and between the momentary and the average price of provisions. Temple was acquainted with the line of thought in 1765 and was unable to answer it, although he did not accept it.[1] A thorough inquiry, it was thought, showed ' that the standard of wages is naturally fixed at the medium price of provisions. There is a relation between these which gradually and constantly takes place ; else why the present wages of one shilling a day instead of one penny, which was the case some centuries ago. Labour and wages must bear such relation to one another in all wise nations that the wages shall be sufficient to render the married state so easy as to encourage the young of both sexes to obey that first and great command, increase and multiply.' But Adam Smith's was the most careful and most influential statement of the revised version. Briefly put,[2] he held, first, that the demand for labour was independent of its supply, so that, the causes which determine the extent of the demand remaining constant, an increase in the number of labourers would necessarily reduce the wage obtained by each, and *vice versa* ; and, secondly, that the supply of labour always tended, through changes in the amount of population, to adjust itself to the demand for it existing in any period in such a way that each labourer would get enough and just enough to enable him to live, and with his fellows to bring up a sufficient number of children to maintain this adjustment. Stated still more crudely, Adam Smith's position was this :—regard the amount of the subsistence for the labouring class as fixed : then they will multiply up to that number which will be just

[1] *Op. cit.* pp. 13–14. Temple's attempted answer is no answer.
[2] See book i. chap. viii. (sp. pp. 61, 63, 70–2, 76—Everyman ed.).

able to exist permanently upon that amount of subsistence; and this adjustment will be maintained not
through restriction of marriages so much as through
infant mortality increasing or decreasing according as
wages are low or high. And these forces will operate
although the demand for labour is not fixed; the result
during a period of changing demand will merely be more
complex. Consequently, if the demand or subsistence
for the labouring class is artificially reduced by a tax[1]—
if, in other words, every labourer's real wages are thereby
reduced—the result will simply be to lessen the supply
of labour and so to raise real wages again. Therefore
the employer will pay both the natural wage and the
tax—the tax ultimately falling, as Adam Smith thought,
on the landlord as regards agricultural labourers, and
on the consumers of non-necessary commodities as
regards others.

The classical political economy thus took over from
the commercial ideas of the eighteenth century and
carried on for the instruction and employment of the
nineteenth, the doctrine that a tax on necessaries
raises wages. And it is noteworthy that the importance
of what it borrowed was much greater than that of the
explanation which it added. This is clear in many
ways in Adam Smith. His theory logically involved,
for instance, that a tax on necessaries would only be
shifted to wages after ten or fifteen years. But he did
not explicitly recognise this; he always spoke most
dogmatically and unqualifiedly on the point; and he
did not argue against taxes on necessaries on the ground
that they were grievous to the poor during that period.[2]
Similarly, the most essential feature of Adam Smith's

---

[1] Book v. chap. ii. part ii. art. 3 (ii. 346-7), and art. 4 (pp. 352-3).

[2] Another minor logical weakness of Adam Smith's theory
was that, admitting as he did that taxes on luxuries used by the
poor only reduce their use of these and do not affect wages, he did
not see that a tax on necessaries might equally, so long as the poor
used any luxuries, simply also reduce their use of these and so not
affect wages.

attitude was the same as that of the less-guarded doctrine,
—namely a conception, not fully explicit, of labouring
people as a class apart, not only living a different life,
but subject to different forces from people of means.
Finally, his theory was as a whole so complicated that
it is improbable that it increased the influence of the
doctrine to any extent in the eighteenth century.
What Adam Smith did was to give the sanction of a name
which had great weight with certain kinds of people to
a view which was already influential.

A new force was thus added to the opposition to
Excise duties on necessaries. The old compassionate
objection in the interest of the poor, which we have
noticed in 1730 and 1732, did not find much expression
in the controversial literature of this period,[1] but when
tax debates begin to be again serviceable in 1776, it is
clear that, far from having weakened, it had become
more dominant. Other distributive grounds of objection to taxes on necessaries do not appear to have
had any general influence.[2] The result was that

[1] The increase in the malt tax in 1760 called forth a pamphlet
by J. Massie, *Reasons* . . . (8228, g. 31) in which he opposed it in
the interest of the poor. ' When I consider how much the common
working people of England have contributed by their industry and
courage to make this nation rich and happy, and how slender a
portion of these national benefits come to their share, I cannot
help being grieved at the thought of measures which will make
that small portion less,' p. 3. Massie denied that the tax would
increase the poor man's wages, but it is doubtful if he was always
consistent in this point. (See *Ways and Means* . . ., 1757, 104, c.
15, p. 2.) For his other pamphlets and life, see D.N.B. Thomas
Mortimer represents the same compassionate attitude : *Elements*,
1772, pp. 453, 459 ; and it is referred to in Lord North's speeches
of 1769 and 1775 (Cobbett, 1769, 16, p. 608, 1775, 18, p. 623, and Sir
Henry Cavendish's *Debates*, i. 388).

[2] Occasional assertions of the distributive unfairness of taxes
on necessaries are :—*Some Considerations upon Taxes* . . . [1750 ?]
T. 13^x (7), p. 9 (poorest pay more in proportion than the rich) ; Sir
John Nickolls (Dangeul), *Remarks on the advantages and disadvantages of France and of Great Britain in regard to Commerce* . . .,
1754, 1138. a. 5, p. 260-1 (' the poor and the rich pay the same
sum ')—apparently appropriated by Postlethwayt (inconsistently)
in *Great Britain's Tax System*, 1757, p. 160. The doctrine that

two negative and inconsistent principles—the one of commercial, the other of social policy—joined together to place the negative maxim that taxes should not be on necessaries in the position of a first principle of tax policy. The opposition view of Walpole's day had become the orthodoxy of Lord North's. But the new orthodoxy had not answered the old,—it had merely displaced it ; nor had it achieved the repeal, although it had so far prevented much increase, of taxes on necessaries.

The first general characteristic of this period was therefore the growth of opposition to taxes on necessaries. The second was the development of opinion unfavourable to direct assessment of means or income, and favourable to the continuance of the distributively inequitable Land Tax. In this result also, commercial ideas played an important part.

The Land Tax was both so partial and as time passed so much less productive than a real pound rate would have been,[1] that proposals for a new direct assessment

necessaries should be exempted, in the form given to it by Montesquieu in 1748, was also occasionally cited in England.   Referring to an Athenian tax, Montesquieu wrote : ' La taxe était juste, quoiqu' elle ne fût point proportionelle ; si elle ne suivait pas la proportion des biens, elle suivait la proportion des besoins.   On jugea que chacun avait un nécessaire physique égal ; que ce nécessaire physique ne devait point être taxé ; que l'utile venait ensuite, et qu'il devait être taxé mais moins que le superflu ; que la grandeur de la taxe sur le superflu empêchait le superflu.'   De L'Esprit des Lois, Livre xiii. § 7.   See N. Forster, op. cit. pp. 52–3, n. ; and Lord Kames, op. cit. pp. 458–9. Kames did not really make the idea part of his view of the English tax system.   It requires some political theory such as Benthamite utilitarianism to give it a basis.

[1] Estimates about the middle of the century as to the average real rate of the Land Tax are : An Essay on the inequality of our present Taxes . . ., 1746, 104. d. 8 (3), pp. 9–11—Land Tax, supposed to levy a fifth of the yearly value of lands, does not raise a tenth, perhaps not a twelfth ; Some considerations . . ., 1750 ? T. 13ˣ (7), p. 4—' In many counties which are reported to be moderately taxed, their land tax generally amounts to 2s. 8d. in the £ at a 4s. tax ' ; Nickolls (Dangeul), Remarks . . ., 1754, 1138. a. 5, p. 268— reassessment would double the yield ; Thoughts . . . with a proposal for raising a supply for the current service . . ., 1756, 104.

were frequently made.[1]   But such proposals had not sufficient weight to overcome the pressure of opposing interests.   On the one hand, experience suggested that a new attempt at an income tax would again fail to reach men of personal estates, and would result merely in a heavier burden on landed men ; and those landed men who were rated very low in the Land Tax had no wish to be brought up to the ordinary level.[2]   On the other hand, the interest of commercial and moneyed men, who escaped so largely in the Land Tax, was against any attempt at a general direct tax, and commercial proposals for a new assessment were usually directed towards reassessment within the landed class alone.[3]

But opposition to an income tax based on the interest of classes was reinforced by the influence of opinion which condemned such a tax, assuming it could be achieved, as essentially objectionable. It is important to realise clearly the character of the objections to which such controlling weight was given. The principle that taxation should be distributed in proportion to income was not repudiated ; on the contrary, it was formally affirmed by the chief objector, Adam Smith.[4] The grounds of condemnation were

c. 46, p. 6, equal Land Tax at 4s. per £ would yield £5,000,000 (in place of £2,000,000). Different places paid very different rates. See *Essay* of 1746.

[1] *e.g.* [Wm. Wood], *A Letter to an M.P.* . . ., 1717, 8132. a. 65, pp. 9–11, for reassessment on land only ; *An Enquiry* . . ., 1738, 104, n. 9, p. 75 ff., for an Income Tax ; *Essay* of 1746, p. 39, for a true Income Tax with exemptions and abatements and allowances for children ; *Thoughts* of 1756, p. 6—for equal tax on lands and funds and debts, but not on traders ; *Gentleman's Magazine*, 1763, 33. 524–5, article on an Essay recommending *inter alia* an equal tax on the general income of the kingdom ; Thomas Mortimer, *Elements*, 1772, 29. d. 13, for reassessment among landlords ; Whitbread's proposal, 28th November 1777, for a new assessment for 1s. of land tax, Cobbett, *Parl. History*, 19, 467–8.

[2] See Dowall, ii. 102 ; *Some Considerations* (1750 ?), pp. 4–6, 8 ; *Gentleman's Magazine*, 1766, 36, 522.

[3] *e.g.* Wood's *Letter* of 1717 and *Thoughts* of 1756.

[4] His first canon of taxation.

non-distributive ; they were based chiefly on commercial ideas, and were employed chiefly by the commercial classes in their opposition to the Income Tax of the Great War.[1] The first ground was that a direct tax on means or income involved, in the striking phrase of Adam Smith,[2] 'an inquisition more intolerable than any tax.' Writing in the thirties, Adam Smith's teacher, Hutcheson, had argued against this trading prejudice. All the harm which periodical inquisition would involve would be the detection of a few broken merchants, which would prevent their opportunities of defrauding their creditors.[3] But when Adam Smith in his turn came to lecture, he reversed the teaching.[4] 'It is easy,' he said, 'to lay a tax upon land, because it is evident what quantity every one possesses, but it is very difficult to lay a tax upon stock or money without very arbitrary proceedings. It is a hardship upon a man in trade to oblige him to show his books, which is the only way in which we can know how much he is worth. It is a breach of liberty and may be productive of very bad consequences by ruining his credit ; the circumstances of people in trade are at some times far worse than at others.' This condemnation was repeated even more sharply in the *Wealth of Nations*,[5] and it was adopted by Lord Kames as one of his rules to be observed in taxing.[6] In practice such taxes were 'altogether arbitrary and uncertain.' The second ground for condemning direct taxes on income was that a tax on profits and interest on capital is either illusory because shifted, or is so inimical to national prosperity that it should not be tolerated. This idea attained weight from the sanction of Sir James Steuart

---

[1] See below for 1798–9, and Smart, *Economic Annals*, pp. 52–3, 466, 469–70 for 1802 and 1816.
[2] *Wealth of Nations*, Everyman ed. ii. 349.
[3] Francis Hutcheson, *A System of Moral Philosophy*, 1755, ii. 341.
[4] Adam Smith, *Lectures on Justice Police Revenue and Arms*, ed. Cannan, 1896 (from notes of 1763), pp. 239–40.
[5] ii. 349, 330.   [6] *Sketches of the History of Man*, 1774, i. 476.

and Adam Smith, but it was put forward much earlier.
It no doubt drew support from the success of the public
creditors in insisting on the exemption of the funds
from taxation,[1] and it was sometimes argued that it
was impossible to tax the interest of money, since the
rate of interest would merely rise in proportion to the
tax.[2]   Steuart's objection was on the ground of
economic policy.[3]   Merchants, he held, ' ought to be
allowed to accumulate riches as fast as they can ;
because they employ them for the advancement of
industry ; and every deduction from their profits is a
diminution upon that so useful fund.' Adam Smith
emphasised the same aspect of the objection, and by
his insistence on the dependence of industry on capital
—an insistence which fitted in with the trader's conception of himself as the chief source of national
prosperity—gave it immense importance in the minds of
those whom he influenced. If the interest of money
were taxed, the capital might, and he suggested would,
be transferred abroad ; for although land is a subject
which cannot be removed, stock easily may, and ' the
proprietor of stock is properly a citizen of the world
and is not necessarily attached to any particular
country.' The resulting loss of capital would tend so
far to dry up every source of revenue both to the
sovereign and to the society—for it is stock that main-
tains industry, cultivates land and employs labour.
The payment for risk and management apart from
interest on capital, Adam Smith regarded as untaxable.[4]
    The importance which was thus attached to certain

---

[1] *The State and Conditions of our Taxes considered, or a proposal
for a Tax upon Funds* . . ., 1714, T. 1990 (20) ; *Reasons for taxing
the Public Funds*, 1716 (*Somer's Tracts*, xiii. 755) ; *Considerations
on the necessity of taxing the annuities* . . ., 1746, T. 1143 (10).
    [2] *e.g.* [Robert Nugent] *Considerations upon a reduction of the
Land Tax*, 1749, 104. d. 43, p. 25. For grounds on which the exemption of the Funds from taxation was defended, see *e.g.* Wood's *Letter*
of 1717, p. 11, *seq.*, and *A Serious Address to the Proprietors of the
Public Funds*, 1744, 8225. b. 5.
    [3] *Inquiry*, ii. 499.
    [4] *Wealth of Nations*, Everyman ed. ii. 329–31.

administrative and economic effects of taxes not only
led to this condemnation of a tax which would be
equitable in distribution, but resulted in the approval
of the existing Land Tax, which was distributively
inequitable.   The magnification of non-distributive
criteria into the supreme test of taxation appeared
most clearly in two pamphlets of 1749 and 1751,
attributed to Robert Nugent, which dealt with the
question of reducing the rate of the Land Tax after
the War of the Austrian Succession.[1] Nugent argued that
' as the benefit of taxes to the public results only from
the clear income, and the evil to individuals extends
not only to the gross produce but to every other
expense and loss incident and consequential; that tax
is most beneficial to the public and least hurtful to the
subject which produces a large sum through a cheap
ollection and which is free from every other eventual
charge.' And as the Land Tax cost little to collect,
was certain, and did not injure trade like taxes on commodities, he opposed its reduction. Less extreme
statements of the same idea were frequent.[2] In his
lectures Adam Smith pointed out that the Land Tax,
although inequitable, had considerable merit—it did
not involve any arbitrary proceedings or disclosures,
it was levied without much expense, and it did not
affect the price of commodities and so obstruct industry.[3]
These advantages were insisted upon with still greater
emphasis in the *Wealth of Nations*[4]; the Land Tax
was perfectly agreeable to all the canons of taxation
except the first (which defined distributive equity).
Adam Smith also pointed out that a further advantage
of the tax was that, unlike a proper assessment on

[1] *Considerations* of 1749, p. 7, and see *Further Considerations*, . . .
1751, 104. d. 42.
[2] *e.g.* Nicholls (Dangeul), *op. cit.* pp. 267–8 ; Postlethwayt,
Dictionary, ii. 11 *seq.*, quoting Nugent ; Steuart, *Inquiry*, ii. 561 ;
Kames, *op. cit.* i. 466 ; Mortimer, *op. cit.* p. 443.
[3] *Lectures*, pp. 239, 240, 241.
[4] *Wealth of Nations*, Everyman ed., ii. 309–10.

means, it was a fixed charge and put no discouragement upon improvements—an advantage which appealed strongly to Arthur Young and made him oppose any reassessment of the tax.[1]

In fact, of course, the real justification for maintaining the Land Tax in its stereotyped condition was that by long continuance it had come to be a rent charge rather than a tax. This was recognised by the end of this period. A writer in the *Gentleman's Magazine* in 1776[2] pointed out 'that the one real objection to reassessment was that many purchasers have given larger sums for estates lowly assessed than they would have given if the Land Tax had in general been more equal'; and to meet it, he suggested that the reassessment should be deferred to the commencement of the nineteenth century and then repeated every twenty-five years. The same answer was made next year to Whitbread's proposal in the House of Commons for a new assessment,[3] and in making the tax perpetual in 1798 (at the 4s. rate below which it did not fall after 1776) Pitt contended that it would be unjust to interfere with the tax, and that he was merely proposing to recognise explicitly an already accepted economic fact.[4] The abolition of the tax would not only have been unfair as between different landowners, but it would have amounted to a gift to the landlord class at the expense of the rest of the community.

---

[1] *Political Arithmetic*, 1774 (288. c. 13), pp. 7–8; repeated in part ii. 1779 (104. a. 81), pp. 11–12; and cf. Eden (afterwards Lord Auckland), *Four Letters to the Earl of Carlisle*, 1779, E. 2098 (8), pp. 89, 108.

[2] 46, 162.

[3] Cobbett, *Parl. Hist.* 19, 467–8 (speech of Lord Ongley). For other recognitions of this fact, see Eden, *op. cit.*, p. 108, and John Young (a Scotch pastor), *Essays*, E. 2076 (1), vii. on Taxations, p. 126. Sinclair, who opposed Pitt's bill of 1798, objected that there was no foundation for the expectation, on which estates were said to be valued, that Parliament would perpetuate the existing Land Tax. *History of the Public Revenue*, part iii. 1790, p. 112.

[4] *Ibid.*, 33, 1363–5; see speech for opposition by Lord Sheffield, 1374. A division in Pitt's favour was 105 to 13.

The two primary elements of the eighteenth-century theory of taxation were, therefore, negative—maxims defining what to avoid. On the one hand, avoid direct assessment on means or income ; on the other, avoid taxes on necessaries and the poor. The way was thus cleared for the third and positive element of the theory —the approval of taxes on commodities other than necessaries, and particularly on luxuries. In the seventeenth century such taxes were approved as one out of several justifiable modes of taxation, but in this period the disposition of opinion raised them to the position of the one satisfactory kind of tax.[1]

The great majority of the tax records of the time testify to the general acceptance of this doctrine.[2] It was so much part of the common stock of ideas that it is with astonishment that the reader comes now and then upon a proposal for some other tax than one on luxuries or on non-necessary expenditure. The new taxes which were in fact imposed in the period were, as we have already noticed, predominantly of this type.

[1] The Land Tax, although accepted, was yet considered radically defective, as being partial, and would not have been imposed anew in that form.

[2] For Walpole's view, see above ; *Gentleman's Magazine*, 1732, ii. 813 ; Thomas Downes, *A Scheme plainly demonstrating how several thousand pounds may be raised yearly to the Government* . . ., 1732, 8227. aa. 47 ; Hutcheson, *op. cit.* ii. 340–1 ; *An Essay on the Causes of the decline of the Foreign Trade* . . ., 1744, 8246. h. 1, pp. 43 *seq.*, 51 *seq.* ; Cobbett, *Parl. Hist.* 1748, 14. 153 *seq.* ; [Josiah Tucker], *A Brief Essay* . . . *with an Appendix containing a plan for raising one only Tax on the consumers of Luxuries*, 1750, 2° ed., 104. h. 10, sp. p. 123 *seq.* and 145 *seq.* ; [Josiah Tucker], *Elements of Commerce and Theory of Taxes*, 1755, 522. l. 9, pp. 169–70 ; David Hume, *Essay on Taxes*, 1752 ; Nickolls (Dangeul), *Remarks* . . ., 1754, pp. 255 *seq.*, 269 ; Postlethwayt, *Great Britain's True System*, 1757, p. 318 *seq.* ; *Proposals for carrying on the War with vigour, raising the Supplies within the Year* . . ., 1757, 8132. c. 71, pp. 11 *seq.* ; *Thoughts* . . . *with a proposal for raising a Supply for the Current Service* . . ., 1756, 104. c. 46, pp. 6, 12, 18 (and cf. *An Essay on the inequality of our present Taxes*, 1746, 104. d. 8 (3), p. 38) ; *Gentleman's Magazine*, 1762, 32. 21 ; [N. Forster], *An Enquiry* . . ., 1767, p. 50–2 ; Mortimer, *Elements of Commerce, Politics, and Finances*, 1772, p. 459 *seq.* ; Kames, *op. cit.* i. 468 *seq.* ; Arthur Young, *Political Arithmetic*, 1774, pp. 12–15, 214, 263–4 ; Adam Smith, *Wealth of Nations*, 1776, Everyman ed. ii. 376–81, 308.

The advantages which were considered to belong to taxes on luxuries—to take the more ideal form of the satisfactory tax—were four. The first and second were, of course, the negative ones that direct assessment of means was not involved, and that, necessaries being avoided, the poor were not burdened, and cost of production was not increased. The third in a peculiar degree expressed the eighteenth-century point of view. It was that, since no one was subjected to the tax unless he chose to consume the luxury, the tax was voluntary or optional; the individual was his own assessor; and thereby taxation according to ability—not ability measured by some rigid and necessarily incomplete standard, but by each man's knowledge of his own circumstances—was achieved. Even Adam Smith was impressed with this advantage of taxes on luxuries. 'Every man's contribution is altogether voluntary, it being altogether in his power either to consume or not to consume the commodity taxed.' The author of a scheme of 1744 considered that through his system of taxes on the consumers of luxuries 'all persons tax themselves voluntarily, than which nothing can be easier or more equal'; and Tucker held that no man could complain of such taxes, 'as it would be his own voluntary act and deed to rate himself in this or that class.'[1]

[1] *Brief Essay*, 1750, p. 165. It may be remarked that the claim that luxury taxes are optional was not pointless, although it was exaggerated. It is sometimes contended that the very conception of a tax implies compulsory levy and precludes option or voluntariness. But this is not so. In fact, all taxes are optional or conditional, but some, of which a tax on a luxury is one, are much more optional or conditional than others. A Poll Tax is conditional on residence within the county levying the tax—a condition or option not easily or lightly evadable; an Income Tax on residence *plus* the receipt of an income of a certain amount—also a very onerous option; a tax on a necessary such as tea, on residence *plus* the use of tea—a fairly though less onerous option; a tax on liqueur, on residence *plus* the use of liqueur—a not very onerous option. What the eighteenth century rhapsodist did not always realise was that you must have some constraint or onerousness in your option; if you merely say to people, we should like you to pay as much as you can afford, you would get very little. The constraint involved in taxes on luxuries was the dislike of foregoing the use of the taxed article.

That even taxation should be consistent, at its best, with the principles of liberty was certainly very satisfactory. The fourth advantage was that taxes on luxuries acted in a general way as sumptuary laws to restrain riotous living,[1] and, in the view of some writers, could, by proper adjustment, be made effective to combat particular evils. Josiah Tucker was specially vigorous in proclaiming this policy, but in only one actual tax, to be discussed below, did sumptuary policy attain the level of a definite purpose of taxation. The first and second of these advantages applied equally to taxes on merely non-necessary commodities, the third less fully, but the fourth hardly at all.

The most important luxury taxes were Customs duties on imports, which were increased several times in this period as the most suitable means of raising additional revenue. In 1748, for instance, Pelham required to secure a loan of about six millions, and decided upon an additional 5 per cent. poundage on imports. He contended that it would be paid easily, would be burdensome to none, and would no way affect the poorer sort of our people. 'As in this nation we have the good fortune to want nothing from abroad that is absolutely necessary for the subsistence of the poor, they cannot be in the least affected by this tax'; while it would hardly be felt by the better sort of people.[2]

Besides being for the most part taxes on luxuries, Customs duties had the additional advantage, on which much store was set by eighteenth-century writers, that, like other taxes on commodities, they were paid by the subject gradually and insensibly, being levied directly only on a small number of merchants, and included in the prices of commodities. This also seemed to favour

---

[1] *An Essay on Ways and Means* . . . 1726, 8245. b. 37, pp. 9, 16; *Essay* of 1744; *Essay* of 1746; Tucker, *Brief Essay* of 1750, pp. 127, 130, 134, 165; *Elements* of 1755, pp. 169, 170; *Proposals* of 1757, p. 13; *Gentleman's Magazine*, 1762, 32, 21; Mortimer, *Elements*, 1772, pp. 459–60.
[2] Cobbett, 14, 153.

liberty.[1] But, not unnaturally, the advantage did not appeal to the merchants, whose trade was restricted, and their protests and proposals form a minor but excellent illustration both of the assertiveness of the commercial class, and of the eighteenth-century view of taxation. Their general standpoint was put clearly in 1717 by Wm. Wood, Secretary to the Customs.[2] The prosperity of the land and of the whole nation depended on extensive foreign trade, and hence Customs should be low, for the encouragement of the merchant, 'who deserves all favour as being the best and most profitable member of the commonwealth.' The duties, however, were high, no general reductions were made, and Walpole, against bitter opposition from the commercial classes in 1733, attempted to make the system of collection more stringent. Proposals then began to appear for the substitution of other taxes in place of Customs.[3] The object of Decker's scheme of 1743, and of another of 1744, was to take off Customs duties, and so do away with smuggling, vexation and search, and enable trade to be carried on with half the stock. Far from heeding such counsel, however, Parliament proceeded to increase the duties further. The answer to the protest of the merchants, that the additional poundage of 1748 would be the finishing blow to trade and manufactures, was that, while it was no doubt desirable to respect the maxim that as a trading nation

---

[1] Hume, *loc. cit.*; Blackstone, *Commentaries*, 1765, i. 306; Kames, p. 469; A. Young, p. 14; A. Smith, *Lectures*, pp. 242-3 ('taxes upon consumption, therefore, which are paid by the merchant, seem most to favour liberty and will always be favoured by this government'); *Wealth of Nations*, ii. 377. Montesquieu had put the point epigrammatically; 'L'impôt par tête est plus naturel à la servitude; l'impôt sur les marchandizes est plus naturel à la liberté, parce qu'il se rapporte d'une manière moins directe à la personne.' *Esprit des Lois*, livre XIII. § 14.

[2] *A Letter to a Member of Parliament . . .*, 1717, 8132. a. 65, pp. 19-20.

[3] *An Enquiry into the causes of the Increase and Miseries of the Poor of England*, 1738, 104, n. 9, pp. 18, 77, 80; Decker, 1743, pp. 12, 21; *Essay* of 1744; Horsley, *Serious Considerations*, 1744, 104. d. 8 (2); *Essay* of 1746, p. 38; Tucker, *Brief Essay*, 1750.

'we ought not to supply the public expense by taxes which affect our commerce or manufactures,' in fact, it was not possible, since the alternatives were still less acceptable.[1] 'That it will be a little inconvenient to our merchant importers, that it will add a trifle to the price of those goods that are re-exported to a foreign market . . .; that it will enhance a little the price of such of our manufactures as are made up in whole or in part of foreign materials—are consequences, and bad consequences too, which can neither be denied nor prevented. But these consequences . . . are not near so bad as those which would have necessarily ensued from any other tax' that could have been thought of.

But although Parliament was not impressed with the supposed disastrous consequences of Customs duties, it was prepared to listen when a new form of luxury tax was propounded which would be free from the disadvantages of which the merchants complained. This was a tax levied directly on the users of the luxurious commodity. Proposals for such taxes were made in 1718, 1726, and 1732 [2]; a minor suggestion of Decker's pamphlet of 1743 was that the tea duty should be replaced by a sort of licence tax to be paid by every family which drank tea [3]; the *Essay on the Causes of the Decline of Foreign Trade* of 1744, perhaps also written by Decker,[4] elaborated the same idea in great detail;

[1] Cobbett, 14. 177, 180, 170, 181, speeches of Samuel Martin Henry Fox and James West.

[2] [Abel Boyer], *Animadversions and Observations* . . . (with) *a new proposition to raise money for the use of the public,* 1718, 8223. d. 22, p. 46 *seq.* ; *An Essay on ways and means,* 1726, 8245. b. 37 ; Downes, *Scheme,* 1732.

[3] P. 8.

[4] For a discussion of the authorship and references to other discussions, see Seligman, *Incidence,* p. 84, n. 4. It is perhaps insufficiently noted that the difference between the proposals of the pamphlets of 1743 and 1744 is precisely analogous to the difference between the two parts of the pamphlet of 1743 itself, which puts forward, in front of the house tax scheme, a minor plan for abolishing the tea duty by imposing a tax on the actual users of tea analogous in idea to the more elaborate taxes of the 1744 pamphlet. The argument drawn from the difference between the schemes does not therefore seem of great weight.

and Tucker, Fauquier,[1] and Postlethwayt all approved
of taxes on the ultimate consumer rather than those
levied first on the trader.   The *Essay* of 1744, for instance,
proposed 'that all persons using, wearing, or drinking
the following articles of luxury (coaches, plate, jewellery,
sedan-chairs, wine, spirits, tea, &c.), be obliged to take
out a licence yearly, paying each one subsidy for each
article, of three half-pence in the pound only on the
computed income they should have to support the
station in life they voluntarily place themselves in by
the article of luxury they use, wear or drink';[2] thus a
person keeping two coaches and six for his own use
would be assumed to have an income of £8000, and be
charged £50 on that account.

For the scheme it was claimed, *inter alia*, that it
exempted the poor, was voluntary, equitable, useful
as a sumptuary law, and that its greatest advantage
was that it would enable all Customs duties to be taken
off, and that it had itself no ill effects on trade.[3]   The
virtues of these taxes, however, were greatly exaggerated
by their advocates, who failed to see that they did not
get rid of, though they probably modified, the restriction involved on trade, that they were difficult to
administer, and that they ran counter to the special
virtue of Customs duties—gradual and imperceptible
payment by the ultimate tax-payer.   It was on these
grounds, among others, that Adam Smith did not
make any great account of them.[4]   At the same time,
they indicated some new sources of luxury taxation,
and Parliament from time to time had recourse to
some of them.   Thus in 1747 a tax was imposed on
pleasure carriages, and in 1756 another on plate (which
however was repealed as a failure in 1758, and replaced
by a licence duty upon the manufacture [5]), and in the

---

[1] *An Essay on Ways and Means* . . . 1756, E. 2213 (3), p. 23
seq.

[2] P. 44.   [3] Pp. 51–3.
[4] *Wealth of Nations*, ii. 357–9.   [5] 31 Geo. II. c. 32.

last quarter of the century a considerable number of additions was made to the list. These taxes, along with the earlier house and window tax, were grouped together by Pitt as the Assessed taxes.[1]

The fourth and last element of the tax doctrine of this period was the acceptance of two other purposes, besides that of the provision of revenue, as grounds for the imposition of taxes. The one was the purpose of trade policy in the Customs duties; the other, the purpose of sumptuary policy in the spirit duties.

Practically no change took place during this period in the Customs policy which had taken shape in the seventeenth century and to which Walpole had given the finishing touches. There were prohibitions and duties on the export of English raw materials, protective duties on directly competing imports, and differential duties and regulations in connection with shipping and the Colonial trade. In these, revenue was subordinated to considerations of trade policy. On the other hand, there was the bulk of the duties on imported super-fluities, which, besides discouraging imports which would compete for English expenditure and worsen the balance of trade, also produced a large revenue. The pamphlet literature shows that the trade policy involved, although it did not pass without criticism, was generally accepted in its main features. The protests of the merchants against high duties were not primarily directed to questions of trade policy at all; and although Decker was inclined to generalise the disadvantages of duties into the principle 'that all prohibitions are in general hurtful,' yet he admitted that 'there may be cases where necessity will call for them,' and that his scheme was not without difficulties. 'I see very clearly that there must be some regulations upon some certain species of goods which may be imported from abroad and would interfere with our own manufactures; as well

[1] Dowell, ii. 187–8.

as upon others where regard must be had to treaties.' [1]
Joseph Massie, writing in 1757, [2] drew attention to this
difficulty, of which he believed few of those who approved Decker's scheme were aware. 'The misfortune,'
he said, 'is that none of these desirable things are to
be come at without repealing those laws which have
hitherto protected our trade and manufactures and made
us a wealthy and powerful people.' 'The truth of the
matter is that an open trade would be the ruin of Great
Britain. Hutcheson [3] thought that import duties were
often necessary to encourage industry at home though
there were no public expenses, and Hume, [4] although
he repudiated the idea of a favourable balance of trade
and condemned trade policy which was based on national
jealousy, was careful to point out that all taxes upon
foreign commodities were not to be regarded as prejudicial or useless, 'but those only which are founded
on the jealousy above-mentioned.' 'A tax on German
linen encourages home manufactures and thereby multi-
plies our people and industry. A tax on brandy increases
the sale of rum and supports our southern colonies.'
On the eve of the publication of the *Wealth of Nations*,
Mortimer [5] and Kames [6] were still insisting in detail
on the principles of mercantile trade policy. And the
influence of Adam Smith's attack was limited during the
eighteenth century. [7] The main alteration in duties
connected with that influence, Pitt's commercial treaty
with France, [8] implied the abandonment of ideas of the

[1] *Op. cit.* p. 22, and 104. d. 8 (1), p. 29.
[2] *The proposal commonly called Sir Matthew Decker's scheme for
one general tax upon houses laid open* . . ., 1757, 104. d. 22, pp. 2, 3, 6.
[3] *Op. cit.* ii. 341.   [4] Essay on the Balance of Trade.
[5] *Op. cit.* pp. 114–123.   [6] *Op. cit.* pp. 488–519.
[7] On the question of Adam Smith's influence, see John Rae,
Life, pp. 60–1, 153–4, 284–94, 349–55, 383–6. It lies outside my
purpose to investigate the question in detail, but a point for consideration is whether Adam Smith had much influence on opinion
regarding protection of particular industries.
[8] See Dowell, ii. 189–90 ; Hewins, *English Trade and Finance*,
pp. 145–155 ; and an excellent account in J. H. Rose, *Wm. Pitt and
the National Revival*, chap. xiv. The text is given in Cobbett, *Parl.*

balance of trade, but on the English side, where there was no real fear of the competition of French woollens and cottons, it did not raise the most acute free trade issues.[1] Indeed, in one aspect, very present in Pitt's mind, the Treaty was an instance of trade policy—the purchase for our rapidly developing manufactures of access to a good foreign market. And in the region of opinion even one who was so much influenced by Adam Smith as William Eden, the negotiator of the French Treaty of 1786, declared in 1779 [2] that taxes should not be imposed on exports 'except in very few articles when it may be found expedient to make a tax operate in the nature of a prohibition or to favour some particular manufacture.'

Over the greater portion of the seventeenth century the important purpose of the taxes on spirits, which were mostly imported, was simply to raise revenue. From the time of the Civil War they paid both Customs and Excise duties. But in the second half of the century the question of home production was in considerable evidence, and to encourage it stringent differential duties were gradually imposed against the imported commodity.[3] Under James II. it paid Excise of 1s. 4d.

Hist., 26. 233 seq. See Pitt's speech of 12th February 1787, ibid. 26. 381 seq.

[1] Contrast the reception of the French treaty with that of Pitt's Irish commercial proposals of 1785 (see J. H. Rose, op. cit. pp. 246–66). Also note, e.g., North's alteration of the glass duties in 1777 and his avowed principle of a high protective duty on the manufactured import so as to preserve the home industry ; Cobbett, Parl. Hist., 19. 245–6 ; and see G. B. Hertz, The Manchester Politician, 1750–1912, §§ ii. and iii.

[2] Four Letters to the Earl of Carlisle, 1779, E. 2098 (8), pp. 88 seq. and sp. pp. 91–2. Adam Smith's qualified approval of an export tax on wool did not appear till the 3rd edition of the Wealth of Nations in 1784, see ii. 142 seq. and sp. pp. 148, 149. Eden's Letters are said to have had a great success (D.N.B.). The third contained a résumé of Adam Smith on taxation.

[3] At the Restoration, home-made strong water or aqua vitae paid 2d. per gallon, while foreign spirits made of wine or cider paid 4d., and foreign strong waters perfectly made 8d. (Dowell, ii. 25), in addition to an import duty of £4 per hogshead. By an Act

per gallon on single and 2s. 8d. on double brandy (in addition to Customs) as compared with 6d. per gallon on the English article; from 1689 to 1693 importation was prohibited [1]; and by 1713 the Excise duties were 3s. 8d. and 6s. 8d. on foreign as against 4d. to 8d. on home spirits.[2] Under cover of this protective system, attempts were further made for a time to secure that the increasing home distillation should, 'for the advantage of tillage,' make use of English grain. Thus in 1690 the Excise on malt-spirit was fixed at 3d. per gallon, while spirit distilled from other English material was to pay 1s. 2d. and from foreign material 10d. per gallon.[3] But this policy restricted the success of the manufacture and it was modified in 1699.[4] The general aim of the policy, however, was realized to the full and the English production is said to have nearly quadrupled between 1684 and 1714.[5] Revenue and industrial development were, therefore, the sole purposes of the spirit taxes of the early eighteenth century. They were not intended in any degree to restrict or prevent consumption, although the desirability of adopting such a policy had occasionally been urged.[6]

of 1670, 22 Chas. II. c. 4, brandy was classed as the last mentioned. 1 Jas. II. c. 5 increased the rates to those given in the text.

[1] 1 Will. and Mary, c. 34, § 6; clause repealed by 5 Will. and Mary, c. 2.

[2] That is my calculation from the numerous Acts. Imports paid Customs in addition. The rates varied considerably between 1693 and 1713.

[3] 2 Will. and Mary, sess. 2, c. 9. The figures given assume that the duties of this Act are in addition to, not in place of, pre-existing duties.

[4] 10 Will. III. c. 10 and note c. 4. Cary had foretold in 1691 that this would be the result, see 'Reasons for repealing the statute for distilling on corn,' Add. MSS., 5540, f. 34.

[5] Lecky, England in the Eighteenth Century, chap. iv.

[6] See debates of 1st March 1670 on a proposal to prohibit the import of brandy, A. Gray, Debates, i. 215 seq. Sir Robert Howard is reported thus: 'As for brandy, we have death along with it; it burns us up. Our hot waters are sent to the Indies, good; and suppose we have no brandy in the world, cannot we live without it?' (p. 217). But the proposal was neither made nor discussed primarily on sumptuary grounds. Sir John Knight said: 'If it destroys men's bodies, then prohibit the use of it totally, both foreign and

But a terrible conclusion awaited the industrial success and the neglect of warnings. Spirits became very cheap and in the second quarter of the century an appalling outbreak of spirit-drunkenness took place, of which a graphic account will be found in Lecky.[1] 'Drunk for a penny, dead drunk for two-pence,' is the legend. A petition of the Justices of Middlesex declared in 1736,[2] 'that the drinking of Geneva and other distilled spirituous liquors had for some years past greatly increased, especially among the people of inferior rank; (that it had) destroyed thousands of his Majesty's subjects and rendered great numbers of others unfit for useful labour and service, debauching at the same time their morals and driving them into all manner of vice and wickedness.' In that year Parliament took the matter in hand and agreed to Sir Joseph Jekyll's resolutions, that the low price of spirituous liquors is the principal inducement to the excessive and pernicious use thereof, and that, to prevent this, duties should be imposed.[3] The Act[4] imposed the prohibitive duties of, first, £1 per gallon on retailed spirits, and second, £50 a year on the retailer—*i.e.* duties on the sale to poor people. The opposition to the Bill fully admitted the evil and the need for some such remedy, but protested against a prohibitive duty, partly on the ground of the vested interest of distillers and retailers, and partly on the view that the moderate use of spirits was not disadvantageous and should not be prohibited to the poor if it was not prohibited to the rich. Pulteney's suggestion was for a moderate duty sufficient to prevent the inferior sort of people being able to make much use of it. The reply of the supporters of the Bill was

home made.' In 1695, Davenant argued in favour of imposing a high duty to suppress the consumption of spirits, which he said was a growing vice among the common people. Characteristically he pointed out that the loss of revenue would be recompensed by increased revenue from wine and other liquors. *An Essay on Ways and Means* . . . 1695, 1028. h. 1 (1), pp. 137–8.

[1] *Loc. cit.*   [2] Cobbett, *Parl. Hist.* 9. 1032–3.
[3] *Ibid.* p. 1033.   [4] 9 Geo. II. c. 23.

that the only way to prevent excess was to put the liquor quite out of the people's reach.[1] Such is the beginning of the modern English spirit duty.

As it turned out, Pulteney's plan would probably have been more effectual. The attempt to crush out the consumption failed completely, Jekyll's Act being contravened wholesale.[2] It was repealed in 1743, and moderate duties imposed, with the two objects, first, of raising revenue, and second, of lessening the consumption and getting the trade within the effective grip of excise control.[3] The Bill was bitterly denounced in the Lords as a mere means of raising money which would do nothing to prevent or reduce drunkenness. Carteret put the case for the Bill most clearly. It was in practice impossible, he said, to stop the consumption entirely; all that could be done was to proceed by degrees to restrict the excessive use of the liquor and at the same time to raise revenue out of it ; they were bound to begin with a low duty, otherwise the clandestine sale would continue unchecked.[4] More careful provisions were also enacted for the regulation of retailing.

The policy defined by Carteret was maintained henceforth.[5] The regulations as to sale were improved and extended,[6] and from time to time the duties were increased, with the double object of raising money and repressing consumption.[7] Pitt, for instance, in increasing the spirit duties in 1794,[8] declared that it

---

[1] See debate of 8th March, Cobbett, 9. 1037 *seq.*

[2] Lecky, *loc. cit.*   [3] 16 Geo. II. c. 8.

[4] Lords Debate, 22nd February 1743, Cobbett, 12. 1193 *seq.*

[5] For the literature of the subject, see Lecky, *loc. cit.*, and note also Josiah Tucker, *An Impartial Inquiry* . . . 1751, 522. g. 4 (4).

[6] Sp. by 26 Geo. II. c. 13.

[7] 1751, 24 Geo. II. c. 40 ; 1762, 2 Geo. III. c. 5 ; 1780, 20 Geo. III. c. 35 ; 1790, 31 Geo. III. c. 1 ; 1795, 35 Geo. III. c. 11, 12 ; 1797, 37 Geo. III. c. 14. Adam Smith noted that 'it has for some time past been the policy of Great Britain to discourage the consumption of spirituous liquors, on account of their supposed tendency to ruin the health and corrupt the morals of the common people' (*Wealth of Nations*, Everyman ed. ii. 372). North's view of the duty in 1780 is a little doubtful according to Cobbett's brief report, 21. 166.

[8] *Ibid.* 30, 1359–60 ; the wording of the Debrett report is different, but the result is the same.

was desirable that the duty should be as high as possible without affording such advantage and temptation to smuggling as might operate as a premium to the illicit trader and tend materially to injure the revenue; and in 1796,[1] in justification of another increase, he emphasized the point more strongly : ' the consumption is so pernicious that with respect to this article no man could wish that there should be any limits to the duty, so far as is consistent with the means of safely collecting it.' The experience and discussion of the second quarter of the century thus resulted in the embodiment of a sumptuary purpose in the taxes on spirits.

A short discussion of Adam Smith's theory of taxation will bring out the general features of the eighteenth century doctrine which we have been considering, and at the same time define the place which Adam Smith holds in the development of English opinion on taxation. It has sometimes been supposed that the publication of the *Wealth of Nations* brought to the world a new revelation of the principles of taxation, and that it immediately affected the policy of the Chancellors of the Exchequer. But this is a serious misconception; the only respect in which it bears some relation to the facts is on the subject of trade policy in the Customs. Apart from that, what Adam Smith did was to expand the commercial view of tax questions which we have been following, and to attempt to systematize and rationalize it by bringing it into relation with the distributive theory of the seventeenth century which Walpole expressed. He gave a wider intellectual sanction to a set of opinions already very influential. Apart from Pitt's commercial treaty of 1786 and Peel's and Gladstone's reform of the tariff between 1842 and 1860, no important change in English tax policy is connected with Adam Smith's influence; on the contrary, all the large changes since his day, such as the imposition of the Income Tax in 1799,

[1] *Ibid.* 32, 1260,

have been made independently or in spite of the influence
of his ideas.[1]

The most important characteristic of the eighteenth
century view of taxation was the excessive emphasis
which it laid on non-distributive criteria of a good tax
system. It did not begin with the question how the
burden of the necessary supply should be distributed,
and thence proceed to the question of the best taxes
by which to attain this result ; it began rather by saying
that this sort of tax or that sort of tax must not be
employed, arrived, by a process of elimination as it were,
at some form of tax which on non-distributive grounds
was permissible, and then proceeded to consider its
distributive justification. This was also the most important characteristic of Adam Smith's view and the
somewhat veiled process of his thought. It is significant
that three out of the four famous canons should be
non-distributive ones. The dominant ideas in his
mind were three. First, direct assessment of means
and hence an Income Tax should not be adopted because
of the inquisition involved, specially on the commercial
classes, and because of the effect on capital.[2] Second,
taxes on necessaries (or on wages) are bad, because they
increase the price of labour. Third, hence taxation
should be raised upon non-necessary consumption or expenditure. The only important difference
between the controlling ideas of Adam Smith's doctrine
and those of the general opinion of his time was that,
while the popular condemnation of taxes on necessaries
was based on the view that they involved a grievous
burden on the poor man as well as on the view that

---

[1] Dowell (ii. 168–70) and Rae (*Life of Adam Smith*, pp. 294,
320–1) argue that North got the suggestion for taxes on men-ser-
vants, auctions and houses of 1777 and 1778 from the *Wealth of
Nations*. This is probably true in the narrow sense ; but such taxes
were on the lines of those generally approved independently of and
prior to Adam Smith.

[2] Because the stereotyped Land Tax did not involve these and
other non-distributive disadvantages he accepted it in spite of its
injustice.

they were not paid by the poor but raised wages, Adam Smith condemned them (and so avoided inconsistency) merely on the second ground.[1]

One result of this over-emphasis was that distributive problems were glossed over in taxes on luxuries or non-necessaries. On the one hand, the exemption of the poor was impliedly accepted as desirable, but, with rare exceptions, no direct repudiation was expressed of the doctrine that every one is under an inherent obligation to share the burden of taxation. On the other hand, the distributive justification of these taxes was rather a matter of faith than of demonstration, and, as we have seen, much distributive virtue was attributed to the primarily non-distributive characteristic of optional or voluntary payment.

The contribution which Adam Smith, as a student and a man of systematizing mind, made to the doctrines of the time was to remove them out of this comparatively isolated condition and bring them into relation with the theory of tax distribution. He attempted to adapt the seventeenth century theory to the new school of doctrine. As, however, he accepted without criticism all the most important elements of that theory, his structure lacked strict logical coherence at parts. But in all probability this did not impair it in the eyes of his contemporaries; for them the essential point was that the thinker sanctioned and supported the standpoint with which they were familiar.[2]

Adam Smith's theory of distribution has to be gathered together from different parts of his sections on taxes. It set out, however, simply enough, with three general positions with which we are familiar. First, every one should pay taxation; second, distribution ought to be in proportion to income (revenue); third, a tax to be just must be general—it must fall on

---

[1] The references for this paragraph are given in the earlier parts of the chapter.

[2] See *e.g.* Eden, *Four Letters to the Earl of Carlisle*, 1779, p. 88 *seq.*

all the three sorts of income, rent, profits and wages.[1] Adam Smith accepted the assumption of the seventeenth and eighteenth century that taxation is made up of non-compensatory taxes, and discussed each tax by itself. At this point there entered the first extraneous factor. A tax on all income is ruled out because taxes on profits and wages are condemned on non-distributive grounds which have been discussed.[2] There is therefore left the tax on expenditure or consumption. 'The State not knowing how to tax directly and proportionately the revenue of its subjects, endeavours to tax it indirectly by taxing their expense, which it is supposed will in most cases be nearly in proportion to their revenue.'[3] Here entered the second non-distributive factor. Expenditure on necessaries must not be taxed, since that would merely raise wages.[4] Hence we are reduced to taxes on non-necessary expenditure (Adam Smith uses the term luxury instead of non-necessary, but in the sense that 'consumable commodities are either necessaries or luxuries.')[5] Next, it was not essential, he argued, that all non-necessary expenditure should be taxed so as to give equitable distribution according to expenditure or income.[6] In particular, he held it unnecessary that all imported luxuries should be taxed, and was in favour of restricting Customs duties as well as Excise to 'a few articles only of the most general use and consumption.' His idea was the somewhat vague one, which ruled in the seventeenth century, and the fallacy of which Petty had pointed out, that (to take the instance given by the latter) 'in the proportion that men drink, they make all other expenses.'[7] Finally,

---

[1] *Wealth of Nations*, ed. Cannan, ii. 310, Everyman ed. ii. 307. [In the remaining notes to this chapter, I shall use the contractions C. and E. for the *Wealth of Nations* in these editions.]

[2] C. ii. 331–3, 351–4, 356–7 ; E. ii. 329–31, 346–49, 351.

[3] C. ii. 354 ; E. ii. 351.   [4] C. ii. 354–5 ; E. ii. 351–3.

[5] C. ii. 354 ; E. ii. 351–2.   [6] C. ii. 367 ; E. ii. 364

[7] *Ibid.* Adam Smith's statement is : 'The revenue which is levied by the duties of excise is supposed to fall as equally upon the

by regarding beer as a luxury, and not, as was usual, as a necessary,[1] he obtained a reconciliation between the theory that all should pay taxation and the maxim that taxes should not be on necesssaries.

The best illustration of Adam Smith's view of the distributive justification of a tax system such as he approved occurs in his section on Taxes on Consumable Commodities.[2] 'The duties upon foreign luxuries imported for home consumption, though they some-times fall upon the poor, fall principally upon people of middling or more than middling fortune. Such are, for example, the duties upon foreign wines, upon coffee, chocolate, tea, sugar, etc. The duties upon the cheaper luxuries of home produce destined for home consump-tion fall pretty equally upon people of all ranks in proportion to their respective expense. The poor pay the duties upon malt, hops, beer, and ale upon their own consumption; the rich upon both their own consumption and that of their servants.' Such taxes had, of course, disadvantages, and they offended against the fourth canon, which required that the amount received by the State from a tax should be as nearly as possible equal to the amount paid, directly and indirectly, by the subjects.[3] But the qualifications which Adam Smith felt compelled to admit in regard to their distributive equity were merely that they make the parsimonious man contribute less and the profuse

contributors as that which is levied by the duties of customs ; and the duties of excise are imposed upon a few articles only of the most general use and consumption.'

[1] C. ii. 355 ; E. ii. 352. Beer was in fact both a necessary and a luxury to the poor. The *Essay* of 1746, *e.g.*, proposed that, in abolishing duties, those on beer, ale, cider, and spirituous liquors should be retained 'as some restraint upon the idleness and luxury of our meaner people' (p. 38). For other notes on the luxuries of the poor, see *Proposals* of 1757, p. 46, and Arthur Young, *Political Arithmetic*, 1774, p. 212. The point illustrates the difficulty of giving a de-finition to 'necessary' and 'luxury' which will be both serviceable and accurate. The usual eighteenth century assumption that the poor did not pay taxes on luxuries was in some degree incorrect. Cf. Massie, *Calculation of Taxes*, 1756, 8226. b. 15.

[2] C. ii. 370 ; E. ii. 367-8.   [3] C. ii. 379-83 ; E. ii. 377-80.

man more than his proportion, and that the absentee escapes altogether[1]; and any inequality due to the former of these difficulties he considered 'much more than compensated by the very circumstance which occasions that inequality—the circumstance that every man's contribution is altogether voluntary.'[2] And on the whole 'the inconveniences which are perhaps in some degree inseparable from taxes upon consumable commodities fall as light upon the people of Great Britain as upon those of any other country of which the government is nearly as expensive. Our state is not perfect, and might be mended, but it is as good or better than that of most of our neighbours.'[3]

It is needless to discuss the steps of this theory in detail, and more important to notice the character of Adam Smith's influence upon the taxation of the poor in the last quarter of the eighteenth century. In spite of the fact that he favoured above all things taxes on luxuries, and therefore might be supposed to have made for easy taxation or exemption of the poor, his influence did not in the circumstances of the time have this character. In the first place, the time was one of financial pressure, and by his condemnation of an Income tax Adam Smith lent his weight against that resource, and so made it more difficult to avoid taxes on necessaries;[4] and by his insistence on non-distributive criteria, and by his lack of a compensatory view of taxation, he gave no support to its continuance when it had once been imposed. The debates of the year 1816[5] pass judgment on any claim of Adam Smith's to

[1] C. ii. 378–9 ; E. ii. 376.   [2] C. ii. 379 ; E. ii. 377.
[3] C. ii. 383 ; E. ii. 381.
[4] A point to be noticed in the problem of the influence on Pitt of Lord Shelburne as against Adam Smith, is that in 1785 Shelburne pointed out to Pitt, in conversation of which a memorandum is extant, ' the impossibility of placing the finances of the country on a really satisfactory basis in keeping with the newest financial ideas without having recourse to an Income Tax.' Fitzmaurice, *Life of Shelburne*, 1876, iii. 440–1.
[5] In very brief and incomplete outline, the situation in 1816

greatness as a thinker on tax (as against tariff) questions. In the second place, the controlling authority in tax matters was dominated by the sentiment of landed men ; and by condemning taxes on necessaries, not as against the interest of the poor, but as disadvantageous to industry, and as falling really on the middle class and the rich, Adam Smith almost invited the House of Commons, in so far as it understood him, to continue and increase taxes on necessaries when money was scarce, and certainly did not condemn them in the one way which that House would have felt. In the third place, he tacitly admitted that the proper subjects of taxation, as he saw them, might easily be exhausted,—a natural result, though he did not see this, of over-emphasis on non-distributive criteria of taxes,—and when this happened, improper ones, he said, must, if necessary, be adopted [1]—a doctrine which North and Pitt were all too prone to depend upon. And, not only did he thus grant absolution in advance upon departure from

was as follows. At the conclusion of long and exhausting wars which had piled up taxes on commodities, both necessaries and luxuries, as well as on income, the Government desired to retain the Income Tax for two years at the rate of 1s. per £ (as against the war rate of 2s.). The opposition, led by Brougham, denounced the tax, specially on the score of inquisition, with the righteous indignation which is apt to be felt by those who have the authority of great names to support them. The sad thing was that the supporters of the Government, even those like George Rose who felt most clearly that the discontinuance of the Income Tax meant the sacrifice of the interest of the poor, had no framework of ideas familiar to their time with which they could effectively explain and defend their position. In a scene of great excitement the Government was defeated by 238 to 201. Not all the majority, however, felt comfortable about their votes two days later; and the Government decided to give up also the War Malt Tax, which fell chiefly on the poor, although financially their action was difficult to defend. For this reading it is only possible at present to refer to the debates themselves (Hansard); see specially those of 20th February 1815 (read Vansittart, Baring and Rose), 12th February 1816, 13th February (London petition), 18th March (read whole), 20th March (on discontinuance of War Malt Tax and recriminations over vote of 18th—read whole). See also Seligman, *The Income Tax*, pp. 106–114; Smart, *Economic Annals*, p. 462 seq.; and *Longman's Political History of England*, xi. (1801–1837), pp. 172– .

[1] C. ii. 390 ; E. ii. 388.

the straight path of justifiable taxation, but instead of indicating an Income tax as the most pardonable offence, he definitely indicated taxes on necessaries. ' Such taxes, though they raise the price of subsistence and consequently the wages of labour, yet they afford a considerable revenue to government which it might not be easy to find in any other way. There may therefore be good reasons for continuing them'[1]; and ' the taxes upon the necessaries of life may be no impeachment of the wisdom of that republic (Holland) which, in order to acquire and maintain its independency, has, in spite of its great frugality, been involved in such expensive wars as have obliged it to contract great debts.'[2] The commercial tradition which Adam Smith represented opposed both taxes on income and taxes on necessaries, but of the two it disliked taxes on income most. And finally, by his acceptance of the usual idea that the rich man and the poor man pay to the tax on beer roughly in proportion to their incomes, he lost a great opportunity of advancing clearer thinking on the question of the actual distributive result of taxes on commodities. It is therefore not too much to say that Adam Smith's influence in practice made for and not against taxes to which the poor contributed.

We shall have occasion to discuss Adam Smith's ideas again from another point of view, but we may conclude this appreciation of what may be called his theory of taxation in the narrower sense, by noticing two points in it which have had a certain influence on opinion in the last half century.

As we have seen, Adam Smith laid it down that the standard of equitable distribution is proportionality to income—this was his interpretation of taxation according to ability; and there has been a certain tendency to accept this interpretation as the result of deep insight and mature consideration on his part. I am not con-

[1] C. ii. 359; E. ii. 356.   [2] See note 1 above, p. 147.

cerned here to discuss the principle itself, but it is of some historical interest to notice that there is no reason for trusting Adam Smith's conclusion on this ground. Income as the rough standard of taxation was a seventeenth-century conception, as we have seen, and it was frequently referred to in the eighteenth century before Adam Smith.[1] It was a vague commonplace, and that is its character in the *Wealth of Nations* also. Adam Smith does not discuss, for instance, whether different kinds of income should all pay the same rates ; there is no reason to believe that he ever seriously considered the kind of problems which came to the front with the imposition of the Income Tax in 1799.[2] And it would have been astonishing if he had ; taxes on commodities were by themselves too inexact an instrument to suggest the question or make its discussion useful. His attempt to justify distribution according to income was of little speculative value ; it was based on the analogy, which is false in important respects, that ' the expense of government to the individuals of a great nation is like the expense of management to the joint tenants of a great estate.'[3] And indeed Adam Smith did not always strictly adhere to his own standard. A tax on house rent, which he approved, would in general, he believed, fall heaviest on the rich ; but, he added,[4] ' in this sort of inequality there would not, perhaps, be anything very unreasonable. It is not very unreasonable that the rich should contribute to the public expense, not only in proportion to their revenue, but something more than in that proportion.'

---

[1] *e.g. Enquiry into causes of the increase . . . of poor*, 1738, 104. n. 9, p. 82—proposal for single Income Tax : ' that the taxing everyone according to his yearly income is the nearest rule that can be gone by to measure his ability, I believe will be readily granted by all ' ; *Essay on the inequality of our present taxes*, 1746, 104 d. 8 (3) —proposal for single Income Tax with abatements and exemptions, p. 38 *seq.* ; *Gentleman's Magazine*, 1763, 33. 524–5, proposal for Income tax with taxes on luxuries.

[2] See below. [3] C. ii. 313 ; E. ii. 307.

[4] C. ii. 326–7 ; E. ii. 324.

The second point is that Adam Smith's systematisation of tax principles implied the idea that the only purpose of taxation is to raise revenue for state services, and his influence has been in the direction of supporting the dogma that no other purposes should be involved in taxes. This was, of course, a natural presumption of the *laisser faire* attitude and the distrust of state intervention to which Adam Smith inclined; and it gained support from the particular instance of Customs duties, which, since he rejected the trade policy involved in the duties of the time, he held should be imposed simply for revenue.[1] But it was also the result of a mistaken or inadequate systematisation. In a few minor cases Adam Smith himself advocated the adoption of extra-revenue purposes in taxes. Thus he suggested that the Land Tax should as a matter of good agricultural policy be so adjusted as to penalise leases which either exacted a heavy initial payment in place of a larger annual rent, or prescribed the mode of cultivation to be followed;[2] and he favoured a special tax, which was certainly not mere ordinary taxation for revenue, to be imposed on ground rents beyond the ordinary rent of land.[3] But the inadequacy of systematisation was much more serious in regard to the actual tax system of Adam Smith's day, which included not only the purpose of trade policy in the Customs, but also that of sumptuary policy in the spirit duties.[4]

[1] C. ii. 367 ; E. ii. 364.   [2] C. ii. 315–7 ; E. ii. 312–3.
[3] C. ii. 328–9 ; E. ii. 326.
[4] Adam Smith was certainly prepared to accept the sumptuary purpose of the spirit duties, though it is not clear what importance he attributed to it ; C. ii. 374–5 ; E. ii. 372.

VIII

1776-1799

THE essential differences between the period which we have been discussing and that to which we proceed depend on the simple fact that the former was a period of comparatively easy finance, while the latter was one of severe financial pressure, in which great difficulty was found in providing the necessary revenue for the American and French wars.[1] In round figures, the national revenue amounted in 1714 to five and a half millions and in 1776 to ten and a half millions, while the annual debt charge had increased only from three millions to four and a half millions. By 1799 the revenue had risen to thirty-two millions and the annual debt charge to seventeen millions.[2] Had it not been that industry and agriculture were advancing at an unprecedented rate, and that the yield of the old taxes was automatically expanding, the country could scarcely have supported the strain ; and, as it was, enormous increases in taxation had to be made.

The significance of this necessity from the point of view of tax policy, was that it descended at a time when men had come to a very general agreement about

---

[1] The cause of the financial pressure of this period was, of course, not merely the fact that expensive wars had to be provided for in it, but also the fact that, as a result of the system of funding war deficits, interest on the larger part of the cost of former wars had still to be paid. It is to be remarked also that the finance of 1714–76 became less easy in the later years, and that the division at 1776 might, for purely financial purposes, be carried back perhaps to 1756.

[2] *Return of Public Income and Expenditure*, 1869, i. 50–53, 174–7, 220–1.

the proper way to raise money upon the subject for the service of the state. There had come into existence a revised and improved canon, in which it was possible for an enlightened generation to take a comfortable pride. But the canon had grown strong during a period when no clamant need existed to test it; it was not a canon embodied in the system of taxation. The test came in this period. Much money was needed. Here was the opportunity to live up to the accepted principles. The Chancellors of the Exchequer made the attempt; and they failed. Yet because the canon was influential, and the test which it failed to meet one of mere practicability, they did not cease to adhere to it. They did not understand its weakness, and in contravening it they merely appealed to necessity. When the proper subjects of taxation are exhausted, it is necessary to resort to improper ones. Therefore the distributive justice or injustice of the ' improper ' taxes was not made a controlling question. The gulf between opinion and policy became wider. It was an opinion so superficial as this, and a practice so demoralisingly inconsistent with opinion, that the eighteenth century bequeathed to the nineteenth.

The accepted doctrine was, of course, that taxes should be imposed on luxuries, or at least on non-necessaries. Such taxes were voluntary and did not involve direct assessment of means—advantages which were so much assumed as essential that it was only the challenge of direct assessment in 1798 and 1799 that elicited much direct reference to them.[1] More immediately present to men's minds was the advantage that the necessaries of the poor were thus exempted from taxation. The most striking characteristic of opinion in this period was the widespread acceptance of this principle that taxes which affect the poor should, if possible, be avoided. It was proclaimed again and again by North and Pitt;

[1] See below, also the debates on the Legacy Duty Bills of 1796.

it was assumed by the great majority of pamphlets and throughout the long debates on the Triple Assessment and the Income Tax. So common was the assumption that in most cases no trouble was taken to explain or defend it. Thus Pitt proposed that the relief which it was in his power to give in 1792 ' should apply peculiarly to that class to whom on every account it ought first to be extended—I mean the most necessitous and the most industrious part of the community.' [1] But there is a sufficient number of indications to show that the grounds on which the principle was held were unchanged —they were, first, that taxes on necessaries (or on wages) raised wages and were injurious to trade and industry ; and second, that they were grievous to the poor, whose lot was hard enough without the added burden of taxes.

It is clear that the trading objection to taxes on necessaries, based on the theory that they were not paid by the poor but were shifted to wages, had considerable influence in this period. It was accepted by Eden and other pamphleteers.[2] One of these, a merchant of London who in 1784 proposed a single

[1] Cobbett, *Parl. Hist.* 29. 828–9. For other instances of the unexplained acceptance of the idea that the poor should be exempt, see Pitt, 1784, 24. 1009–10 ; 1789, 28. 162 ; 1797, Debrett, *Parl. Register*, 66. 276–7–8 ; Lushington, *ibid.*, 544 ; Geo. Rose, *A Brief Examination into the Increase of the Revenue . . .*, 1792 *to* 1799, 1799, B. 524 (7), pp. 31–2.

[2] Eden, *Four Letters*, 1779, pp. 93–4; John Berkenhout, *Lucubrations on Ways and Means humbly addressed to Lord North*, 1780, 104, c. 13, p. 61—' the moment the war is at an end, you will abolish the taxes upon candles, soap and leather ; taxes which originated in the false system of raising money on the necessaries of life ; taxes which depress our manufactures more than all the rest, parish taxes excepted . . .' ; Francis Dobbs, *Thoughts on the Present Mode of Taxation in Great Britain* (dedicated to Pitt), 1784, 8225 b. 33, pp. 3–4, 8–9 ; successful competition with other nations ' is impossible whilst the necessaries of life are higher here than in other countries— for according to the sum necessary to support the manufacturer, so must be the price of his labour.' ' There is but one possible remedy, and that is to take away every tax that in any shape touches on the necessaries of life ' ; H. G. Macnab, *Letters addressed to Wm. Pitt* (against the Coal tax), 1793, 8223. c. 54, pp. 54–5, 95, 96. Sinclair discussed the theory in his *History*, but did not accept it, part iii. 1790, p. 127.

window tax which was to exempt poor cottagers (on the model of Decker's House Tax), cynically pointed out that this exemption, which he first of all described as a 'pleasing consideration,' was 'in reality only an imaginary indulgence, as the wages of the poor must always be regulated by the inconvenience to which they are subject and the rate of their accommodations, therefore every advantage they receive must centre with their superiors.' [1] The theory was probably common now, as before, among the very vocal commercial and manufacturing classes; and most significant of all, it was put forward by North in his budget speeches as one of the reasons for avoiding taxes on necessaries. In 1776 [2] he laid it down that 'taxes in all countries where necessity did not compel should as much as possible be laid on luxury and the elegant conveniences of life, but much more where the strength of a nation chiefly depended on its trade and commerce.' In every operation such as the present, luxuries ought to be taxed, both because the first weight ought to fall on the rich and opulent, and because every tax which might in its consequences tend to affect our manufactures so as to enhance their value to foreign purchasers

---

[1] *Considerations . . . with a Plan for consolidating into One Rate the Land and all other Taxes . . . By a merchant of London,* 1784, 1102, h. 11 (9), pp. 14–15. The only instance I have noticed in this period of an attempt to reconcile the compassionate and trading objections to taxes on necessaries occurs in *Thoughts on Taxation,* 1798, 1103, h. 52 (see pp. 20–3, 35–6). ' It is well known that a tax on beer, salt, soap, leather, etc., and the high price of provisions must add to the necessary expenses of the labourer, and that to enable him to subsist some addition must be made to his wages . . . '; but ' many are the victims that fall a prey to want and disease before their wages are augmented in proportion to the increase of their expenses ; so that, though the labouring part of the community do not ultimately pay the tax when once it has found its proper level, yet till that takes place they feel the burden of it more severely than any description of men, as it must be defrayed out of the funds necessary for their immediate subsistence or the maintenance of their families . . . ' p. 35–6. After the war, Brougham and the economists of the *Edinburgh Review* took pains to elaborate this position, see *e.g.* June 1818, 30. 86–7.

[2] Cobbett, 18. 1318 ; cf. 19. 243.

ought, if possible, to be avoided.' But it is probable that the compassionate objection to taxes on necessaries in the interest of the poor was much more influential in Parliament. It was to this feeling that Pitt seemed always to appeal, and I have noticed no instance of his use of the trading objection. So on the one occasion during this period when serious opposition is recorded against proposed taxes on necessaries (1790–91),[1] the ground alleged was the hardship to the poor,—'the laborious peasant and industrious mechanic,'—a class of the community, one Peer affirmed, 'which more than any other was entitled to the attention and protection of the House.'[2] At the one extreme was the sentimental and philanthropic attitude of William Drake,[3] who declared that 'when he saw beneath the roof of penury a steady loyalty and a willingness to obey our laws, he wished he was as rich as Crœsus in order to be the instrument of cherishing the distressed and comforting the afflicted. He advised the Chancellor of the Exchequer to abstain from his intended tax on malt, and open a public subscription book for the poor, desiring that he might be put down for 200 guineas.' At the other extreme was the appeal of Lord Loughborough,[4] which might almost have been taken for a demand for equitable distribution. He denied that the burden involved on the poor would be light, and pointed out that 'the pressure of every burden was felt in proportion to the weakness of him who bore it.' 'Few of their Lordships, he was afraid, could form an adequate idea of the effect of any additional duty on a necessary of life to the poor.' The tax would amount to 5s. a year on a poor man. 'What would their Lord-

[1] The opposition was against the Malt Tax, and was partly in protest against the heavy taxation of that product and of brewing ; also against increasing the price of a liquor which was the great safeguard against the extended use of spirits. See 16th December 1790, 20th December, 27th December (H. of L.); Cobbett, 28. 1014 *seq.*, 1170 *seq.*, 1195 *seq.*

[2] Earl of Kinnoul, pp. 1195–6.

[3] P. 1172. [4] Pp. 1204–5.

ships think of a capitation tax to that amount. . . ?
Would they not reprobate the idea as unjust, oppressive
and cruel ? ' It was natural, indeed, that it should
be the plea for compassion on the poor that should
influence Parliament in objecting to taxes on necessaries
—for Parliament was dominated by the sentiment of
the landed class which instituted the Speenhamland
allowances in supplement of wages in 1795, and to
which neither Adam Smith's reasoning nor the interest
of the trader in low wages was likely to make much
appeal.[1]

A large number of taxes was imposed or increased
in this period in accordance with the doctrine that
taxes should fall on luxuries. North regarded his
impositions on carriages, cards, dice and newspapers
in 1776 and male servants in 1777[2] in this light.[3]
A carriage, ' though an object of convenience, was in
another light a luxury, because none kept them but
such as were really or nominally rich.' Of the same
type was Pitt's tax on pleasure horses in 1784. He
considered his addition of 1785 to the tax on male
servants as a tax falling chiefly on the opulent and
extravagant;[4] and newspapers (the tax on which he
increased in 1789 and 1797) were, he said, ' certainly
to be considered as articles of luxury ' and a fair object
of taxation.[5] Similarly both North and Pitt regarded
imports such as wine and tobacco as luxuries and as
such fit objects of taxation. North, for instance,
increasing the tax in 1781, said that ' if he knew what
luxury was, tobacco came within that description '
(although it was used chiefly by the common people).[6]

---

[1] See L. Stephen, *Utilitarians*, i. chaps. i.–iii., and Dicey, *Law and
Opinion in England*, pp. 101–2, 106–10, and Lecture V. *passim*.
[2] For short accounts of and references to the Statutes imposing
these and other taxes, see Dowell, ii, under years cited.
[3] Cobbett, 18, 1318 *seq.*, 19, 244.   [4] *Ibid.*, 25, 552–3.
[5] *Ibid.*, 33. 433–4, 28. 211.
[6] *Ibid.*, 21, 1370. Cf. Pitt on Tobacco, 1795, 32. 563.

Customs duties were increased many times.[1] Finally, a number of taxes which, though not falling on luxuries, had certain similar features, were accepted and justified by a variant of this doctrine. Such were deed stamps and legacy duties. They exempted the poor and were regarded as evidence of the wealth and ability of the person paying them. One of several increases in the former was made by North in 1776. 'He thought from the easy manner of collecting the stamp duties and the benefits supposed to arise to the parties from such transactions at the time, that deeds would bear an additional stamp of 1s.'[2] In taxing bills of exchange in 1782 he denied that there would be any hardship, since the bill was an evidence of wealth.[3] So in 1795 Pitt justified an increase of the assessed taxes and the imposition of small legacy duties, chiefly on the ground that 'they attached to property, and would be felt only by the higher and richer orders of the community.'[4]

But such taxes were not nearly productive enough to meet the needs of the time, and so a first departure had to be made from the strictest form of the ideal tax.

---

[1] The attitude towards Customs may be gathered from North's speech of 1779. He proposed a surcharge on the net produce of customs and excise, but made certain exemptions. 'The brewery was exempted, because beer was a great article of consumption with the lower orders of the people ; and if agreeable to the committee he would exempt soap, candles and leather from the surcharge.' *Ibid.*, 20, 166.

[2] *Ibid.*, 18, 1319.   [3] *Ibid.*, 22, 1157.

[4] Debrett, *Parl. Register*, 60, 599 (the volume numberings given here are those of the backing of the B.M. copies, in 289 f.), and cf. Cobbett, 32, 562. Pitt added : 'and it was with peculiar propriety that in a war which had for its basis the security of property, those persons who were happily possessed of wealth should peculiarly contribute to its support.' There are very fairly reported debates on the legacy duty bills which illustrate excellently eighteenth-century views of taxation, but the subject (from the eighteenth-century standpoint) is not important enough to justify the amount of space they would demand. The proposed duty on succession to landed property was rejected. See Debrett, 61. 347 *seq.*, 362, 602, 643, and Lauderdale's protest, Cobbett, 32, 1155

A series of taxes on objects of general use or expenditure was imposed, which diffused the burden more widely than taxes on luxuries, and yet in general exempted the poor. Such, for instance, were the inhabited house duty of 1778 (exempting houses up to £5 rental), the receipt tax of 1783 (exempting receipts up to £2), the calico tax and the increase in the graduated window tax of 1784 (exempting houses under seven windows), the taxes on maid-servants and shops of 1785 (shops under £4 rental exempted), and the tax of 1796 on horses kept for industry. We have a brief summary of North's speech on the inhabited house duty, which he justified thus :[1] 'It was necessary to provide a productive tax ; it was difficult to fix on any that would not be in some degree unequal ; (but) he wished to avoid burdening the lower ranks ; it was not easy to come at the real property of individuals ; but one ground of judging of this, which prevailed in all nations, was by the expense at which they lived ; and this, though it might not answer in every single instance, was yet a very good general rule.' Taxes on houses 'were proper and eligible, as they were visible signs of ability to pay them.' The other taxes of this class were defended as equitable in the same way. Two of them, the receipt tax and the shop tax, were attacked by the commercial classes as being partial against them, and evoked much discussion. The former, imposed by the coalition government of North and Fox, was justified by Fox as a tax in proportion to expenditure. 'There could not be a better way of coming at the expenditure than by taxing the receipts, or in fact taxing the payments made.' It was natural to suppose that a man of £2000 a year would pay double what would be paid by a man of £1000 a year. In addition, it was not compulsory, it was optional : 'you were not compelled to take a receipt.'[2] The opposition had no difficulty in showing

[1] Cobbett, 19, 872, omitting the connecting *that's*.
[2] *Ibid.*, 11th June 1783, 23. 1001. See also budget speech of

that the tax was unequal (accepting Fox's view of its incidence), since the trader had more money trans- actions than the propertied man of equal income; but what is of interest is rather the standard which Fox desired to conform to. It was the same standard which, Pitt contended, justified the shop tax. It would really fall, he thought, on the customer, and so roughly on general expenditure. The point at issue between him and the opponents of the tax was simply whether this view of the incidence of the tax was correct.[1]

The distributive inequality of a tax on an object of general use was not generally recognised. The minor point alone was urged that the parsimonious wealthy man escaped too lightly.[2] Apart from the alleged inequalities of the receipt and shop taxes, the only general objection made came from the commercial classes, who protested against manufactures being made subject to taxation. Their influence was very con- iderable. They caused the defeat of Pitt's Irish policy in 1785,[3] they induced him to withdraw a proposed extension of the coal tax in 1784,[4] and to repeal, against his own judgment, the calico tax in 1785 and the shop tax in 1789; and they opposed, but without success, his adoption of Walpole's excise methods of collecting the wine and tobacco duties.[5] A pamphlet on the calico

Lord John Cavendish, p. 933, speeches of Wray, Beaufoy and Pitt, pp. 998, 1004, 1015, and Alderman Newnham's motion for repeal, 4th December 1783, 24. 97 seq. Pamphlets were numerous, e.g. 8228. ccc. 21, 712 f. 1, and E. 2147 (2).

[1] See debates of 1786 ibid., 25, 1165 seq. They were continued yearly. See Pitt's speech in the last debate, 2nd April 1789, 27. 1343. Pitt was basing his case on Adam Smith (Wealth of Nations, ed. Cannan, ii. 337).

[2] Three Essays on Taxation of Income, 1799, B. 707 (6); cf. Keith, An Impartial and Comprehensive View of the Present State of Great Britain, 1797, B. 711 (1), p. 54. Keith also said that the poor and the industrious man paid too high a share, but did not explain it.

[3] See J. H. Rose, Wm. Pitt and Nat. Revival, chap. xi.

[4] 1784, Cobbett, 24. 1027–8, and 1215.

[5] Wine, 5th May 1786, ibid., 25. 1434–9, and debates of 7th June and 26th June (H. of L.); Tobacco, 10th June 1789, 28. 157, 24th June (p. 179), 15th July (p. 231). Pitt gauged the changed state of feeling since Walpole's day. ' So much were former prejudices

tax[1] was indicative of their standpoint. It was entitled *Manufacturers improper subjects of taxation*, and
contended that, since Britain's hope of maintaining
her place among the nations depended on her manufactures, anything tending in any degree to enhance
prices or burden the merchant who exported them
was to be condemned. This was a quite partisan
contention, and both Fox, who advocated repeal, and
Pitt repudiated the doctrine that manufactures, as
manufactures, were improper objects of taxation.[2]
Pitt, however, said that ' the opinions, however originat-
ing, however infused or however founded, of so large,
so useful and so respectable a body of men as the
cotton manufacturers, nay even their prejudices and
errors, were to him objects of such serious consideration
that he would not put his own sentiments in competition with them when the point in question was
such as could with any safety be given up.'[3]

But taxes on luxuries and on objects of general
expenditure were, taken together, also insufficient to
provide the required revenue, and so a second and
altogether more serious infringement had to be made of
the accepted ideal of the tax system. The old taxes on
necessaries (beer, salt, candles, leather, coal, soap) were
not only not repealed, but they were increased. The
malt tax was increased in 1779, 1780 and 1790 ; the salt
tax in 1780, 1782 and 1798 ; the soap tax in 1782, the
candle tax in 1784, and the tea and sugar duties several
times ; while, apart from Pitt's reduction of the tea duty in

against this mode dissipated that he did really expect on the present
occasion . . . he should have but very few if any dissenting voices
against this proposal.'   Fox repeated the old arguments.   ' He
would never agree to any regulations which bartered away freedom
and the constitution for revenue.'   The Cider Tax of 1763, repealed
1767, was opposed on the same kind of ground, but with more
reason. *Ibid.*, 15, 1307 *seq.*, and 16, 206–7.
     [1] B. 707 (1).   The tax on printed goods was retained.
     [2] Cobbett, April 20, 1785, 25. 478, 480, 483, 485, 490.
     [3] P. 483.

1784 to prevent smuggling, the only reductions were those made by Pitt in 1792, when he took off the additions of 1784 and 1790 to the candle and malt taxes, and completed the exemption of houses with less than seven windows from the window tax.[1] The use of tea and sugar, which are included in this list, was rapidly extending among the poor in this period, and they were gradually taking on the character of necessaries in which they were usually regarded in the nineteenth century. This was recognised in Parliament, and it was admitted that in taxing them, taxes were being laid on commodities which at least bordered on necessaries.[2] Beer, however, did not at this time cease to be looked upon generally as a necessary.

The way in which North and Pitt introduced their proposals for taxes on necessaries was very significant.[3]

[1] For all these, see Dowell, ii., under years.

[2] The extending use of tea and sugar is illustrated by an attack in 1777 on the growth of extravagance among the poor—*An Essay on tea, sugar, white bread and butter, country ale-houses, strong beer and Geneva, and other modern luxuries*, 1777, 8275. aaa. 10.   J. H. Rose (*Wm. Pitt and Nat. Revival*, p. 182, citing *Farmer's Letters*, 197) says: 'Arthur Young found that the use of tea had spread into the homes of cottagers; and he classed as extravagant those villages which owed their refreshment to China, and commended the frugality of those which adhered to home-brewed ale.' In 1795, Pitt increased the tea duty as falling on a luxury and therefore a proper object of taxation. Fox protested. 'With regard to the poor, he feared that tea had of late years made a great part of their consumption' (Cobbett, 31. 1317–18). Debrett reports Fox as saying that 'tea and sugar were now in such common use that he feared they were necessaries of life' (54. 316). Next year, Pitt admitted this tacitly. On 7th December 1796 he proposed to increase the tea duty again; but exempted the coarser kinds of tea as a common beverage of the people, and with regret increased the Sugar Tax, which also affected the people of the lower classes. Debrett, 63. 265–67. On the other hand, Sinclair the historian regarded sugar as a most eligible subject of taxation. 'It is a luxury of life that might undoubtedly be dispensed with.' *History of the Public Revenue*, part iii. 1790, p. 186.

[3] The reports of speeches in this period vary very much in character. Only the most important speakers were reported at length, and this was not always the case even with them. Also it is probable that few of the speeches given at length were reported verbatim. They were probably written up from very full notes of the line of argument and of the significant words and phrases. But granted that, I do not see any substantial reason for distrusting

They did not assert that everyone should pay taxation and that such taxes would fall equally as between rich and poor ; neither, on the other hand, did they repudiate these doctrines.   Their attitude was one of distress and apology.   As Pitt said in 1784,[1] with reference to a proposed tax on coal which was later withdrawn, ' it was painful to him to tax that without which we could not subsist.'   Similarly he was ' seriously concerned ' to have to tax candles, a necessary of life ' as indispensable with the poorest as with the richest family in the kingdom.' [2]   They excused themselves on the ground of pressure for money and the paramount need for ' productive ' or ' substantial ' taxes.   To quote Pitt again : ' the truth was, that nothing but the urgency of the present exigence should have driven him to this and several other resources.' [3]   And to be productive, taxes must, they argued, touch the body of the people, who are the great consumers [4]—not considering such a possibility as an Income Tax.   And finally, they put in a plea in mitigation, that the added burden would be a very small one—' so trifling a burden,' North remarked in reference to the salt tax of 1780, ' that no person, however poor, would have cause to complain.' [5]   Pitt's answer to the opponents of the malt tax addition of 1790 was similar.   He could not believe ' that so very small an addition to the duties on malt already paid (about a farthing a gallon on the better sort of beer) could be attended with serious consequences to any description of persons, rich or poor.' [6]

The truth was, of course, that without being able

them ; and, particularly when employed as a whole, and not merely for the expressions of a single speech, their testimony seems to me conclusive.   For practical purposes, it is inconceivable that the reports with which I am concerned, viz. those of financial speeches, were invented by reporters.   See Tierney, 27th December 1798, Cobbett, 34. 148.

[1] Cobbett, 24. 1027.   [2] Ibid. pp. 1028-29.   [3] Ibid.
[4] e.g. North, 1781, ibid. 21. 1363-64 ; Pitt, 1784, 24. 1026. Cf. Fox, 1783, 23. 1002.
[5] Ibid. 21. 168.   [6] Ibid. 28. 1174-75.

to say that the poor man ought not to bear a share in
taxation, they desired for compassionate or trade reasons
to avoid taxes on his necessaries. And yet they did
not hold this opinion firmly enough to prevent its
contravention in practice. Two results of some importance followed. First, taxes on necessaries ceased
to be put to any real test of distributive equity. They
were not imposed because the poor should pay taxation ;
on the contrary, they should not be imposed at all. The
question whether they laid an equitable share of the
burden on the poor, therefore, did not arise. Only
necessity justified taxes on necessaries — they were
' improper taxes.' Thus the condition of opinion con-
spired against any advance in the understanding of the
distributive effect of such taxes, or any recognition of
the necessity for a compensatory Income Tax or the
like, even on the theory that the poor should pay taxation
in proportion to income. Secondly, opinion on taxation necessarily lost in authority. Certain taxes ought
not to exist, but they did exist and grew heavier. The
doctrine that necessaries should not be taxed ceased
to be a rule to be followed—it became a rule to be
followed when circumstances permitted ; and yet it
remained, as we have just observed, the only test to
which taxes on necessaries were subjected. ' In instances
when the sums wanted will admit of it, the objects of
taxation should ever be property and the luxuries of
life,' said North.[1] Pitt expressed the same idea in
other words when he declared productiveness to be
the first consideration in imposing taxes. That apology
for a theory was even regarded by George Rose as worth
embroidering in his defence[2] of Pitt's financial policy
from 1792 to 1799 on this ground : ' It is a principle
of taxation, equally permanent and politic, to spare, as
far as is consistent with the productiveness of the taxes
to be imposed, the great body of the people, those

[1] 1777, *ibid.* 19. 243.
[2] *A Brief Examination* . . ., 1799, B. 524 (7), p. 31.

inferior ranks from whose labour and industry the wealth
of the country is chiefly derived.' But its real meaning
was expressed more truly by the opposition leaders, whose
speeches bring out very clearly how general was the
attitude to taxation which North and Pitt represented.
Fox pledged himself to support Pitt on his proposed
taxes on necessaries of 1784. 'Indeed, so sensible was
he of the necessity of raising taxes that there were
hardly any taxes the rt. hon. gentleman could have
proposed that he should have thought himself, from
the situation he had held, entitled to oppose.'[1] So,
on another necessaries budget in 1790, Sheridan[2] said :
'As for the taxes proposed, the rt. hon. gentleman's
situation was at present so difficult that it was almost
unjustifiable to oppose any taxes.'

One other explanation requires to be added to make
the situation clear. The doctrine that taxes should not
fall on necessaries was not only not respected in fact,
but it was based on positions which did not have in them
the quality of coerciveness. This was obviously true
of the first ; for the objection to taxes on necessaries
on the ground that they raised wages and injured trade
was merely one out of several non-distributive objections to taxes, and it clashed, in particular, with objections to direct assessment. But it was also true of the
second. The desire to exempt the poor on compassionate
grounds was in a measure sentimental and superficial.
It is necessary to guard against exaggeration on this
point, for the sentiment did without doubt stimulate
the Chancellors of the Exchequer to a real attempt to
find taxes which did not fall on the poor—those which
we have discussed, and the Triple Assessment and the
Income Tax to which we proceed, make this clear. But
while it is true that the desire influenced practice, it is
equally true that it did not control it ; no attempt was
made to live up to it completely, or indeed even to discuss
the means which would make that possible. This was

[1] Cobbett, 24. 1032.   [2] *Ibid.* 28. 1011.

partly due to unwillingness to face direct taxation,
whether because of a real fear that it was impracticable
or on account of doctrinal prejudices or of mere self-
interest ; but it was also due partly to the fact that
compassion for the poor could not uproot from men's
minds the idea that after all it was just that the poor
man should pay taxation. That implication of the
freeholder view of society constituted the background
of opinion all through the eighteenth century, as a great
mass of evidence testifies ;[1] and it could not be over-

[1] In addition to sections on Walpole and Adam Smith, see *The
man's mistaken who thinks the taxes so grievous* . . ., 1755, 8132. c. 27,
p. 11-12. 'Is it not the duty of the meanest of His Majesty's subjects
to lend their utmost assistance in time of danger in common with
their masters . . . should our enemy prevail will not our manufactures be destroyed and our people made slaves to foreigners ? '
Proposals of 1757, 8132. c. 71, p. 49, and cf. p. 12. 'Every person
ought to contribute somewhat towards the support of the government by which he is protected'—referring to the poor man.
Blackstone, *Commentaries*, 1765, i. 117 *seq.* and 297. *Reflections on
the present high price of provisions* . . ., 1766, 8247. df. 37 (1), p. 22.
' For as every man is bound to contribute to the public revenue in
proportion to the benefits he receives from the public protection,
so no man has a right to complain whilst particular care is taken in
the imposition of taxes that they are not unequally laid.' 'Every
one who desires to enjoy the sweets of society is ready to pay toward the defence of himself and his fortune.' Thomas Mortimer,
Elements, 1772, p. 458. The people 'should remember that all the
subjects are bound in one common bond to support the civil government under the protection of which they enjoy inestimable rights
and privileges ; and that it is the indispensable duty of every individual to contribute in a due proportion to the national expenses ;
for, as an elegant Italian author observes, " Every individual in paying taxes deposits a part of his property in the public treasury in
order to preserve the remainder and to enjoy it securely."' Kames,
Sketches, 1774, ii. 464 (viii. § 2 at end). Thomas Percival, *An
Inquiry into the principles and limits of taxation as a branch of moral
and political philosophy*, 1785 (Memoirs of the Literary and Philosophical Society of Manchester), T. 276 (6), *passim*. Sinclair, *History*,
part iii. 1790, p. 128, which brings together various feelings regarding the taxation of the poor. Adam Ferguson, *Principles of Moral
and Political Science*, 1792, ii. 434. John Young, *Essays*, 1794,
E. 2076 (1), vii., on Taxations, p. 133. 'Nothing can be more reasonable than that all who enjoy the protection of government should
contribute according to their ability for its support.' Burke,
Regicide Peace, 3rd Letter (ed. Payne, p. 208). 'None on account
of their dignity should be exempt ; none (preserving due proportion) on account of the scantiness of their means. The moment

thrown by, though it was not easy to reconcile with, any mere plea for compassion. The two attitudes moved on different planes—the one was an appeal, true or false, to justice—to the essential conditions of life ; the other was an appeal to sentiment, and was relatively superficial. And therefore, although men avowed the desire to exempt the poor, yet they regarded this not so much as an act of justice as a concession to misfortune ; and if they were unable always to grant the exemption, the failure was ground for regret and distress or even apology, but could not be regarded as an injustice. This was the unconscious logic of the Parliamentary mind.

A change in the tone of one of Pitt's budget speeches at the very end of this period illustrates this, and shows how close to the surface was the idea that everyone was under an obligation to pay taxation. In a supplementary budget of 1798,[1] subsequent to the imposition of the Triple Assessment, Pitt proposed *inter alia* to double the salt tax (to yield half a million a year) ; and, besides explaining that it would lay no larger a yearly sum than half a crown on each labouring family, and referring to the extraordinary exigencies of the times, he justified his proposal by appealing to the common interest of the whole nation in the war. 'I am still more confirmed in the justice of this tax, and I am still more persuaded that the very order of people I am speaking of will be satisfied of that truth, when they are informed that persons of the highest rank are not, either with respect to their property, their liberty, or their happiness, so interested in the preservation of this country and the happy constitution under which they live as the lower

a man is exempted from the maintenance of the community, he is in some degree separated from it. He loses his place as a citizen.' Cf. also pp. 219–20.

[1] *Parl. Register* (Debrett), 68. 66–67, substituting *or* for *and* before 'their happiness.' The report in Pitt's collected *Speeches*, iii. 293–95 is differently worded, but brings out, though not so clearly, the same points. Pitt made the same point in 1805 on another increase in the Salt Tax : see Cobbett, *Parl. Debates*, 4th March 1805, iii. 697.

and labouring classes of the community. If they want to be convinced of this truth, let them look to the situation of those countries which have been overrun by the French.' He also pointed out that the poor had been for the most part exempted from the taxes lately imposed—a rudimentary recognition of the compensatory method of distributing taxation between rich and poor which implied no real understanding of the distributive character of taxes on necessaries.[1]

It is from the basis of this state of opinion and policy that we can alone understand the character of the third and most striking departure which was made from the eighteenth-century view of a good tax system. The circumstance was again financial need. At the end of 1797 Pitt came to the conclusion that the immense yearly addition which was being made to the national debt had become a menace to the credit of the State, and decided to recommend Parliament to break with the system of providing new taxes only for the interest of the deficit. He proposed that a large portion of each year's deficit should be provided within the year. Only a direct assessment, however, could yield the desired sums. Consequently, in 1798 a tax known as the Triple Assessment was imposed, from which it was estimated that four and a half millions a year would be obtained. But this tax was widely evaded, and next year it was replaced by an Income Tax of 2s. in the £, which was estimated to produce seven and a half millions

---

[1] I have only noticed one real recognition of the compensatory idea in this period. Thomas Percival in his *Inquiry*, p. 23, said: 'To apportion the taxes with all possible impartiality is essential to their having the full force of moral obligation. Yet this is the most arduous office of the financier; and when a kingdom is under the pressure of accumulated debts, can perhaps be accomplished only by such a modification of the whole system of revenue as shall compensate the unavoidable excesses in some cases by equitable exemptions in others.' But he did not develop it, nor did he realise the distributive result of taxes on commodities in general use. Cf. Keith, *loc. cit.*

a year, and which did produce about six millions.[1]   The
nineteenth century may be said to have opened, so far
as matters of taxation are concerned, with Pitt's Income
Tax of 1799; and if we properly grasp the state of opinion
in that year, we have not only understood the eighteenth-
century view of taxation, but we have obtained a clue
to the way in which tax questions were approached for
the ensuing fifty years.

The first point to be observed regarding the Income
Tax is that it contravened the doctrine that revenue
should be raised through taxes on expenditure, and
not by direct assessment of means.[2]   It involved 'an
inquisition more intolerable than any tax,'[3] it would
lead to fraud, it was far from optional,[4] it fell on profits
and so diminished reproductive stock.[5]   It was a 'forced

[1] Altogether the best and fullest account of these taxes is given
in *The Income Tax*, 1911 (pp. 57–115), by Professor Seligman, who
for the first time has made use of the pamphlet literature of the
subject. As explained in Chap. III., I am unable to accept Professor
Seligman's view of the relation of the Income Tax to the direct taxes
of the seventeenth century. See also Dowell, ii. 212–14, 215–16.
I hold myself relieved from going over the history in detail.

[2] The best statement of the attitude outside of Parliament was
by Francis Newbery, a Commissioner of Taxes, *Thoughts on
Taxation*, 1799, T. 1647 (6), who considered optionality, particularly,
' as of the very essence of taxation in a free country.' 'If . . . one
of the first characteristics of a free constitution be security of person
and dominion of property, how can an impost which is inevitable and
compulsory, and which therefore militates against the dominion
of property, be consistent with freedom ? . . . How can freedom
exist when its characteristic quality is gone ?' (pp. 9–11). Cf. in
Parliament, Tierney, 31st December, 1798, Debrett, 69. 492–93.
For contemporary pamphlet discussion of the doctrine that taxes
should be on consumption, see *e.g.* Lauderdale, *Plan for altering the
manner of collecting a large part of the public revenue*, 1799, T .1649 (6),
pp. 12–14, and *Three Essays on Taxation of Income*, 1799, B. 707 (6),
p. 28 *seq.*

[3] *Parl. Register* (Debrett), 14th December 1798, M. A. Taylor, 69.
247–48, Wm. Smith, 69. 263–64 (quoting Adam Smith), 31st December, Nickolls, 69. 486. Cf. Petition from City of London, 22nd
March 1802, 79. 256–58. For a moderate statement of the commercial view not pushed to the length of opposition to the bill
in the circumstances of the time (1798), see Baring, 69. 260–61.

[4] *e.g.* Duke of Bedford, 8th January 1799, *ibid.* 69. 563.

[5] Hobhouse, 4th December 1798, 69. 128. ' It was a tax which
would strike with peculiar force at industry and the fruits of industry, while indolence was left untouched and encouraged . . .

contribution.' It was to be regarded as a temporary sacrifice to meet a great emergency.[1]

Nothing could show more clearly the dislike and distrust of direct assessment than the first plan which Pitt adopted for his emergency tax. The Triple Assessment was a half-way house between taxes on expenditure and a direct tax on income. It was an attempt to raise a large sum by a single tax and yet retain as much as possible the character of the accustomed taxes of the time. Direct assessment of means and inquisition were avoided [2] (except as regards claims for exemption and abatement) by basing the contribution of the tax-payer, not upon his income or property, but upon his payment in a previous year to the assessed

The merchant is accustomed annually to convert a part of his profits into capital. If the tax-gatherer calls for a portion of those profits, he must devote less to the increase of his reproductive stock. Thus the progress of our trade would be obstructed.' Quotes Sir Jas. Steuart: 'As to the pure profits on trade,' 'although they appear to be income yet I consider them rather as stock, and therefore they ought not to be taxed.'

[1] Triple Assessment, Pitt, 24th November 1797, *ibid.* 66. 278 ; Income Tax, 3rd December 1798, Pitt (less definite), *Orations of William Pitt*, Everyman ed., p. 279 ; Repeal 1802, Addington, 5th April, Debrett, 416 (Cobbett, 36. 448). The fallacious argument that by reducing the spending power of the rich the yield of the taxes on expenditure would suffer and, employment being lessened, the poor would be affected, was not of much importance. It had been discussed and refuted in 1779, when Pulteney (*Considerations . . . on the means of raising the necessary supplies*, T. 1118 (9)) suggested raising the whole supply within the year by a tax of 1½ per cent. on fortunes (capital). The objection was then made, by Burke among others (Cobbett, 20. 168), but in his Budget speech North, followed by Pulteney, pointed out the fallacy—the tax would be spent by the State. It reappeared, however, in 1797–99. Lauderdale gave countenance to it (*A Letter on the present measures of Finance*, 1798, T. 1649 (5), pp. 23, 36) ; Rose made careless and inconsistent use of it (*Brief Examination . . .*, 1799, p. 33) ; the Duke of Bedford put it forward as an objection to the Triple Assessment, 5th January 1798, Debrett, 66. 655 ; and see Hobhouse, 4th December 1798, 69. 127. Not much notice was taken of it. See Pitt, 14th December, 1798, 69. 267, and *Thoughts on Taxation*, 1798, 1103. h. 52, p. 62. As noted before, the argument had a certain local validity.

[2] Purposely, of course ; see Pitt, 24th November 1797, Debrett, 66. 274 ; 14th December, p. 456; and cf. *e.g.* Nickolls, 3rd January 1798, p. 526.

taxes, *i.e.* upon his expenditure on servants, house rent, carriages, and the like. But, on the other hand, the tax was not optional; for it was based on expenditure in the past, which is as rigid and unalterable a standard as it is possible to invent. It was, therefore, not left to the tax-payer to reduce his contribution by reducing his expenditure.[1] The Triple Assessment was an attempt, and as it turned out an unsuccessful attempt, to get a tax on income [2] (with exemption up to £60 and abatements) but on the basis of past expenditure.

The Income Tax was not imposed, therefore, because it was considered a better tax than those on expenditure, or in order to remedy any inequality in the existing distribution of taxation. On the contrary, it was imposed in the face of severe condemnation of direct assessment by the current doctrine of the age, which, although not shared in its full extent by Pitt,[3] was so general and powerful that the tax was repealed in 1802 and 1816 in spite of financial difficulties.[4] But, on the other hand, it is equally important to notice that the Income Tax was regarded as an emergency tax because of this condemnation, and not because of its distributive

---

[1] This was one of the chief grievances; *e.g.* 4th December, Nickolls, 66. 335; Plummer, p. 343—'If a tax to be raised was upon luxuries, an opportunity ought to be afforded to persons to retrench those luxuries'; 4th January, Hobhouse—the only justifiable scheme of taxation is such a tax—whether upon carriages, horses, or any other article—as will 'never interfere with . . . the right of the individual to subject himself to that share of the burden which in his own judgement his fortune and condition in life will allow,' p. 558; Lords' Protest, Cobbett, 33. 1299, §. 4, p. 1302.

[2] Pitt, 24th November, *ibid.* 66. 278; 14th December, Fox, pp. 434–35; Pitt, p. 456.

[3] Pitt was not given to expressing unnecessary judgments on abstract questions, and it is not easy to know what exact view he held of the place of an Income Tax in the hierarchy of taxes. But he certainly dissented, along with not a few others, from the extreme condemnation passed upon it by the commercial classes. See Pitt, 14th December 1798, Debrett, 69. 269–71; Bishop of Landaff, *An address to the people of Great Britain,* 1798, 8026. c. 50, p. 2; *Thoughts on Taxation,* 1798, pp. 65–66.

[4] Seligman, *op. cit.* pp. 87–89, 106 *seq.*, and see note ·5, p. 146.

principles. These were widely accepted, and even if they had been modified to meet the one objection of any influence which was raised against them, the tax would still have been condemned as permissible only in the last resort. That is to say, *distributively* the Income Tax was an expression and not a contravention of the typical eighteenth-century view of the equitable distribution of taxation.

The distributive characteristics of the Income Tax (and of the intention of the Triple Assessment) were three.

First, the poor—that is, the great body of the people—were exempt. Only those with incomes of £60 a year and upwards (the middle class and the rich) paid Income Tax. No doubt, though it was never mentioned, one of the reasons for the exemption was that it is extremely difficult to levy a direct tax on the poor. But it is important to notice that it was considered altogether desirable and proper that the poor should be exempted. No complaint was raised against their exemption ; on the contrary, it was held up as one of the chief grounds for accepting direct assessment.[1] The reason, of course, was that exemption of the poor was an accepted maxim of current opinion, and that in the Income Tax the maxim did not conflict, as it did in taxes on expenditure, with productiveness.

Second, it was not because the poor already paid enough taxation otherwise that they were exempted from the Income Tax. This is another way of saying that the Income Tax was not imposed or considered as a compensatory tax, or as part of a compensatory system of taxation. It was looked at by itself, just as taxes were looked at in the seventeenth century and by Walpole and Adam Smith. Hence its repeal was demanded in 1816 with an easy conscience and with scorn for opposi-

[1] Triple Assessment, Pitt, 24th November, Debrett, 66. 277–78, 4th December, p. 317. Cf. Lushington, 3rd January, p. 544, Lord Grenville, 5th January, p. 643. Scarcely mentioned in Income Tax debates. See G. Rose, *op. cit.* p. 32.

tion, and opponents of repeal were so little able to explain and justify their position.[1] If we ask ourselves what answer we should make to-day to a proposal to repeal the Income Tax, we can realise the most striking change in opinion on taxation which took place during the nineteenth century.

Third, the distributive standard adopted for the Income Tax was proportionality to income, with certain minor modifications. The act imposed a tax of 10 per cent. on all income of whatever kind (from land, funds and property of any kind, farming, trade, professions and earnings) over £60 a year. In adopting this principle Pitt simply took over and made precise the seventeenth- and eighteenth-century idea that distribution should be proportionate to income. But although he made it precise for the practical purpose in hand, he did not make it precise as a matter of principle, either in his own mind or in that of others.[2] It remained essentially what it was in the eighteenth century—a somewhat vague idea which was probably sound but was not clearly understood in all its bearings; the more elaborate consideration of the question, which was one of the distinguishing marks of the nineteenth century, was only beginning. It is not to be implied that Pitt thought that the standard he adopted was inequitable in particular respects; on the contrary, he defended it against proposed modifications;[3] but neither he nor his critics had an all-round view of the problems involved.

The minor modifications, which were generally accepted,[4] were: first, certain allowances to the taxpayer in respect of his children—a recognition, in the spirit of the seventeenth and eighteenth centuries, that ability cannot be measured only by some one circumstance, such as income; and second, abatements to

[1] See note 5 above, p. 146.
[2] See discussion of differentiation below.   [3] *Ibid.*
[4] On allowances for children, see interesting short debate on 22nd December 1798, Debrett, 69. 404 *seq.*

tax-payers whose incomes ranged between £60 and £200, the official view of which was not very clear.[1] The practical reason was, no doubt, (1) that if you exempt an income of £60 it is absurd to tax an income of £65 at the full sum, and (2) that it was intended in general to levy a tax on the full income.

The Income Tax, then, was a direct assessment on means, regarded on that account as an emergency expedient, imposing a tax which was not considered as part of a compensatory system of taxation, falling upon the wealthy and middle class, in proportion to incomes, and exempting the poor. This was its significance in relation to the eighteenth century, and the major part of its meaning for the first half of the nineteenth century. But for the nineteenth century it had an additional significance. It raised sharply certain questions about proportionality to income as the standard of distribution (the poor not being in question) which were necessarily slurred over in the eighteenth century, but constituted a considerable subject of debate in the nineteenth.

We are not concerned here to discuss these nineteenth-century questions in detail, but it is necessary to notice briefly how they were approached in 1798 and 1799. Two chief criticisms were then advanced against the justice of taxation in proportion to income. The first, which was supported by influential commercial opinion, was that it was unfair to tax at the same rates landed or funded income, life income, and professional

---

[1] Rose (*op. cit.*, pp. 32–33) described it as based on the 'principle of proportioning public assessments to the ability of different classes.' 'The small earnings of laborious industry are spared altogether ; the progressive rise of the tax saves, in a proportional degree, the moderate incomes of the classes of all the orders below competency . . . .' Auckland (Debrett, 69. 547–48) explained the intention as based on the exemption of incomes 'necessary to actual subsistence,' whence incomes above that amount must be abated to some extent till a point (necessarily arbitrary and disputable) is reached at which the full rate can be applied.

or commercial income.   There should be differentiation
between settled, temporary and precarious incomes.
What modification of proportionality should therefore
be made was, however, not very clear to the critics.
In the debates on the Triple Assessment, we find chiefly
a general protest against crushing the middle class.[1]
A typical statement of the case next year was Tierney's.
All income, he said, was not disposable property; the
professional man or trader had to save from his income,
whereas the man of property had already the continuance
of his secured.[2] A less complacent form of the objection was that the bill taxed indolence and industry
equally.[3] ' It is not asked whether one be not a farmer
who has earned it ($£500$) by the sweat of his brow—or
whether the other may not be a mere miscreant, who
loads the earth with an useless incumbrance.' The only
defined   suggestion   for   a   common   denominator   of
different sorts of income was the rather absurd one of
capitalising them.[4] This proposition derived from the
idea, loosely held and interpreted very differently by
different men, that taxation should be on property or
capital;[5] which, as Pitt pointed out, involved the

---

[1] e.g. 4th December, Debrett, 66. 335–36 (Nickolls), 7th December,
p. 381 (Wilberforce).   But cf. Fox, ibid. p. 622, and Lords' Protest,
Cobbett, 33. 1302, § 4.
[2] Debrett, 69. 492.   [3] Ibid. p. 262, Wm. Smith.
[4] Frend, Principles of Taxation, 1799, T. 1651 (3), pp. v.–xi.
5 seq.
[5] It is as impossible to neglect as it is difficult shortly to explain
the numerous references at this time to the idea that taxation
should fall on property.   The term was used vaguely and differently
by different people.   In its broadest form, it meant little more
than that the poor should be exempt from taxation.   Thus Auckland (5th January 1798, Debrett, 66. 653) and Pitt (p. 456) admitted
that there would be no objection to an equal contribution on the
whole of property; and Pitt spoke of the Triple Assessment as a
surrender of part of our property as a salvage, and said that consumption having failed it was necessary to resort to the ' general
taxation of property ' (Inc. Tax, 3rd December 1798, Orations,
Everyman ed. p. 279, and 14th December, Debrett, 69. 268).   In
the same way, taxes on servants, houses, etc., were sometimes
spoken of as levied on a visible criterion of men's property; and
Addington in reimposing the Income Tax in 1803 (changed in
administrative ways but not in its essential distributive principle),

position that a landowner and a trader, each with
a capital of £15,000, should both pay the same tax

renamed it the Property Tax (see Seligman, *op. cit.*, p. 89 *seq.*). So
used the phrase did *not* mean (1) that the tax should fall on capital
value as against the annual income of property, or (2) that the
value of property owned was accepted as the just standard of
distribution. But, the notion being vague, it was possible to use
it to mean both these things. First, without distinguishing the
points at issue, Pulteney in 1779 proposed a contribution of 1½ per
cent. of each man's fortune to raise the whole supply within the
year (*Considerations*, T. 1118 (9), p. 36); and in 1798 the Bishop of
Landaff approved what he called a tax of a tenth of ' every man's
whole property' for a similar purpose (*Address*, p. 1 *seq.*). Similar
expressions were used by the spokesmen of the commercial classes.
If taxes could not be on luxury they ought to be on property (Lushington, 14th December 1797, 66. 418–19). Second, it was argued in
Parliament, *e.g.* by Col. Wood, Thurlow, and the Duke of Bedford
(Debrett, 4th December 1797, 66. 355–56, 5th January, p. 661; 69.
562 *seq.*), and in pamphlets by Lauderdale and Frend (*op. cit.*), that
property (capital) was the equitable standard of distribution and
that income was not. Pitt answered these two lines of argument
thus : (1) He pointed out that the manufacturers, who had as great
an interest in the defensive contest as others, should not be exempted, and that it was visionary and impracticable to think that
the burden could be laid on the rich alone, 7th December 1797, 66.
387 ; and (2) on the heels of his own declaration that it was necessary
to resort to the general taxation of property, he said (69. 268 *seq.*)
that ' in order to ascertain the capital of the country the only
proper criterion that offers itself is that of income,' and pointed
out that to tax equally a capital of £15,000 which yields the landlord
£500 and the trader £2250 a year would be unjust (p. 272). It should
be noted that the idea that taxation should be on capital ran counter
to the economist's doctrine that it should not, and that the result
would be injurious to the commercial interest of the country—see
e.g. 1796 debates on Legacy Duty bills, *e.g.* Grey, Debrett, 61. 363,
as well as note 5, p. 168.

The explanation of the use of the idea is perhaps threefold.
First, the ruling classes were people of landed property, whose
incomes were property incomes, and to whom, granting that the
poorer classes were exempt, it was easy to think carelessly of taxation
of income and of property as the same thing. The difference rose
sharply in considering the incomes of wealthy professional men
and traders, which were now being generally taxed directly for
the first time for a century. Second, the idea was a useful one
for the commercial classes to take up (see *e.g.* City of London
petition, 1802), in order to condemn the proposed and later the
existing tax. Third, it was possible to support the doctrine on the
ground of the benefit theory of taxation ; which was well known
although not effectively operative on men's thought. It was said
that each citizen should pay in proportion to the protection he
received from Government, which it was asserted was in proportion
to his property. So Thurlow and the Duke of Bedford (*loc. cit.*);

although their incomes were £500 and £2250 respectively.[1]
The whole discussion was indeed lacking in definiteness,
and much complicated by the eagerness of the commercial classes to seize on any argument by which
the hated direct assessment could be vilified. Pitt
made a detailed reply on the subject on 14th December
1798, in which he declined to differentiate.[2] He did
not agree that there was any injustice as between the
property income and the annuity; he was not clear
whether the demand for differentiation in favour of
earned incomes was just, and he did not think it administratively practicable. We must, he said, take
the situation of men as we find them and make one
rule of privation apply equally to all income : ' whether
a man is in the habit of saving a portion of his income
or spending it all, he shall have one tenth less to save,
one tenth less to spend in the year.'

The second and much less representative criticism
was that it was unfair to tax the large and the small
income at the same rate. The tax should be graduated ;
the larger the income the larger the rate (not merely
the amount) of tax should be. What we may call
pseudo-graduation was a common technical device in
English taxation, designed to bring some standard
other than means or income into closer relation thereto.
Seventeenth-century Poll Taxes, the Window Tax and
the Triple Assessment were cases in point. The

the latter added that the heavier taxation of landowners was but
just, since they, being fixed in the soil, got most benefit from the
protection of the State, which, indeed, he implied, in no way helped
the man whose profits depended on his own exertions or expense.
A less general but commoner form of the argument was that it was
specially incumbent on property to contribute in a war chiefly
undertaken for the defence of property (e.g. Bowles, *Two Letters*,
1796, 102. g. 58, p. 32 ; Alderman Lushington, *loc. cit.*).

· A few suggestions were made that the standard of distribution
should not be expenditure or capital or income, but some combination of these. See Hobhouse, 4th December 1798, 69. 127–28, and
Sinclair, 14th December, p. 233.

[1] Pitt, 14th December 1698, Debrett, p. 272.
[2] *Ibid.* p. 274.

abatements in the Income Tax between £60 and £200 were another form of pseudo-graduation; and it was on this analogy that the favourite argument for real graduation was based.[1] What reason was there, it was argued, for stopping the grading at £200 ? In the vagueness of opinion regarding the abatements, the point was of some debating force ;[2] but the real answer, of course, was that whatever the abatements meant, they did not mean the progressive cutting down of incomes. A better form of the argument was Gilbert Wakefield's. He pointed out[3] that the poor man's income is spent chiefly on necessaries, and that as the income increases it is spent more and more on luxuries ; and, he argued, it is only just to take from luxurious more than from necessary income. It is noteworthy that John Ranby, who replied to Wakefield's pamphlet and was far from an extremist in temperament, agreed with Wakefield on this point.[4] But whatever the value of the argument, it did not justify graduation in the sense in which it came to interest the later nineteenth century ; for the special feature of the Death duties is that the rate increases sharply within the range of quite luxurious incomes. In fact, there is every reason to suppose that the demand for graduation at the end of the eighteenth century was only half serious, outside the circle of a few extreme types of mind.[5] Graduation in the modern and important sense is not merely a theory of ability to pay taxation, but a criticism of the social system of inheritance of property, and such criticism was quite untypical, though not unknown, in England at that time.[6] One

---

[1] 31st December 1798, Nickolls, Debrett, 69. 486 ; 8th January, Lord Holland, p. 536; *Thoughts on Taxation*, 1798, 1103. h. 52, p. 64; Frend, *op. cit.* pp. iii.–iv.

[2] See Auckland, Debrett, 69. 547.

[3] *A reply to some parts of the Bishop of Landaff's address . . .,* 1798, 1389. d. 57, pp. 14–15. See *D.N.B.*

[4] John Ranby, *An Examination of Mr. Wakefield's reply . . .,* 1798, 1102. i. 59, p. 19.

  e.g. Paine, *Rights of Man*, part ii. chap. v.   [6] See next chapter.

of the advocates of graduation regarded it as inevitable that Pitt should not have adopted it ; for if he had, ' the rich must have driven him headlong from his station.' [1] Auckland and Rose simply said that it would be revolutionary, a plan for equalising fortunes, contrary to the rights of property.[2]

The theoretical interest in these debates on the principle of taxation according to income is therefore subsidiary. The more precise consideration of the question was only beginning. But this fact constitutes their historical interest on one side : it illustrates the character of the seventeenth- and eighteenth-century idea that taxation should be in proportion to income or revenue. On another side, their significance from the historical point of view consists in this, that they mark a further step in the growing influence of the commercial classes on tax questions. We have already seen that their influence helped powerfully to mould the eighteenth-century view of a good system of taxation. But during that century they escaped their fair share of taxation, and now, with a tolerably effective direct tax, their influence was for the first time brought to bear on the abstract question of distributive equity. The result was to emphasise the problem of distribution as between the wealthy and the middle classes which became one of the distinctive tax problems of the nineteenth century. The distinctive problem of the seventeenth and eighteenth centuries was that of distribution between rich and poor, and the Income Tax to some extent diverted attention from that problem to the other which interested the middle class more directly.

The nineteenth century opens, therefore, on the one hand, with (1) an Income Tax which was considered in its main features distributively just and yet as a

[1] Frend, *op. cit.* p. iv.
[2] Auckland, *loc. cit.* ; Rose, *op. cit.* p. 33.

mere temporary expedient for an emergency, (2) much less temporary but still 'improper' taxes on necessaries which contravened the maxim that the poor should be exempt and whose distributive effect was on that account very little considered, and (3) taxes on luxuries and objects of expenditure other than necessaries, which alone were approved as exempting the poor, distributively equitable and administratively tolerable; and on the other hand, with (1) the doctrine that everyone should pay taxation, overruled, as regards the poor, on compassionate or trading grounds, (2) the rough principle that taxation should be distributed in proportion to income, (3) the theory that this was achieved by the third species of taxes just mentioned, and without the conception of a compensatory system of taxation. In addition, it took over Customs duties arranged for purposes of trade policy and spirit duties designed to check consumption as well as to raise revenue.

IX

SOCIAL THEORY IN THE EIGHTEENTH CENTURY

THE tax opinion of the eighteenth century contained, in addition to relatively technical doctrines, three more fundamental and characteristic elements all connected with the problem whether the poor man should pay taxation. The first was the theory that everyone, including the poor, should pay taxation as a matter of inherent political obligation ; the second, that the poor should be exempted on grounds of compassion ; the third, that taxes on the poor are not really paid by them but increase the price of labour. During the last two chapters we have been interested chiefly in the influence of these ideas on concrete tax opinion and policy ; but we shall realise their significance more fully if we attempt, in continuation of Chapter V., to bring out their relation to the political philosophy by which they were all dominated and conditioned.

The social attitude of the eighteenth century was not based only on one political theory, but it was nevertheless based predominantly on one political theory. This was the ' freeholder,' non-functional conception of society. Men entered into society in order to secure themselves in the rights which individually belonged to them ; the state existed to provide this security ; the rights to be secured were theoretically ' natural ' rights, in practice conceived as the more general and characteristic rights guaranteed by English law ; and all men having rights to be protected, which, though different in extent, were essentially similar in kind, every man was a free man and a citizen.   The basis of political obligation was that the state was necessary to, and in effect did, protect men's rights.   Men were born not to functions or service but to rights or enjoyments. They were born freeholders or free merchant adventurers.

The more abstract political speculation of the century illustrates very clearly the predominance of this conception of society.   On the one hand, it was put forward in the strict Lockean form by writers like Blackstone, Kames [1] and Thomas Percival of Manchester.[2] Blackstone, for instance, who began to lecture on English law in Oxford in 1753, and the first volume of whose *Commentaries* was published in 1765, explained in his introductory sketches on the basis of law and government [3] that the individual possessed some ' absolute ' rights—chiefly those of personal security, personal liberty and private property — which appertained to him merely as an individual, independently of his membership of society ; but that no absolute duties pertained to the individual (at least such as law could explain or enforce)—all duties were relative only ; and that, ' the principal aim of society is to protect individuals in the enjoyment of those absolute rights which were vested in them by the immutable laws of nature.'   Blackstone's essential justification for the existence of a propertied aristocracy, had he thought it necessary to discuss such a question, would therefore have been that they had natural or absolute rights to property like other people, and not that they governed England or did anything in particular for any one or anything but themselves.[4]

[1] For Blackstone and Kames, see references below.

[2] Thomas Percival, *op. cit.* 1785, pp. 2–3, and *Appendix*, T. 189 (2), note A on property.

[3] *Commentaries*, vol. i., 1765, pp. 47–48, 118–21, 134–36.

[4] At the same time Blackstone was, of course, far from thinking that the landed gentry fulfilled no functions.   See pp. 7–12.

On the other hand, the freeholder conception was equally involved in the speculation of those who, prior to Bentham,[1] attempted to add to or substitute for Locke's theory a vague utilitarian explanation of rights, such as that the right of private property is beneficial to society. This was the position of the philosophers Hutcheson,[2] Hume[3] and Paley,[4] the economists Adam Smith and Sir James Steuart, and the Whig lawyer Sir James Mackintosh.[5] These thinkers had no idea of a connection between rights and functions. Adam Smith, for instance, discussed at one point the causes of the subordination of classes in society,[6] and all he saw was, first, that birth and fortune seemed to be the two circumstances which principally set one man over another, and, second, that the reason for subordination seemed to lie in the need for the defence of great private properties. The sixteenth century theorist would have said that subordination and great properties existed so that the subordinate classes might be well and justly governed. And finally the freeholder conception dominated the feeling of those who were led, by the implications which the French Revolution emphasised in Lockean ideas, to repudiate the doctrine of natural rights, and with Burke

[1] Bentham's importance was for the nineteenth century, although his ideas were worked out in the eighteenth and on the basis of its speculation ; and it would be misleading either to treat him briefly as an abstract and uninfluential thinker of the eighteenth century or as the inspiration of a powerful school of political opinion which had then no existence. It is therefore more convenient to neglect him here. It may be noted, however, without going into the question, that Bentham did not get rid of the implications of the freeholder theory of society nor give any place to ideas of function. See Halévy, *Radicalisme Philosophique*, vol. i., *La jeunesse de Bentham*.

[2] *A System of Moral Philosophy*, 1755, i. 253, 285, 293, 309, 317–22, 327, 352–3.

[3] *Treatise of Human Nature*, 1738, book iii. part ii. §§ 1–3.

[4] *The Principles of Moral and Political Philosophy*, 1786, book iii. chaps. i. ii. and iv.

[5] *A Discourse on the study of the law of nature and nations*, 1799 (Introductory Lecture to Law Course), 518. k. 23 (1), pp. 38–42.

[6] *Wealth of Nations*, ed. Cannan, ii. 202–5, Everyman ed., ii. 199–202.

to canonise the actual property and other rights which tradition had sanctified in England.[1] Even Burke, in spite of his splendid inconsistencies, did not succeed in any direct way in embodying ideas of function in his defence of the English social order. He made men feel the complex and organic and traditional character of a real society, but he advanced very little in comprehension of the structure of his organism.[2]

Now it followed directly on this conception of society as held together by the protection of individual rights, that all men, rich and poor, should pay taxation —that is, share in the cost of the protecting organisation. The logical alternative, as Burke said,[3] was loss of citizenship. 'The moment a man is exempted from the maintenance of the community, he is in some sort separated from it. He loses the place of a citizen.' This was the doctrine which, as we have seen, underlay even the sentiment in favour of exempting the poor from taxation; and we can also realise how essential it was in the thought of the century from the answer which Lord Kames, one of the judges of the Supreme Court in Scotland, attempted to give to an attack made upon it from the standpoint of functional ideas. Kames [4] argued in the usual way that 'as every member of the body politic is under protection of the government, every one of them . . . ought to pay for being protected.' But this proposition, he continued, was controverted by the author of *L'ami des hommes* (Mirabeau), who maintained 'that the food and raiment furnished to the society by husbandmen and manufacturers are all that these good people are bound to contribute; and supposing them bound to contribute more (*i.e.* to

---

[1] See *e.g.* Wm. Vincent, Dean of Westminster, *Sermons*, 1817, i. 263 *seq.* (xiii., 'That property is sacred,' 1798).

[2] See e.g. *Reflections on the French Revolution*, ed. Payne, pp. 58–62, 69–73, 111–14.

[3] *Regicide Peace*, ed. Payne, Third Letter, p. 208.

[4] *Sketches of the History of Man*, 1774, viii., Finances, § ii. at end (722, k. 18, p. 464),

pay taxation) it is not till others have done as much for the public.' Kames' real answer was that the question whether men performed services for their society had nothing to do with their paying taxation—they ought to pay in virtue of the protection they receive. But he also tried to meet Mirabeau on his own ground; and the result affords a good illustration of the unfamiliarity of functional ideas. On Mirabeau's argument, he pointed out, lawyers and physicians ought to be exempted as much as husbandmen, and especially those who earn the largest sums, because they are supposed to do most good. And, he added, 'the luxurious proprietor of a great estate has a still better title to be exempted than the husbandman, because he is a great benefactor to the public by giving bread to a variety of industrious people.' Mirabeau was suggesting in effect that the wealthy non-labouring classes did nothing; Kames answered by saying that they spent their incomes. But, as we have said, Kames' view of society was not a functional one which demanded public service of the individual, and it was not really on that basis that he justified the taxation of the poor man.

It is significant that the two typical criticisms of this view of society, which were made in the eighteenth century, were scarcely realised to be criticisms of the political theory itself and did not result in overthrowing it. They merely raised the doubt whether the poor man could, in fact, be regarded as properly within the circle of freeholder citizens. The first criticism was expressed, in relation to taxation, in the compassionate desire to exempt the poor man in spite of the principle that every one should pay taxation—a desire which we have seen was very influential in Parliament in the last quarter of the century. It stood for the feeling that rich and poor were not taxable citizens of the same uniform kind. The poor did not simply have in smaller

quantity the same rights as those enjoyed by the rich ;
the non-labouring propertied class was very conscious
of the difference between its own life and that of the
labourer. But this recognition did not lead to a re-
examination of the basis of class distinctions. The
'rights' conception of society barred the way. The
difference between rich and poor was no one's fault ; the
nature of things had worked out so ; and to attempt
to alter it would be to tamper with rights which constituted the basis of society.[1] The result, so far as the
freeholder theory had influence on men's thought,
was first, that class differences were accepted, on the
basis of a theory which had no place for them, as fundamental and in the nature of things, and yet without
any justification or explanation why this should be so ;
and second, that the propertied classes, judging life from
the standpoint of rights enjoyed and taking their own
ample means and freedom from labour as a standard,
often felt that the poor were objects of pity and compassion because they had to toil and because their
means were scanty. This result was attested by Burke
and condemned with passionate contempt in a memor-
able passage.[2] 'The vigorous and labouring class of
life,' he wrote in 1797, 'has lately got from the *bon ton*
of the humanity of this day the name of the " labouring
poor."' 'Hitherto,' he continued, 'the name of
Poor (in the sense in which it is used to excite compassion) has not been used for those who can but for those
who cannot labour . . . ; but when we affect to pity as
poor those who must labour or the world cannot exist,
we are trifling with the condition of mankind. It is
the common doom of man that he must eat his bread
by the sweat of his brow, that is by the sweat of his
body or the sweat of his mind. I do not call a healthy
young man, cheerful in his mind and vigorous in his

---

[1] See *e.g.* Vincent, *op. cit.*, Sermon xvi., 1792, 'That there must
always be a class of poor ' ; and cf. Paley, *loc. cit.*
[2] *Regicide Peace*, pp. 219–20.

arms—I cannot call such a man *poor*; I cannot pity my kind as a kind, merely because they are men.' This was a fine protest against the sentimentalism which pretended to judge the essential conditions of life from the standpoint of a favoured minority; its weakness was that Burke did not clearly realise that the ultimate object of his condemnation was the view of society which regarded the minority not as a class which possessed rights as a condition of its performance of functions, but merely as individuals specially favoured by fortune.

The second criticism of the freeholder conception of society and of the theory that every one should pay taxation was expressed indirectly and by implication in the commercial and economic doctrine, that the poor man cannot be taxed,[1] and more widely in the new political economy of the second half of the century. Economic speculation made it very clear that society was not made up of independent freeholders in any sense. It emphasised the direct economic dependence of men on one another, and showed that the great mass of men worked and produced not for themselves but for others. But two circumstances prevented this line of thought from having its full effect on political theory. The one was the weakness of the economic speculation in its own field; the other was the influence on the minds of the economists of the Lockean philosophy. Thus, in regard to the propertied classes, the economists saw clearly enough that their wealth and income depended on their ownership of property, and not on their own labour or service, and they therefore treated them as rendering no labour or service, or, in the phrase of Sir James Steuart, as 'idle rich consumers.'[2] They consumed

---

[1] As we have seen, the doctrine was not always held in this extreme form. But it often was; and pushed to its logical conclusion and from the point of view of its human and political significance, this is what was involved in the theory that a tax on wages or on necessaries raises wages. See discussions and references in Chaps. VI.–VIII.

[2] *Inquiry*, book v. chaps. ii.–iv. *passim*; *e.g.* ii. 494. The landlords were the chief 'idle rich consumers' for the economists,

and did not produce. It was, of course, of importance to emphasise the fact that the propertied man *may* consume without producing, but it was an extremely narrow view of life to assume that men do not produce because they do not get paid for their work. Yet this was the tacit assumption which the classical political economy made regarding the English governing class. It did not include its work any more than it included the work of women not employed in industry, in what it chose quite arbitrarily to call ' economic ' goods ; and, as a practical consequence, it ignored such work. Indeed, taking over and expanding the Lockean basis of self-interest as the motive of social organisation, it had no proper place for service which had no direct motive of individual advantage to him who performed it. The propertied class was treated, therefore, simply as possessed of rights, the exact nature and value of which the economist discussed at length. But not only so. It did not occur to him to question the justification for such rights. He treated it as natural that some men should possess them ; his study assumed such rights as data. Consequently, on this side the new political economy made no breach in the freeholder, non-functional view of society. On the contrary, it fortified it by embodying it as an assumption of a new and very vital field of inquiry. In regard to the labouring classes, its relation to the freeholder theory was equally important,

and it is not necessary for the purpose of this chapter to discuss their view of the owners of stock or capital. It may be noted that the commercial classes were apt to look on the landed class as merely spenders of wealth. See e.g. *The Nature of the present excise* . . . , 1733, 104. d. 19 ('Such as live upon the fat of the land, and contribute in no degree to the service of the public, but, on the contrary, by their luxury and exorbitant consumption of foreign commodities confound our trade and turn the balance of it against us '—p. 28), and cf. [Nugent] *Considerations upon a reduction of the Land Tax*, 1749, 104. d. 43 (' Landed men are, by themselves, of advantage to the public only in what they spend ; traders are of advantage by what they spend and by what they gain ; and the gains of trade exceed the expenses of the trader. A rise of rents can only be through an increase of employment . . . '—p. 20).

but less defined. The fact about the labouring classes which it emphasised was that they were a factor of production. This alone made it difficult to fit them into the conception of a society of freeholders ; and the economists made it more difficult still by treating these classes also as motived simply by self-interest—*i.e.* as working simply to advantage themselves, and not at all with the desire to perform service which also advantaged others—and yet as necessarily obtaining in general only a bare subsistence. This conclusion was again due to faulty analysis in the directly economic sphere, but its result in relation to political theory was more significant. The idea that the test of citizenship is the enjoyment of rights was not given up, but society was conceived as divided into classes, one of which had so little in the way of enjoyment of rights, and was so essentially a means or instrument to the advantage of the other classes, that its position, if it were to be described in the terms of the freeholder political theory, could only be said to be outwith the pale of citizenship. In taxation, the result was the idea that, broadly speaking, the poor are not taxable citizens.

No political theory could have such widespread influence on social opinion as the freeholder theory had in the eighteenth century, except by representing some real and important aspect of the state of contemporary society. And the freeholder theory did represent such an aspect—namely, the fact that the rights which the governing class in particular possessed were rights attaching not to an office but to ownership of property. They received incomes whether or not they performed services in return. But the theory also misrepresented the state of society, for it treated this legal meaning of the right of property as its whole significance. The theory ignored the fact that the governing class did perform services in society, and that it was not composed merely of ' idle rich consumers.'

This other aspect of English society was represented by the second but much less important political theory which influenced the social attitude of the eighteenth century. It was a theory of class duty and of the mutual dependence of classes, and was expressed in general terms by all kinds of men,[1] but was voiced chiefly by the Church, which at all times, though to what extent I am unable to say, insisted on a functional theory which treated rights not as their own justification but as the conditions of duties. Three instances may be taken which stretch across the eighteenth century. Swift's teaching, in a sermon on mutual subjection,[2] was that every man, in the station appointed to him by God, was obliged to act toward the good of the whole community. ' He who doth not perform that part assigned him toward advancing the benefit of the whole, in proportion to his opportunities and abilities, is not only a useless but a very mischievous member of the public ; because he taketh his share of the profit and yet leaves his share of the burden to be borne by others

[1] e.g. *An Enquiry into the causes of the encrease and miseries of the poor of England*, 1738, 104. n. 9, chap. iii., on great men's leaving their country estates ; *A view of the internal policy of Great Britain*, part ii., 1764, 1250. a. 44, chap. on landed gentry and nobility, p. 219 *seq.* (' This rank of independent men, whose duty it is to think for and direct the busy and laborious below them, who in return labour and toil for their ease and accommodation, should be careful to preserve among them the science of arms and war,' etc.); C. Varlo, *Schemes*, 1775, 112. d. 19, Preface, p. iii. ; John Young, *Essays*, 1794, E. 2076 (1), pp. 13, 15, 35, and cf. pp. 86–87 (Young, who was an able thinker of conservative cast of mind, illustrated the difficulty of the time in giving functional ideas scope against ideas of rights, specially rights of property. He realised clearly that government was a special and difficult business, for which the ordinary worker, although power and authority (he held) ultimately resided with him, was little fitted, and that the landed class performed this business ; and yet he described equal representation as unjust on the ground that as the owners of the largest rights the landed men should in reason have the largest say in settling the laws, which would affect their rights more than those of others) ; John Ranby, *An Examination of Mr. Wakefield's reply to the Bishop of Landaff*, 1798, 1102. i. 59, justification of system of hereditary power and honours, pp. 55–56 ; Stanhope, *Life of Pitt*, iii. 166, Pitt's view of the landed class.

[2] *Prose Works*, ed. Temple Scott, iv. 112–14, 116–17.

. . .' The wise man should assist with his counsels, the great with his protection, the rich with his bounty and the poor man with his labour. Even princes depend for every necessary of life upon the meanest of their people, and are but the greatest servants of their countries. The prince cannot say to the merchant, I have no need of thee ; nor the merchant to the labourer, I have no need of thee. The poor are generally more necessary members of the commonwealth than the rich, ' which clearly shows that God never intended such possessions for the sake and service of those to whom He lends them, but because He hath assigned every man his particular station to be useful in life. . . .' In a more theoretical form the same idea was embodied in Dean Tucker's *Treatise concerning Civil Government* (1781), in which, in opposition to Locke, he defends the need for and explains the natural origin of rank and station in society on the ground of mutual dependence and the need and ability for the performance of different functions.[1] On the same lines, Thomas Gisborne, a clergyman-squire and well-known preacher of evangelical sympathies, published in 1794 *An Enquiry into the duties of men in the higher and middle classes of society in Great Britain, resulting from their respective stations, professions and employment,* in which he set out in great detail what he conceived these duties to be.[2] Among chapters on the duties of peers, members of the House of Commons, naval and military officers, justices of the peace and other classes less definitely of the propertied order, there is one on the duties of private gentlemen ' who follow no profession and live upon the annual incomes of their estates ' : first, as landowners—to encourage a race of honest, skilful and industrious tenants, to see to the full cultivation of the ground and the maintenance of their estates in good condition ; second, as invested with various offices and trusts of a public nature ; and

---

[1] *Treatise,* 1781, 522. g. 6 (3), pp. 3–4, 137 *seq.*
[2] 8406. gg. 9. See *Dict. Nat. Biog.*

third, as bound to the performance of numerous private and domestic duties.

As a protest against a mere ' rights ' view of society this teaching was of great value ; it humanised class relationships and differences. But its limitations were equally important. It was substantially an attempt, as we said of the sixteenth-century theory, to moralise the *status quo* without understanding it at all fully or applying strict standards of criticism to it. Gisborne did not inquire, for instance, whether the duties which he required of the private gentleman who lived on the income of his estate were in any way commensurate with his wealth or his ability to perform services. In other words, while he related the rights of the governing class to duties, he did not study or criticise the relation or ask whether the rights were an adequate or excessive provision for the duties performed. This, of course, was a very complex and difficult, as well as fundamental, question, and it is not strange that Gisborne did not tackle it. But the result was greatly to qualify the force of the teaching and to make it easy to treat the sharply defined legal rights as in practice unrelated to the loosely defined moral duties, and as justified, on the lines of the freeholder theory, simply as rights. This was no doubt one of the reasons why the non-functional view of society was so much more influential on the political and social thought with which we have been concerned.

One other but still less influential qualification to the predominance of the freeholder theory remains to be noticed. It consisted of a critical or revolutionary application of ideas of function to the existing English system and appeared in the last quarter of the eighteenth century both before and after the French Revolution. Briefly, like Mirabeau, it demanded of the landed classes what function they fulfilled in the scheme of things ; and it answered that they performed none, that landlords were sinecurists, 'an unessential class,' mere consumers of rent, drones.

Men of very different types and with very different plans took up this position. Wm. Ogilvie, Professor of Humanity (formerly of Philosophy) at Aberdeen University, published in 1781 an *Essay on the right of property in land*,[1] in which he advocated the breaking up of large properties into small farms for peasant proprietors. He contended that this was justified on grounds both of natural right and public advantage ; and in a section on ' the abuses and pernicious effects of that exorbitant right of property in land which the municipal laws of Europe have established ' he pointed out that the income of landlords came to them and increased without effort of theirs, and described it as a tax on the cultivators of the soil, the salary of sinecure offices.[2] He contrasted their position with that of the clergy, whose tithe was often complained of :[3] ' If considered as the reward of duties to be performed to the public, the incomes of the clergy, after admitting all that spleen has advanced against that order of men, must appear by far better earned. How slight indeed, in themselves, and how negligently performed are those duties which the state seems to expect at the hands of landholders in return for their affluence.' In spite of all this, however, the landlords were to keep the rents (thereafter fixed) of their divided-up estates,[4] and continue, apparently, to be mere sinecurists ; moreover, in a very conciliatory preface addressed to English landholders, Ogilvie suggested that England stood least, if at all, in need of the application of his ideas.

A more interesting advocate of functional ideas, from the standpoint of taxation, was John Gray, a political writer only known, apparently, by his pamphlet of 1785,[5] entitled *A Plan for finally settling the Govern-*

[1] 1027. c. 4.   [2] Pp. 44–45, 47.
[3] P. 46.   [4] Pp. 145–46.
[5] 8145. c. 38 (London, 1785).

ment of Ireland upon constitutional principles. He dealt with the problem how to provide Ireland's share of the cost of defensive services under a scheme of constitutional connexion with England, and devoted himself to contending that it should be raised on the landlords alone. The argument, which he applied equally to England, was that there are three essential or necessary services—the provision of food, of clothing and housing, and of defence; and that the landlords, who under feudal conditions had performed the third of these services, had gradually freed themselves from it, and from an essential had degenerated into an 'unessential' class, a class of mere idlers maintained by the labour of others. But it was a first principle that every one should contribute his proportionable share to the public prosperity; no man should be maintained by the sweat of the brow of another without rendering some equivalent. Make the landlords, then, give up at least some portion of the tax they levied on society to pay for the defensive service which they had shirked; and adopt some system to prevent the needless augmentation of unessential classes, of whom the landlords were the chief but not the sole instance.[1] Sinclair, the historian, discussed Gray's pamphlet in 1790 more sympathetically than might have been expected.[2] He allowed it had much plausibility and admitted at least that 'nothing would be more politic than to instil it into our possessors of land that they are the natural defenders of the country at home . . . and that if they become languid and effeminate and abandon the posts which it is their duty to maintain they will be an unnecessary and useless class, and ought alone to defray those public charges which their own deficiency may occasion.'

Better known are the views of the post-Revolution writers like Paine, Godwin and Gilbert Wakefield.

---

[1] Gray included artists, clergy, lawyers, etc., among the unessential classes, which, however, he did not desire totally to suppress; pp. 15, 77.

[2] *History of the public revenue*, part iii., 1790, p. 114-15.

Paine regarded the aristocracy as mere consumers of rent, drones, who governed the country in their own selfish interest, and suggested a plan for preventing the accumulation of property through succession by primogeniture, and proposed a graduated tax on income, which arrived at 20s. per £ at the twenty-third thousand.[1] Godwin's communistic *Enquiry concerning political justice* (1793), passed the same judgment on the wealthy classes, and Wakefield,[2] in the bitterness of a fine if hypersensitive soul, likened the governing propertied class to the master of the Ass in the Fable which refused to fly with him from the enemy—'for what is it to me who my master is, since I shall but carry my panniers as usual ? '

All these writers pointed out very justly that the governing class was maintained by the labour of others, and demanded in effect what function it fulfilled in return. But when they asserted that it performed no function, they were flying in the face of obvious facts. It was a real and important question whether the functions were well performed or were an adequate return, but to contend that the English landed class of the eighteenth century made no return was absurd. This view was analogous to the narrow view of life which regarded economic production, as ordinarily defined, as the only kind of service or function required by men in society. These writers, indeed, took the same view of the facts of social life as the economists ; it was on the ethics that they differed. The economists saw no objection to ' idle rich consumers ' ; these critics, like their successors in the nineteenth century, saw every objection. On the facts, moreover, they were both in error to a large but undefined extent. To such a degree did the freeholder theory of rights blind men both to the needs and to the facts of national life.

---

[1] *Rights of Man*, part ii., 8006. bbb. 23, pp. 29, 83, 86, 111–12.
[2] *A Reply to some parts of the Bishop of Landaff's address*, 1798, 1389. d. 57, p. 37.

INDEX

Note.—For taxes on particular commodities or objects of expenditure, see under Assessed Taxes, Customs, Excise, Stamp Duties, Necessaries, Luxuries.

For Product Safety Concerns and Information please contact our
EU representative GPSR@taylorandfrancis.com Taylor & Francis
Verlag GmbH, Kaufingerstraße 24, 80331 München, Germany